THE DEATH OF TOLSTOY

WILLIAM NICKELL

Cornell University Press *Ithaca & London*

THE DEATH
OF TOLSTOY

RUSSIA ON THE EVE,
ASTAPOVO STATION, 1910

Frontispiece: Vladimir Chertkov photographs Tolstoy as he reads his mail with Valentin Bulgakov, May 19, 1910. This image was captured by Thomas Tapsell, a professional English photographer hired by Chertkov; Chertkov shot a similar picture of Tapsell photographing Tolstoy in the fields of Yasnaya Polyana.

Copyright © 2010 by Cornell University

First published 2010 by Cornell University Press

Printed in the United States of America

Library of Congress Cataloging-in-Publication Data

Nickell, William, 1961–
   The death of Tolstoy : Russia on the eve, Astapovo Station, 1910 / William Nickell.
       p. cm.
   Includes bibliographical references and index.
   ISBN 978-0-8014-4834-8 (cloth : alk. paper)
   1. Tolstoy, Leo, graf, 1828–1910—Death and burial.
   2. Tolstoy, Leo, graf, 1828–1910—Appreciation—Russia.
   3. Russia—Intellectual life—1801–1917.   I. Title.
   PG3395.N53 2010
   891.73'3—dc22   2009049661

Cornell University Press strives to use environmentally responsible suppliers and materials to the fullest extent possible in the publishing of its books. Such materials include vegetable-based, low-VOC inks and acid-free papers that are recycled, totally chlorine-free, or partly composed of nonwood fibers. For further information, visit our website at www.cornellpress.cornell.edu.

Cloth printing   10 9 8 7 6 5 4 3 2 1

Contents

Acknowledgments

I wish to thank Irina Paperno, Eric Naiman, Reginald Zelnik, Hugh McLean, Michael Denner, Donna Orwin, and Olga Matich for their invaluable advice and encouragement in the writing of this book. I also thank Evgenii Bershtein, Shawn Elliott, Robert Wessling, Molly Wessling, and Maryse Meijer. Financial support allowing research for this book was provided by the International Research and Exchanges Board, The Vice Chancellor for Research at the University of California, Berkeley, and the Gary Licker Research Chair at the University of California, Santa Cruz. In the final stages of work I received the wonderful support of Deanna Shemek and Tyrus Miller. The staff at the Tolstoy Museum in Moscow provided tremendous assistance and good will, but I owe a special note of gratitude to Valentina Stepanovna Bastrykina, without whose willing help and invaluable advice I could never have completed this project.

Chapter 2 has previously appeared in *Tolstoy Studies Journal* XVII (2006). Chapter 4 has previously appeared in Russian translation in *Novoe literaturnoe obozrenie* 44 (2000). Both are reprinted here by permission of the editors.

THE DEATH OF TOLSTOY

Левъ Николаевичъ Толстой
† 7 ноября 1910 г.

1. Postcard commemorating Tolstoy's death on November 7, 1910.

Introduction

Death is the beginning of a new life.
    —FROM TOLSTOY'S *Calendar of Wisdom,* November 7 entry

On the Eve

In the middle of the night of October 28, 1910, Lev Tolstoy closed the door to the room where his wife of forty-eight years was sleeping, packed his things and left his home, never to return. At the age of eighty-two, the most famous living Russian embarked on a final journey that would become one of the great legends of the twentieth century.

Tolstoy had already been assigned literary immortality by his contemporaries, been called the "second tsar" because of his political influence, and given rise to a worldwide religious movement; now, in the last ten days of his life, he would once again demand the world's attention and call the conventions of Russian politics, religion, and everyday life into question. His journey would cover only a short distance but would traverse the sacred and the profane, the epic and the mundane. He would be pursued by secret police, a battalion of journalists, emissaries of the Russian metropolitan, his family and his followers, and the entire Russian public, who tracked every development in the newspapers. When he died, thousands of workers would strike and students would take to the streets in protest; his name would be exalted in eulogies and mired in scandal. As the Russian public read, wrote, and spoke about what all this meant, they in turn created their first great modern mass-media event. Tolstoy could not have written a more compelling novel, and in the hundred years that have followed, the story has lost none of its power to intrigue and provoke.

Late in life Tolstoy wrote that his favorite books were those without authors: the Bible, epics, collections of proverbs, and folklore. His last days would become such a story—one that insisted on being told and retold and would be created and recreated collectively. The unfinished quality of the narrative—an enigmatic departure for an unknown destination, a portentous journey cut short by death—invited all to imagine how it might have ended and to expand on the possibilities of what it *could* mean. Unanswered questions and narrative gaps allowed readers to tell their part of the story, suggesting how they felt it should progress and what they wanted it to mean. In this sense Tolstoy's journey to an obscure railway station in the remote town of Astapovo is a modern epic, conveyed to us by that heir to oral tradition, the modern media. It is this public phenomenon that is at the center of this book, which attempts not to provide closure to a single narrative of Astapovo but instead to open it back up as the multivoiced tale of tales that it is.

From its very onset the telling of this story undergoes a mitosis-like fragmentation and self-propagation. We begin with one version, as Tolstoy himself records in his diary how he awoke in the night, disturbed by the sound of his wife searching through his papers, and made his decision to leave.

> "I fell asleep and again, like the previous nights, I heard the opening of the door and footsteps.... On previous nights I didn't look at my door, but this time I looked up and through the crack I see bright light in the study and rustling. It is Sofia Andreevna searching for something, and probably reading. The day before she asked me not to lock the door. Both of her doors are open, so she can hear the slightest movement on my part. Day and night my every word and action have to be made known to her and are under her control. Again footsteps, careful opening of the door, and she passes. I don't know why, but this produced a feeling of unrestrained revulsion and indignation. I want to go back to sleep, but I can't. I tossed and turned for about an hour, lit the lamp, and sat up. The door opens and Sofia Andreevna comes in, asking "about my health" and surprised that my light is on, which she sees in my room. The disgust and indignation grow; I gasp for breath, take my pulse: 97. I can't lie down and suddenly make the final decision to leave. I write her a letter and begin to pack the most essential things, only to get away. I awaken Dushan, and then Sasha, they help me pack.[1]

The last action, awakening others in the house, immediately produces variants of the story. Dushan Makovitskii, a Slovakian doctor and devoted Tolstoyan, had lived at Yasnaya Polyana for six years as Tolstoy's physician and assistant. He had long kept detailed notes of everything that happened in Tolstoy's life, and he continued this fastidious practice now.[2] Aleksandra L'vovna, or Sasha, was Tolstoy's youngest daughter, also a devoted follower of her father. She was keeping her own record of daily life at the estate and left multiple accounts of her father's last days: notes in a log, a more complete account in her diary, and a third version in a memoir. Varvara Feokritova, the typist for Sofia Andreevna who shared Aleksandra's room, was also awakened. She too was keeping a "Tolstoy" diary and began to document what was taking place. In its earliest moments, one story had already become four.

From these accounts we can put together a detailed picture of each step that followed. Makovitskii took Tolstoy's pulse again: it was 100. Tolstoy told his daughter what had motivated him to leave now and where he was going; he would probably visit his sister at Shamordino convent, but if he changed his mind would send a telegram via his associate Vladimir Chertkov under the name T. Nikolaev. He was nervous and hurried to gather his things (of which we are given a detailed list); there was a particularly anxious moment as they retrieved a large trunk from near his wife's bedroom. They agreed to depart from the stable instead of the house to keep things quiet. Tolstoy himself then went to the stable to wake the coachman; on the way he lost his hat in the dark. He spent a long time looking for it with an electric flashlight but couldn't find it. It was damp and muddy outside; leaving the stable, Tolstoy met Makovitskii, Aleksandra, and Feokritova carrying his luggage: the trunk and a large bundle with a plaid blanket and a basket. Makovitskii had another of Tolstoy's hats in his pocket and gave it to him. They returned to the stable, with Tolstoy lighting the way with the flashlight. "He walked ahead of us, pressing the button on the flashlight every now and again and then immediately turning it off. Father always felt bad wasting the product of human labor, and for such innovations he felt especial admiration and he was sorry to expend the stored-up battery power. So we moved along, now in total darkness, and then every little bit under the direction of the lamp, which Father, feeling bad, would immediately shut off."[3] Tolstoy helped the coachman prepare the wagon. He put on a long peasant coat over a cotton jacket, said goodbye to Aleksandra and Varvara, and the group set out. The road was muddy, and the driver proposed heading for the main road, with the groom leading the way with the lamp. Tolstoy preferred taking the road through the village.

Makovitskii stayed close by Tolstoy's side and meticulously recorded everything he saw. When he was absent, others began to fill in the gaps in his account. At Kozelsk he went to check on the timing of the train stop and returned to find Tolstoy speaking with a student on the platform: the young woman with whom he spoke subsequently wrote an account of their conversation, which was duly printed in the Moscow newspapers.[4] The same pattern would hold in the days that followed. When Tolstoy went for a walk by himself at the Optina Pustyn monastery, his path (to the southwest corner of the grounds and then into the woods) was reported to Makovitskii by a worker, who had in turn learned it from a comrade. His movements on the grounds of Shamordino and Optina were also observed and reported by monks, some in public accounts, some in private reports to church officials in Petersburg. Tolstoy's followers Aleksei Sergeenko and Vladimir Chertkov soon arrived and joined

Makovitskii in recording each word and action. When Tolstoy fell ill, six doctors kept detailed medical records. A small battalion of reporters extended this record to the entire setting of Tolstoy's death, noting every movement in the station and reporting every aspect of the story to their editors, who also adopted the logbook method, simply listing the telegraphic dispatches of the correspondents in chronological order in their newspapers. Everything related to this story was treated as newsworthy, and in many papers more than half of the editorial space was devoted to its coverage. The Russian government also joined in this performance; secret agents had begun following Tolstoy on the train to Astapovo, and they filed regular encrypted reports to government offices in Petersburg until Tolstoy was buried ten days later.

From all these records we know practically everything that Tolstoy did: what he ate, how he moved, whom he met, what he said, how he was feeling, and, from his notebooks, even a bit of what he thought. All this documentation adds up not to one story, but to many. Tolstoy himself participated in this process as well. Even as he rushed to make his escape from Yasnaya Polyana, he wrote three versions of his parting letter to his wife:

> October 28, 1910.
> My departure will upset you. I am sorry about that, but understand and believe that I could not behave any differently. Besides everything else, I can longer live in the conditions of luxury in which I have lived, and I am doing what old men of my age usually do: leaving worldly life to spend the last days of my life in solitude and quiet.
> Please understand this and don't come after me if you find out where I am. Your arrival will only make your and my situation worse, but it will not change my decision. I thank you for your honorable forty-eight years of life with me and ask that you forgive me for everything for which I might be guilty before you, just as I with all my soul forgive you for anything about which you might be guilty before me. I advise you to make peace with the new circumstances in which my departure will leave you and not to have unkind feelings for me. If you want to inform me of something, tell Sasha; she will know where I am and will send me what is necessary; she cannot say where I am, because I made her promise not to speak about this to anyone.
> —Lev Tolstoy[5]

The two preceding drafts, however, are somewhat longer and contain elements that do not appear in the final version, including the following passage that speaks directly to what would become one of the great mysteries of Tolstoy's departure: "Most people leave for monasteries, and I would go to a monastery if I believed that which they believe in monasteries. Not believing this, I am simply going into solitude. It is necessary for me to be alone."[6]

The omission of this passage created one of those gaps in the story that would stimulate the mass interpretive energies provoked by his departure.

Looking back on this now, we are struck by how few these gaps are in number, but also by how gaping they become in consequence. The public would be given vast quantities of information about Tolstoy's departure but no clear sense of how it all fit together. One feels at times that Tolstoy has lent his own novelistic touch to this process, withholding information, hinting at variant conclusions, moving simultaneously toward multiple outcomes.

At the same time, if we look closely, we find unanticipated coherence. We can, for instance, look back over the diaries of Yasnaya Polyana and find a clear and steady progression in Tolstoy's resolve to leave. What came as a shock to the world at the time is not at all unexpected from this point of view. Tolstoy had spoken and written of his desire to leave for years, and in the period leading up to his departure did this with increasing frequency. According to Makovitskii, he had discussed crossing the Russian border numerous times in 1909–1910, taking particular interest in learning how he might do so incognito.[7] In late September and early October 1910 he repeatedly discussed his desire to leave home while out on his daily horseback ride with Makovitskii.[8] In late October such talk became still more focused. Mikhail Novikov, a peasant in whom Tolstoy saw a model of virtuous everyday life, visited on October 21; Tolstoy promised him that he would not die at Yasnaya and intimated that he was planning to leave soon and live his last days in a place where he would not be known. On October 25 Aleksandra L'vovna recorded in her diary a substantive conversation with her father about his possible departure. "I went to see Father. He was sitting in the armchair at the desk and not doing anything. It is strange to see him without a book in his hands, without a pen—it's unusual. 'I am sitting and daydreaming,' he told me, 'daydreaming about how I will leave. Will you really want to go with me?' asked Father. 'I wouldn't want to be in your way—maybe at first, so that it would be easier for you to leave, I wouldn't go with you.'"[9] (This is precisely the plan they subsequently used.) That same day Tolstoy wrote in his "Diary for Myself Alone" of his "sinful wish" that Sofia Andreevna would give him an excuse to leave. "That's how bad I am. But thinking of leaving and about her situation—and I am sorry and feel that I can't do it."[10] The next day, October 26, he wrote Chertkov regarding his conversation with his daughter and thoughts about leaving, which came to him "in moments of weakness." He called this less a thought than a feeling and asked Chertkov to act as if the reported conversation had never happened.[11] The following day he left.

As in any good novel, however, the motives for this action remain complex and provocative. Despite a great deal of foreshadowing, including much that appeared in widely known publications, the departure itself was nonetheless striking, with all the quixotic verve of a Dostoevskian scandal. Even in Tolstoy's own account it appears as a spontaneous act, for which he will not clearly identify a rationale even to himself. He leaves because his pulse is 97, as if his body has itself decided that it is time for him to go.[12] What motivation lay behind this impulsive response? How does the immediate provocation for his departure conform to the universal law ("what old men of his age" usually do as they approach death) to which Tolstoy refers in his letter?

As the public surveyed this situation, they found themselves stuck on precisely this point. How to harmonize a spiritual journey with an unfortunate family argument? They would argue over the genre of the story—whether it could be read as great drama or should be handled lightly, with polite discretion. Could its elements of melodrama be reconciled with the great national epic that they had believed was taking shape before their eyes? Would editorial gossip make travesty of this desire? Much debate in the press would be carried out between those wanting to know more, and those hoping to know less. The media, meanwhile, fed upon the gaps in the story and relied on a great deal of hearsay in order to fill them. The public record of the event is thus detailed but inaccurate, flawed, and incomplete. And while it is fascinating to see how Tolstoy's contemporaries write the story of what they know, it is equally interesting to see how they write the story of what they do not know, and what they do not want to know.[13] It is here that they take their part in the story.

Russia on the Eve

A young student attending Tolstoy's funeral left the following remarks in his memoirs:

> It is somehow strange. Awareness of the importance of the event, the death of a person, awkwardly mixes with curiosity as to the outward appearance of the deceased, whom you have never seen, and there you are looking at him as if he were alive.... And when I passed by the house, where they were taking leave and where Tolstoy lived, there were lights. They had managed to straighten up the room where the coffin had lain and return it to its usual order. A lot of people are going up to the windows and looking in. I went up as well.... In the neighboring room a gray-haired man was sitting at a small desk reading and writing something, evidently receiving telegrams.[14]

This student might well be the hero of this book. His hesitant intrusion and eye for the periphery, mixing curiosity, reverence, and a sense of spectacle, capture the nature of the collective author that this work describes. As he traverses this hallowed yet disarmingly prosaic ground, his uncertain steps describe the path that the Russian public would take in the early winter of 1910 as it sought to pay its respects to the remains of its most celebrated representative. Parting with Tolstoy would place longstanding practices and ideals in confrontation with the emerging realities of a new age. In this sense Tolstoy was, as Lenin wrote in 1908, "a mirror of the Russian revolution." The changes he reflected at the time of his death, however, were deeper and more widespread than anything the Bolsheviks could have devised. As Tolstoy died and entered the public domain, he left an image of Russia that reveals the broad underlying movements, profound and subtle, of a culture in evolution.

We can explore this image in much the same way that we read literature: finding rhetorical strategies, important metaphors, and organizing symbolic structures. My interest here is in how these last take shape in the moment, in the various newspaper accounts, personal correspondence, police reports, secret circulars, telegrams, letters, and memoirs that compose the story. My approach has been to evoke the moment fully, until the points I wish to illustrate are self-evident, allowing the architecture of my presentation to reveal my interpretive designs. I have allowed my original sources to speak in their own terms as much as possible, emphasizing the historical moment of 1910, rather than that of the early twenty-first century.

This does not mean, however, that we will ask the same questions that were asked in 1910. An item in the November 27 issue of *Novoe vremia* reported that when Tolstoy left he had not intended to take his pen with him and speculated that this signified that he intended to give up writing. Whereas the historical question of whether or not Tolstoy indeed intended to abandon writing or even to leave his pen might be of considerable interest to some readers (he was writing constantly from the time that he left his home), I am concerned with how the pen is used to structure the story of his departure. The *Novoe vremia* piece offers a long, flowery exegesis, in which its abandonment becomes a gesture of renunciation of the highest order, suggesting that Tolstoy knew that death was near. The author of the article, the brother of Prime Minister Petr Stolypin, adopts the interpretive strategy of the ruling circles, who downplayed the political and religious implications of Tolstoy's departure, centering their evaluations of Tolstoy and his death in his past significance as a writer. (The departure was not, in this narrative, the potential advent of a new life lived according to Tolstoy's ideals.) The potential of such "clues" to provide evidence in support of politically nuanced conclusions evokes the odd balance between morality play and whodunit that the departure managed to strike. Such meaning was readily assigned to the most trivial of items attached to Tolstoy's flight.

As Tolstoy surrendered to posterity, the public adopted stewardship of his persona, passionately debating everywhere, in all walks of life. When workers in a railway cafeteria refused to serve a woman who spoke out against Tolstoy a week after his death, they not only argued over his legacy but also suggested to those who read of their exploit that it was worth arguing about. They joined others in making that legacy into a vivid reflection of Russian society in 1910. As various issues were contested—should the press give Tolstoy the privacy he sought, should Sofia Andreevna be admitted to Tolstoy's bedside, could Tolstoy be given an Orthodox funeral—his death provoked Russian society to consider how the power of its institutions (the media, church and state, the doctors, friends and family, the public and the individual) should be balanced.

New technologies amplified this discussion and lent their own duplicitous tenor to these debates. Modern media provided new powers to preserve the historical moment as it passed, but the mass production of national mourning raised concerns about maintaining the integrity of the subject. When Tolstoy's impresario Vladimir Chertkov explained to a newspaper correspondent that he was recording their conversation on a phonograph record because he "valued every word said about Lev Nikolaevich," he gave singular expression to the way in which Tolstoy had become a distributable intellectual property. The journalist was taken aback by the extraordinary measure of Chertkov's conservation efforts, but he himself was an agent of the same enterprise. And although some newspapers took others to task for their heated pursuit of the story, they all treated it as something emblematic and inexhaustibly significant—as the final chapter in a narrative which everyone had read with great interest, and about which everyone had formed passionate opinions.[15] The massive volume of reporting was itself so striking that it became part of the story. On November 20, for example, the editors of *Rech'* reported that all their correspondence concerned only Tolstoy and that it was physically impossible to report all the information they were receiving.

This fascination with Tolstoy did not begin with his death, of course. It is the latent energy of his celebrity that stimulates the media frenzy of his last days and explains the anticipatory efforts of church and state to "police" the story as it developed. The cause for their concern is neatly captured in a 1909 memoir describing how a crowd of people spotted Tolstoy as he walked the streets of Moscow and followed him for an entire afternoon, finally leaving him as he reached his home. As one member of the crowd remembered, they went on their way happy that they "had spent at least a few hours in the presence of the great citizen of the Russian land." Returning home, they continued to size up Tolstoy: "All evening we talked about him, about his immeasurable significance in the history of Russian consciousness, and we got so carried away by this discussion that we even forgot that it was Shrovetide."[16] This shift, from observance of an important Orthodox holiday to observation of Tolstoy, is characteristic of the extent to which national, Orthodox consciousness was being displaced. The "great citizen of the Russian land" (a common epithet in the "Tolstoy days") was the object of a collective fascination that increasingly conflicted with the interests of the Russian church and state. Tolstoy's death and funeral dramatically intensified this tendency. The makeshift deathbed scene at Astapovo and subsequent lying in state in the stationmaster's house, where anyone passing through the station could pay his or her respects, followed by the funeral ceremony featuring the Yasnaya Polyana peasants, lent an unruly democracy to Tolstoy's last days.

This story is also a cultural landmark, in that it was captured in such detail and from so many different perspectives at a time when this was a truly rare phenomenon. We encounter a multimedia, multivoiced, multinational recording of the event that competes with current technologies in its completeness, creating a sort of primitive "world wide web." In this sense Astapovo serves as an important moment of transition between the world that was coming into being and that which was coming to an end. When Bishop Parfenii of Tula was captured by a film crew as he left an interview with Tolstoy's son at Astapovo, the two ages were in direct confrontation: the exit of the old was captured by the entering new, the two having been drawn together by their mutual and conflicting interests in what was transpiring.

The scene at Astapovo demonstrates in many ways that it is often upon the exceptional that modernity first visits its latest inventions. The whole story strikes us as contemporary in many ways: one team of doctors was brought in from Moscow to care for Tolstoy, while another was summoned to deal with Sofia Andreevna's emotional crisis. And though Tolstoy's wish to die on his own terms was honored in many respects, he did not maintain control over his medical treatment.[17] Attempts to capitalize on the writer's death are likewise familiar to contemporary readers: an American firm attempted to purchase Yasnaya Polyana to display its farm equipment, while others planned a vegetarian kitchen at Astapovo as a more fitting Tolstoyan shrine. In the mania surrounding Astapovo, everything relating to Tolstoy was invested with great meaning. So permanent did this fascination seem at the time that plans were proposed to build a railroad line to Yasnaya Polyana, and a wine merchant from Yaroslavl considered building a hotel there.[18] There was also discussion of building a monument to Tolstoy in Red Square, in which he would be depicted as a blacksmith and situated across from Minin and Pozharskii (the latter represented the physical strength of Russia, and Tolstoy would represent its spiritual strength).[19] Even local coachmen entered this industry: when Aleksei Ksiunin visited Optina to investigate the Tolstoy story, two different drivers offered to take him from the station, each claiming to have been the one who had driven Tolstoy there.

The pages that follow explore such banal manifestations of national mourning but also a more profound project. Ultimately the story of Astapovo became an exercise in developing the narrative potential of the modern subject. At first glance the result of this effort may appear to be hero worship and mythomania, but if we read more expansively and include even the most negative perspectives, then something more significant emerges. Tolstoy becomes a cultural epicenter, a locus of abundant contiguity with a broad range of phenomena, and a point of orientation to a changing world. Tolstoy can be read as he himself had portrayed Napoleon in *War and Peace*—not as a "general" organizing culture according to his own will but instead as an emanation of the public will, around which that public organized itself. The "great Tolstoy" is a term invested with meaning not only for those believing in his "greatness" as an artist or moral teacher but also for those who viewed his legacy less favorably. Tolstoy became a cultural endowment, into which each mention of his name was an investment; he was an institution of "greatness" in its quantitative, as well as its qualitative, sense. The public cultivated a collective identity in the sense that it built on this potential of Tolstoy to encompass, signify, and engender what it was to be Russian in 1910.

I rely heavily on the record of this process that has been preserved in the newspapers, which themselves played a tremendous role in its development. To a significant extent the book is a study of the growing power of the media to generate sympathies and produce shared experience. Though I devote a chapter to the question, the conflict of that power with other interests comes into play in the other chapters as well. The potential energy of the dead Tolstoy inspired a frenzy of commemorative efforts that did not always conform to the interests of the family, church, or state and at the same time consistently dominated the very atmosphere of the unfolding events. In descriptions of the scene at Astapovo and the funeral, the presence of the media was noted as often as was the absence of the clergy. Their ability to reproduce that experience in newspapers and newsreels countervailed the efforts of both church and state to divert attention from the event; these latter efforts themselves became a part of the story and were used to build it up, rather than diminish it, as the authorities in Petersburg had hoped. Memoirs and diaries of the Tolstoy family describe how their experience was also consistently mediated by the press; they spent much of their time at Astapovo talking to reporters and reading how their own story was being described in the papers. Pictures taken during the funeral make it clear that this solemn procession came to a halt in deference to the photographers, and some mourners noted that Tolstoy's face had been disfigured in the making of his death masks.[20] As the public gathered to regard both the physical and the symbolic remains of Tolstoy, the media seemed to have greater explanatory power than family, church, or state and increasing authority to define the event according to its own terms.

A similarly contemporary concern described in the book is the advent of modern celebrity and the conflict between the public and the private Tolstoy.

One might wonder if this distinction should even be made, as the Tolstoy family itself was scarcely able to discern between them. When Tolstoy left his home, the boundaries became still more obscure, as the traditionally internal and private family dramas surrounding his death erupted into public view. One writer for a Petersburg newspaper was prompted to lament at the time: "Tolstoy has no personal life."[21] And if his private life ended even before his death, his public life did the opposite. The embalming of his body was described in detail in the press, and the body, once prepared, was immediately placed on public display at the station, where it was viewed by throngs of travelers, many of them just happening to be passing through the station in their travels. Those who missed this opportunity were able to see pictures of the dead Tolstoy in any newspaper they picked up, next to detailed narratives of his final hours, facsimiles of his will, and intimate details of the family drama that precipitated his departure from home. Memoirs of the subsequent funeral at Yasnaya Polyana show that even those who had never met Tolstoy entered his family home (for the viewing of the body) with a detailed knowledge of its key personalities and circumstances. Tolstoy's final days became a spectacle of lost privacy as his family's experience of his death was exposed to and disturbed by public view.

This exposure left the public and political content of private life unusually conspicuous and open to scrutiny. Nowhere is this overlap of public and private more evident than in the vigorous political maneuvering that surrounded the funeral and other public commemorations. While I pay considerable attention in the fourth chapter to the development of a "genre" of public funerals in Russia, the particular circumstances of Tolstoy's death and funeral prove especially revealing of the extent to which the body can become politic.

In the course of the book it becomes clear that Tolstoy the author, even in his final and most compelling tale of escape, was situated firmly in the grip of his audience. Many observers at the time liked to imagine that he had full authority over his life text, a power that he had seemed to exercise quite convincingly as he brought that life to such a dramatic conclusion. One writer suggested that Tolstoy was like Beethoven, who once, after performing one of his sonatas, rushed back to the piano to add the final chord that he had suddenly understood was missing from the piece.[22] Tolstoy's last days, his eulogists argued again and again, provided similar resolution. I, in contrast, living a century later, have found it most interesting to listen to their unresolved debate over what exactly that final chord had been.

Фот. В. Черткова.

Когда испытываешь чувство недовольства всѣмъ окружающимъ
и своимъ положеніемъ, уйди, какъ улитка въ свою раковину, въ
сознаніе покорности волѣ Бога и выжидай времени, когда Онъ
позоветъ тебя опять дѣлать Его дѣло въ жизни.

Серія II № 7.   Левъ Толстой.

2. One of a series of postcards produced by Vladimir Chertkov featuring photographs and proverbs of Tolstoy. This one reads: "When you feel dissatisfaction with your surroundings and your situation, go away, like a snail into its shell, conscious of your submission to the will of God, and wait for that time when he will again call you to do his work in life."

1

The Family Crisis
as a Public Event

And every one that hath forsaken houses, or brethren, or sisters, or father, or
mother, or wife, or children, or lands, for My Name's sake, shall receive an
hundredfold, and inherit everlasting life.
—St. Matthew 19:20

Though buffeted on the eve of World War I by heavy seas, the family ship did
not go down. Yet many who abandoned ship did so with relief, with a sense
of deliverance, and with the hope of embarking on a personal adventure, only
to end in horror.
—Michelle Perrot

When Lev Tolstoy left his house in October 1910, he had
no destination in mind. His immediate objective was to go
somewhere where he would not be found for a few days, then to head further into the "great world," as he called it. At the nearby railway station he
purchased tickets for two different destinations, hoping to cover his tracks.
He had arranged to keep his daughter Aleksandra informed of his journey,
on condition that she tell no one else where he was, and had told her that
any telegrams received from him would be signed not with his real name,
but with "Nikolaev." Thus Tolstoy set forth into the public domain, cast-
ing off his famous name to take on one more befitting the vagrant life he
imagined.[1]

A popular Russian legend holds that in 1825 Tsar Alexander I abandoned
the throne to become a monk in the depths of Siberia, adopting the name
Fyodor Kuzmich. If Tolstoy ever imagined that he could accomplish something similar, he was confronted instead with the realities of the early twentieth century: a long inquiry into his personal life and a public examination
of who he was in the most quotidian sense. When the public set out to find
Tolstoy after he left his home, they were not only looking for him physically,

but were also searching for his identity. Much of this search focused on the Yasnaya Polyana he had left, where, it was believed, the secrets of his home life would reveal the motivations for his actions. Family members, servants, friends, and visitors were interviewed in the hope that they might provide inside information to explain what had happened. When those closest to the events began providing conflicting information, however, it became clear that the private self that was sought had long ago been lost in the morass of Tolstoy's overgrown persona, even in his own home.

If literature was a "second government" in Russia, as it has aptly been described, Tolstoy was without question its tsar in the early twentieth century. He made much of his discomfort with this role, but it did not stop him from also becoming the patriarch of a secular church. "Tolstoyanism" was part of a tremendous industry built around his writing, but it extended far beyond literary celebrity and came to refer to a whole lifeway that found adherents from the 1880s well into the twentieth century. The namesake of this movement had renounced his wealth and privilege to become an ardent moralist, advocating pacifism, vegetarianism, nonviolence, and menial labor, and these views were soon adopted by followers around the globe, many of whom organized communes where they lived on the land and shared their labor. The movement spread throughout the world, including Japan, India, Bulgaria, Canada, and the United States. In Russia it became a significant cultural and political force, producing vegetarian kitchens in major cities and communes throughout the country.

Tolstoy was eminently aware of the pitfalls of having a movement named after him and was quick to tell people that he was not himself a "Tolstoyan." But he also knew very well that many of his actions, including his departure, were deeply "Tolstoyan" gestures and would be interpreted that way by the public. His wife was convinced that most everything he did was "Tolstoyan" and that she had long ago lost the Lyova she had married.

Tolstoy admitted that he felt he had lost himself in the process as well, and comments in his diary after his departure suggest that he too was searching for that same "real" self, which he did not believe he could find at home. Much of his writing over his last years describes a longing for an unmediated, authentic self that could act outside of his own history and representation.[2] His attempted escape would not readily lend itself to this process, however: Tolstoy ventured into the "great world" as a modern celebrity, and his departure only further stimulated the newspapers to narrate. This was a familiar dynamic for all involved. Tolstoy's plowing and bootmaking may have been sincere attempts to ethically center himself in everyday activity, but he knew very well that they had also come to serve as archetypal gestures suitable for quick caricatures of his moral persona. His departure could be read as a closing bow to his audience; as he set forth to "walk the walk" in his

ОДНО ИЗЪ ОТКРЫТЫХЪ ПИСЕМЪ СЪ
ИЗОБРАЖЕНІЯМИ Л. Н. ТОЛСТОГО.
Работы Шерера и Набгольца.

3. Another postcard featuring images of Tolstoy's peasant ways. Ilya Repin, two of whose images are shown here to the right, contributed much to this iconography.

homemade boots, he stepped in the long shadow of his representation, along a path already marked by his persona.

The public search for the real Tolstoy was in fact stimulated by this persona, and it continued, and even intensified, after his death. Family diaries and private letters were quickly published, offering what for that time were considered shocking intrusions into the realm of the private. The public laid claim to these materials as if by eminent domain and found itself arbitrating the family dispute over Tolstoy's legacy. The family acknowledged this authority by producing open letters for the newspapers discussing the execution of his will—appealing to the public to take their part in a rancorous dispute over Tolstoy's papers. The documents that they produced as evidence, however, are marked by such a long-standing anticipation of this intrusion that they can scarcely be read as private papers—particularly where they touch on the issues most relevant to Tolstoy's departure and legacy. Deciding how to best honor Tolstoy's will became an exercise in the hermeneutics of these documents—of determining how they could best yield the information (legal, but also spiritual and psychological) necessary to come to appropriate terms with his legacy. The Russian public found itself orienting not only to the traditionally legitimate claims of blood relations but also to others that were complex and ill-defined, including its own significant interest in the matter. Some wanted nothing of a heritage that denied the patriarchal rights of the family, while others celebrated the bestowal of his gifts on the family of man. This chapter describes how Tolstoy's estate was divided among these public and private allegiances.

News of Tolstoy's departure turned the attention of the startled public first on Yasnaya Polyana. The "great writer of the Russian land" had abandoned one of the most fabled estates in all Russia, plunging his family, and his wife of forty-eight years, into crisis. Speculation over what might have inspired his sudden and secret departure centered on family issues—had there been a decisive argument, perhaps over Tolstoy's refusal to accept the Nobel Peace Prize, or to accept one million rubles for the rights to publish his collected works? This curiosity was piqued by further sensational reports: Sofia Andreevna had responded to her husband's farewell note with dramatic resolve, attempting suicide by twice running from the house and throwing herself into a pond, then declaring her intention to starve herself to death. Reporters were soon snooping around Yasnaya Polyana for clues, and the newspapers were filled with pictures and drawings of the estate, as well as photos of family members and other principal characters. The family members resisted this attention at first, but after two days of closed consultation they realized that their story would be told with or without their participation and decided to release a statement to the press. They recognized that they themselves were in the spotlight, and came to understand their own stake in the representation of the events that were transpiring. On October 31, Andrei L'vovich made an announcement to a reporter for *Novoe vremia,* initiating what was to become a long public airing of the family linens: "This sad occurrence shook our whole family. This is an entirely intimate matter, not suitable for discussion in the press, but unexpectedly for us in the Moscow and Tula papers there appeared descriptions of our family grief, and moreover in a sensational tone, and thus I decided to relate everything I know so that correct information about what has happened at Yasnaya Polyana might appear in *Novoe vremia.*"[3]

Though we now think of Tolstoy's departure from his home as a brief prelude to his death, at the time that it was announced in the newspapers on October 30, 1910, it was viewed as a beginning for Tolstoy.[4] Speculation over where he was headed, what sort of life he would lead there, and what had motivated him to leave initiated a passionate discussion in the newspapers not only of the prospects facing Tolstoy but also of those facing the Russian family. The turn of the century was a time of increasingly vexed attention to the family as it was redefined by radicals and decadents and angrily defended by conservatives and reactionaries. No one had wrestled with the values of the traditional family more tortuously, or publicly, than Tolstoy. From his earliest period as a writer he only thinly veiled the connections of his characters and their struggles to his own life and family, and his two great novels were written during the period of his life that was centered, as he described in his *Confession,* in the life of his family.[5] This was the Tolstoy who fathered thirteen children, eight of whom lived to adulthood, and who made the family estate at Yasnaya Polyana a living representation of the patriarchal ideals reflected in his early novels. The primary narrative lines of *War and Peace* and *Anna Karenina* described families in various stages of happiness, crisis, and reconciliation. At the close of the latter novel, the family is not a "question" but is instead the answer, as Levin/Tolstoy discovers that his place in the universe is precisely beside the home fire, where a new bond with his infant son has helped him recognize the vital importance of the "familiar" in grounding his tormented soul. All this amounted to what Vasilii Rozanov saw as a "religion of the family," of which Tolstoy could be seen as a sort of literary patriarch.

But the family happiness that Levin finds at the end of *Anna Karenina* was a last grasp at a domestic idyll that was on the verge of collapsing in Tolstoy's own life. In the aftermath of his "spiritual crisis" of the late 1870s Tolstoy came to view marriage as an evil that was merely lesser than that of uninhibited sexual abandon, and to believe that the physiological desires it channeled should be sublimated instead into social love and ethical engagement. The most controversial and widely known statement of these views, *The Kreutzer Sonata,* suggested that even the perpetuation of the human species was an illegitimate justification for sexual relations.[6] His continued critiques of private property and class privilege likewise undermined the traditional identity of the family, as they were based on a neo-Christian notion of universal brotherhood rather than blood relations.

These ideas achieved broad circulation in Russia and throughout the world and were restated by Tolstoy in a number of other works and public pronouncements. Rejection of marriage and family became a defining characteristic of Tolstoy's role as a counterculture figurehead. The experience of one avid reader of Tolstoy, described in a eulogistic editorial in late 1910, was shared by many: as a child he had read the *Childhood* trilogy, then in his later years had passed on to the great novels, and finally he had delved into the "forbidden" literature, among which he counted *The Kreutzer Sonata* and "Thoughts on the Sexual Question" as particularly influential.[7] This trajectory was troubling to those who preferred the sentimental domestic idyll of *Childhood* and the Old Testament morality of *Anna Karenina.* The cooling of the home fires in Tolstoy's writing was in some quarters seen to represent the destabilization of Russian society, for which the family had long been considered the foundation.[8] Although over the course of the nineteenth century the ideal of mutual affection began to displace the patriarchal authority that had reigned in the family, the notion that marriage and family were critical components of a healthy society was still largely unquestioned in the ruling circles of Petersburg as Russia entered the twentieth century. The Chief Procurator of the Holy Synod at the turn of the century, Konstantin Pobedonostsev, was particularly vehement in his defense of the family against Tolstoy's ideas, insisting that marriage inculcated mutual tolerance and therefore worked to hold society together.[9]

The Russian family, however, was itself increasingly falling apart: the number of annual divorces rose from 71 in 1860 (around the time of Tolstoy's marriage) to 879 in 1890 (when *The Kreutzer Sonata* appeared), to 3,526 in 1909.[10] In 1910, in fact, a reform of the divorce law, which had for many years been forestalled by Pobedonostev and the Holy Synod, was finally passed.[11] Though Tolstoy did not advocate divorce, he was a symbolic stimulant to this disintegration. Young "Tolstoyans" were abandoning the Church, refusing military service, rejecting notions of property, the authority of the state, and, not least, the sanctity of marriage and the family. While recent scholarship has attributed changes in the profile of the Russian family to rising levels of education, the importation of European intellectual movements, and growing individualism, at the turn of the century there was at times a more myopic focus on Tolstoy as the culprit. Thus, while the public discussion of Tolstoy's departure often focused on mundane concerns, its dithyrambic pitch suggests that people were concerned with much more than the family legacy of the Tolstoys. Russian society was considering its own perspectives on the family happiness that had crumbled at Yasnaya Polyana, and gave rapt attention to each new detail, no matter how shocking or unappealing.

A National Family and Estate

The Russian public did not need an event so sensational as Tolstoy's departure to focus its attention on its most famous citizen and his family estate. Vasilii Rozanov wrote in 1908 that to be a Russian and not to have seen Tolstoy was like being a European who had not seen the Alps.[12] As the title of his article indicated ("A Trip to Yasnaya Polyana"), the experience of seeing Tolstoy was largely wed to that of seeing his estate, particularly after the Tolstoys ceased wintering in Moscow in 1902. A 1903 album marking Tolstoy's seventy-fifth birthday described Yasnaya Polyana as a cultural mecca.[13] Those unable to make this pilgrimage could avail themselves of this album, find reports in the newspapers and journals, admire paintings by Repin and Ge (some of them depicting not Tolstoy but his estate), and even view cinematic documentaries featuring shots of the landscape at Yasnaya. Yasnaya Polyana became part of the currency of Russian culture, not unlike the way Walden entered the

American cultural lexicon.[14] One journalist reporting on the *ukhod* (departure) told his readers that he would not describe the estate because everyone knew it from "hundreds of descriptions and thousands of photographs."[15]

This scrutiny was motivated by curiosity about Russia's most famous person but also by the conflict inherent in Tolstoy's residence at his estate. The sculptor Ilya Ginzburg wrote that when he visited Yasnaya he felt that there was an implicit assumption that he was to scrutinize Tolstoy's daily life, so that he would be able to answer the questions that would inevitably be posed to him: was it true that Tolstoy lived in a well-appointed estate, with servants and the like; and if so, how could these conditions be reconciled with his beliefs?[16] Zinaida Gippius's memoir of her visit to Yasnaya Polyana with Dmitrii Merezhkovskii in 1904 gives as much attention to domestic life as to philosophical discussions with Tolstoy.[17] In his aforementioned article Vasilii Rozanov focuses entirely on the relationship of Tolstoy's moral persona to his surroundings.[18] An album published to commemorate Tolstoy's death (which inferred by its very title, *Yasnaya Polyana: The Life of L. N. Tolstoy,* that Tolstoy's life was metonymically described by his estate) presented a photographic tour of the house, offering readers the opportunity to compare Tolstoy's modestly furnished study and bedroom with the more elaborately appointed bedroom of Sofia Andreevna and the living and dining rooms.[19]

Tolstoy also contributed to this literature. An autobiographical piece entitled "Three Days in the Village" focused on the contrast between life on his estate and conditions in the surrounding villages. One passage described his return home after visiting a dying peasant who was so destitute that he had no bed or pillow on which to die:

> A marvelous pair of horses harnessed to a covered sleigh stands at the porch. The driver is a handsome man in a sheepskin coat and fur hat. My son has come from his estate. Here we are sitting at the dining table set for ten places. One place is empty. It's my granddaughter's. She is not feeling well today and is eating in her room with her nanny. A special meal has been prepared for her: bouillon and sago. At the large dinner of four courses, with two types of wine and two servants and flowers on the table, there are conversations: "Where are the marvelous roses from?" asks my son.[20]

The dinner conversation revolves around the cost of such roses (a ruble and a half each) and the health of a family friend who winters each year in Italy. When someone objects that the journey is difficult, it is pointed out that it is only thirty-six hours on the express train, and that soon it will be possible to fly. Tolstoy does not take part in the conversation about these various comforts but instead describes them from a third-person perspective, distanced and judgmental. Though the press did its best to play up the unexpectedness of Tolstoy's departure, much of his later work foreshadowed it. "Three Days

4. A montage of images of the rooms at Yasnaya Polyana from a 1910 commemorative album. Sofia Andreevna is depicted in the upper right photograph.

in the Village," appearing in the September *Vestnik Evropy,* served as an immediate preamble.[21]

Still, after his departure voices rose in a chorus of clichés describing Yasnaya Polyana as a haven of comfort, a nest of domestic bliss in which Tolstoy had been surrounded by the utmost tenderness and attention to his every need.[22] Sofia Andreevna fostered this image, and reminded the public of Tolstoy's need for *ukhod* in its second sense ("to nurse, care for, or look after"); from this perspective, the Tolstoy home was the epitome of the sort of restful haven that an aging national genius deserved. But reports of Tolstoy confiding his dissatisfaction with his family life to friends and followers also appeared, as did rumors of dramatic family conflicts at Yasnaya, including stories that Sofia Andreevna was prepared to appeal to the authorities to help resolve them.[23] The estate had also become an icon of invaded privacy: one incident that was thought to have possibly provoked Tolstoy's departure was the request of his nephew to land a plane at Yasnaya Polyana. (He was going to bring along the cinematographer Drankov, who would film his historic flight in the presence of Tolstoy.)[24] The phrase that was commonly used to characterize the departure, *ukhod ot mira v mir* ("departure from the world into the world"), aptly described the compromised space surrounding Tolstoy.[25] The world had closed in on Yasnaya Polyana, but his only escape was into the same public sphere that had invaded his private life.

Self-Representations

Tolstoy's family conflicts were private long before they became public, beginning in earnest in the years following his religious crisis in the late 1870s. In the beginning of this period he was largely able to reconcile his new views with his domestic life; in 1882 he still felt it ethically permissible to buy and furnish a house in Moscow. But the ambivalence surrounding this aspect of his life had already begun to take root. In an entry in his diary the previous year he is already testing the idea of leaving his family: "The family is the flesh. To reject the family is the second temptation—to kill yourself. The family is a single body. But don't submit to the third temptation—serve not your family but the one God."[26] Only a short time later, however, Tolstoy came close to succumbing to the former temptation.

Aleksandra Tolstoy was twenty-six years of age when she accompanied her father on his final journey. Her father had come close to leaving his family many times during her life, however—the first time having been the night of her birth in June 1884.[27] Relations between her mother and father reached their first serious crisis at this time, as Sofia Andreevna took issue with Lev Nikolaevich's growing disregard for their financial concerns, while he in turn grew increasingly critical of her lifestyle, which in that period had become especially luxurious. Particularly symbolic of their differences was the decision of Sofia Andreevna to hire a wet nurse for Aleksandra. For Tolstoy, the purchase by a gentry woman of a peasant woman's breast milk was an indefensible luxury. The employment of wet nurses had been a point of contention throughout Sofia Andreevna's childbearing years—Tolstoy had always insisted that Sofia Andreevna nurse their children herself and had relented only in cases of physical necessity, but now Sofia Andreevna had secured a nurse in advance, arguing that, since Lev Nikolaevich no longer managed their financial affairs, she would not be able to do both his work and hers with the new baby.[28]

On June 18, after a heated argument with Sofia Andreevna, Tolstoy left home, intending to go away for good.[29] He turned back, however, over concern for her, as she was about to give birth. When he returned, he found his family whiling away the evening hours playing cards and croquet and retired to his room, where he spent a troubled night considering his situation.[30] So distant were his feelings from his family at this point that he found himself indifferent even to the birth of his daughter, which came in the middle of the night: "Childbirth began; that which in a family is the most joyous and happy transpired as something unnecessary and oppressive."[31] A month later he only regretted that he had not gone away.[32]

Such rifts continued episodically, and although there were times of relative improvement in the Tolstoys' relations, their fundamental disagreement was never resolved. In the beginning Tolstoy imagined that he could reorganize his family life, much as he had restructured the management of his estate. He drafted a sort of personal manifesto describing how the family's wealth and unnecessary furnishings would be given away, and how the house would be reorganized along the lines of a Fourieristic phalanx. The men would live in one room, the women in another, and all would devote their energies to intellectual pursuits and shared labor for the benefit of the poor.[33] In December 1885, after a difficult scene with Sofia Andreevna (which had begun with his announcement that he was leaving her to go to Paris or America, and had ended with him weeping "hysterically"), Tolstoy spent three days writing her a long, programmatic letter, describing to her the possible conditions for their continued cohabitation.[34]

Tolstoy realized, however, that he could not force his views on his family, who did not always want to live on the cutting edge of morality. In January 1883 Sofia Andreevna wrote to her sister: "He is part of the vanguard, going in front of the crowd and showing the way that people should go. But I am part of the crowd, and live at their pace, and together with the crowd I see the torch that every forward-thinking person carries, including Lyovochka, of course, and I recognize that that is the light. But I can't move any faster, as

I am held back by the crowd, and my surroundings, and my habits."[35] Ilya, in his memoirs, asks how it was possible for his family to reconcile his father's views with the values that had been inculcated in them since their early childhood—"with the absolute necessity of eating soup and cutlets for dinner, with speaking English and French, with our preparations for the private school and the university, with learning parts for amateur performances." It often seemed to them not as if they had ceased to understand him, he wrote, but rather that he had ceased to understand them.[36]

The awkward and contentious double life at Yasnaya Polyana divided Sofia Andreevna and Lev Nikolaevich but also the rest of the family and their friends and relations. The Tolstoys' three daughters, and particularly the younger two, became followers and supporters of their father, while the feelings of the sons ranged from warmth for their father (Sergei and Ilya), to calm indifference (Mikhail), to loyal support of their mother (Andrei and Lev). Outside this circle stood the Tolstoyans, who urged their teacher to live according to his own principles, not those of his wife. In addition, there was a wider circle of family friends who were often impartial but tended to be more sympathetic to the position of Lev Nikolaevich. Sofia Andreevna did have her own supporters, whom she persuaded that Tolstoy's ascetic impulses were self-centered, and that he was ignoring the tremendous responsibilities that

5. Tolstoy reads a draft of his article "On Madness" to a circle of Tolstoyans. From left to right are F. A. Strakhov, Valentin Bulgakov, the physician A. S. Buturlin, the skopets A. Ya. Grigor'ev, Chertkov, M. P. Balakin, Dushan Makovitskii, Anna Chertkova, L. P. Sergeenko and the actor P. N. Orlenev. (See chapter 5 for the background to the writing of this particular article.)

he himself had generated (to his family, but also for his various enterprises and for the entertainment of the steady stream of guests he attracted to Yasnaya Polyana). She also liked to remind everyone that Tolstoy's own personal needs could not be met without her indulgences.

Though Tolstoy acknowledged that it would be a sin to abandon his wife and family, he never ceased to be openly critical of their way of life. Where the "plebian" radicals of the 1860s had criticized the values of the upper classes, Tolstoy took the same perspective on his own past and family life. It was self-flagellation, perhaps, but he inflicted wounds on his family as well; the family came to be viewed by Tolstoy's sympathizers as an encumbrance and faced constant moral examination. Daily life at Yasnaya Polyana passed under the watchful eye of the worshipful, the curious, and the media, which was constantly projecting the Tolstoy family life before a worldwide audience. "We lived in a glass house," Tatiana would complain later. The intense scrutiny of the public proved to have a particularly strong effect on Lev L'vovich and Sofia Andreevna and explains much of what was to follow Tolstoy's departure and death. Sofia Andreevna became obsessively mindful of the way her relationship with Tolstoy was represented; at times her actions can only be explained by the tremendous anxiety and paranoia that resulted from these attentions. And though he tried to ignore it, Tolstoy was also sensitive to public perspective on his family life and its contradiction of his ideals.[37]

Life in the Tolstoy household was to a considerable extent "performed," inasmuch as it proceeded under constant observation and documentation. During the summer preceding Tolstoy's departure eight people were maintaining a daily diary of "private life" at Yasnaya Polyana, all of them writing with a public perspective in mind.[38] Such were the circumstances in which the Tolstoy marriage reached its critical juncture in the fall of 1910.

The Crisis of 1910

What has been labeled the "final struggle" for Tolstoy began in the summer of 1910, and it was primarily a dispute between Sofia Andreevna and Tolstoy's colleague Vladimir Chertkov over the boundaries of Tolstoy's loyalties and, to a considerable extent, of his royalties. The opposing parties in this dispute were, during this summer, physically divided into camps: Chertkov was at nearby Teliatniki, Aleksandra L'vovna's estate, along with a whole detachment of Tolstoyan associates, while Andrei and Lev, the two Tolstoy children most loyal to Sofia Andreevna, were visiting at Yasnaya Polyana. Mistrust and animosity between the groups grew over the course of the summer, and by the end of July they were engaged in open warfare over Tolstoy's papers.[39]

Tolstoy had created the conditions for such a division long before, in 1891, when he renounced his rights to all his writings but allowed Sofia Andreevna to retain control over his works written before 1881. While she had continued to publish editions of his earlier and most popular works, including everything written up to and including *Anna Karenina,* the works that had followed had increasingly come under the control of Chertkov, who became Tolstoy's personal publisher, editor, and publicist. This occurred in part because many of the later writings were censored or unpublishable in Russia, and Chertkov, while in exile in England, had established a publishing house there to disseminate these works. Thus there was a clear division between the corpora on several levels—one consisted of literary works that had achieved universal acclaim and acceptance and had been published legally in Russia, while the other consisted largely of religious, philosophical, and political writings that had met with official opprobrium and were ferreted away in illicit libraries, subject to confiscation and destruction. For Sofia Andreevna, the secrecy with which these later works were handled no doubt contributed to the air of illegitimacy surrounding Tolstoy's relations with Chertkov. The illegality of Tolstoy's ideas connected to what she viewed as enemy designs on her family; the intrigues at Yasnaya Polyana were part of a larger conspiracy against national values, for which Chertkov and his cohort had more than once received "due" punishment.[40]

As Tolstoy advanced in years, the question of what would become of his manuscripts after his death became an increasingly vexing point of contention. For Sofia Andreevna, insofar as the question centered on the popular works of her husband, this control would determine the financial security of her family. For years she had been concerned that Lev Nikolaevich would somehow deprive her of her rights to publish these works and was particularly distrustful of the influence of Chertkov in deciding this matter. To make the situation worse, as marital relations between the Tolstoys disintegrated, Tolstoy became increasingly close to Chertkov, who became his spiritual confidant. Sofia Andreevna was particularly sensitive to this issue, because she and Lev Nikolaevich had always been open with each other, freely reading each other's diaries and correspondence. As Tolstoy came to view Chertkov as his literary executor, Sofia Andreevna's authority over his writings, including his diaries, began to diminish. She fought bitterly to maintain her position as a privileged reader, and eventually compelled Tolstoy to deposit the diaries in a bank in Tula. When she demanded access so that she could be certain that the diaries were not being given to Chertkov, Tolstoy refused and she ran to her room, yelling that she had taken poison.

As the conflict over the manuscripts intensified, the Chertkov camp asked Tolstoy to write a will clearly stating who should gain control of them upon his death. This will became the quietus of Tolstoy's domestic life. The Teliatniki camp convinced Tolstoy to compose and sign the document in secret, arguing that the group at Yasnaya Polyana might resort to any means to have it annulled, including having Tolstoy declared mentally unsound. The will was written during a 1909 visit to Chertkov; in July 1910 this version was revised, transferring the rights to his papers to Tatiana L'vovna if something were to happen to Tolstoy's chosen literary heir, Aleksandra L'vovna. Then another clause was added, giving Chertkov editorial control of the manuscripts. It was an allusion to this latter clause, which Sofia Andreevna overheard in a conversation between Tolstoy and Chertkov, that sparked the most acrimonious of all the struggles over Tolstoy's papers during his lifetime.

Evidence of a secret between Lev Nikolaevich and Chertkov confirmed Sofia Andreevna's mistrust of their relationship. She wrote in her diary at the time that she had discovered that they had devised some plot "against me and the family," and she began to protest desperately against their having any contact, finally achieving an agreement that the two would not meet.[41] Sofia Andreevna defended her actions by telling people that her husband had "unnatural" inclinations toward his friend, producing a passage from Tolstoy's early diaries as evidence. The entry in question described his tendency to fall in love with men and the complex feelings he had experienced traveling with a male friend.[42] She showed the passage to a series of people in the family's inner circle, though not always achieving the desired effect: Tolstoy flew into a rage and threatened to leave, while Chertkov's mother, who was visiting her son and had gotten wind of the accusations, responded with an angry letter.[43]

Sofia Andreevna used Tolstoy's early diaries to explain her anxiety over his relationship with Chertkov but also to demonstrate her authoritative knowledge of his private life. For Sofia Andreevna, the diaries represented the intimacy of her marriage, a sacred dominion that had been invaded by Chertkov. If Chertkov had become the primary reader of the diaries (as she had always been before), then in her eyes Tolstoy was essentially writing them "to Chertkov."[44] Tolstoy had become emotionally, if not physically, intimate with Chertkov, who now stood between a husband and a wife whose marriage was strained to its limits. Her leaking of a sensitive passage in the earliest diaries suggested that she knew more than others and had legitimate reasons to stand between the men. The use of the diaries to fight this critical battle is also characteristic. As her relationship with Tolstoy crumbled, Sofia Andreevna fought resolutely to control its representation, which she felt would ultimately be informed by their private papers. These papers were now falling into the controlling hands of her antagonists, the Tolstoyans, who were motivated by similar concerns and thus could not be trusted.[45] Her actions throughout this final period were based in her anticipation of this process of "publication."

The complex identities of the Tolstoy marriage were thus increasingly defined by this strange, public-minded privacy, over which Sofia Andreevna struggled to maintain control. Her own diary from this period criticizes Tolstoy for allowing his self-representations to be filtered by Chertkov, for whom Tolstoy was always *posing* for pictures that were presented as natural and unaffected. On July 31 she described in her diary the false representation that Tolstoy made to his followers when he wrote of the moral difficulties of living in conditions of luxury, and emphatically corrected it: "But Lev Nikolaevich needs this luxury more than anyone. A doctor for his health and care;[46] two typewriters and two typists—for the writings of Lev Nikolaevich; Bulgakov—for his correspondence; Ilya Vasil'evich—a servant to watch after him. A good cook—for Lev Nikolaevich's weak stomach." She also made "corrections" to Tolstoy's own papers: when Tolstoy visited his daughter and wrote to Sofia Andreevna that he missed being home, she underlined the passage in red and added her own annotation: "And it's all a lie, and I am dying alone at home."[47]

The extent to which all this "privacy" was intended for public consumption is revealed most vividly in a lesser-known parting letter between the Tolstoys—this one addressed by Sofia Andreevna to Lev Nikolaevich in late July 1910. In the throes of her despair over the "secret plot" against her, Sofia Andreevna had decided to leave, and wrote thanking Tolstoy for their "former" happiness, wishing him a rather guilt-ridden future of Christian happiness: "Be healthy and happy in your *Christian* love for Chertkov and all humanity, excluding for some reason your unhappy *wife*" (emphasis in original). She also left something more curious but entirely in keeping with the public profile in which she pictured her relationship with her husband—an announcement of her departure for the newspapers, in which she adopted the sensationalist, melodramatic tone popular in the boulevard press:

The Facts Can Be Verified on the Spot

In peaceful Yasnaya Polyana an extraordinary event has occurred. The Countess Sofia Andreevna has abandoned her home, the home where for forty-eight years she has lovingly cared for her husband, giving him her whole life. The cause of this is that Lev Nikolaevich, enfeebled by age, having completely fallen under the harmful influence of Mr. Chertkov, has lost any will of his own, has allowed Chertkov to utter rude words to Sofia Andreevna, and constantly consults him secretly about something.

Having suffered for a month with a nervous illness, on account of which two doctors were summoned from Moscow, the countess could no longer endure the presence of Chertkov, and abandoned her home with despair in her soul.[48]

This press release, written for her own private papers, reveals the extent to which her interior world had become public space. She herself embraced that

6. Forty-eighth wedding anniversary, September 25, 1910. Tolstoy wrote in his diary: "Again a request to stand for a photograph in the pose of loving spouses."

representational industry that she criticized in Chertkov. Throughout the last months of her marriage she attempted to maintain a public image of enduring conjugal affection by arranging for photographers and cinematographers to film her together with her husband. A picture of the Tolstoys taken on the day of their wedding anniversary speaks volumes: Sofia Andreevna looks lovingly at her husband, her arm wrapped through his, while he looks vacantly at the camera, with obvious dissatisfaction on his face.[49]

Living in a world that she perceived as a false construction, Sofia Andreevna often felt that her only recourse was to respond with her own dissimulations. These were made not only to the outside world but also to her husband and family, who became increasingly wary of this practice. In June 1910, when Tolstoy was visiting his daughter Tatiana in order to escape the tensions at Yasnaya, Sofia Andreevna became upset that Chertkov was there with him and sent a telegram asking that he return immediately, as her pulse was racing and she was not well. When it was decided that her telegram was a ruse, Tolstoy replied that he would return several days later. Sofia Andreevna then wrote another telegram suggesting that it really was necessary for Tolstoy to return but signed this one with the name of her secretary, Varvara Feokritova. This was the only way they would pay attention to it, she said. Over the last months of Tolstoy's life she increasingly resorted to such contrivances, which were often of a much more dramatic quality: she would claim that she had taken opium, fire a gun loaded with blanks, or write in her diary that she had thought of throwing herself under a train, à la Anna Karenina.[50] Even this suicidal ideation came to be viewed at Yasnaya Polyana as but another theatrical representation of her conjugal devotion and despair.

Tolstoy, meanwhile, had his own difficulties delineating the space of the self. He felt himself "divided into pieces," as he wrote, in the contest over his papers. As if to define this space, at the end of July 1910, he began a new diary, one that he called "a real diary for myself alone":

> I begin a new diary, a real one for myself alone. Today I must note one thing: that if the suspicions of some of my friends are just, then an attempt has now begun to secure her aim by endearment. For some days now she has kissed my hand, which never used to occur, and there are no scenes nor any despair. May God and good people forgive me if I am mistaken. I do not easily misunderstand what is loving and kind. I can love her quite sincerely. But I cannot love Lev [his third son]. Andrei is simply one of those in whom it is difficult to think that the spirit of God exists (but remember that it does). I will try not to get irritated, but to maintain that resolution. The chief thing is silence. I cannot deprive millions of people of what they perhaps need for their souls. I repeat "perhaps." But if there is even the smallest probability that what I write is needed by men's souls I cannot deprive them of that spiritual food in order that Andrei may drink and indulge in debauchery, or that Lev may swear and...But heaven help them! Do your own duty and do not judge.[51]

This *real* diary begins by describing the *artifice* of Sofia Andreevna's actions and reveals that standing his own ground has become equated, conversely, with silence. But even this diary, for Tolstoy alone, addresses itself immediately not only to God but to an audience of "good people" and to the "millions" who might benefit from his spiritual nourishment.[52] Though Tolstoy did not intend for this diary to be mediated by loyalties to his family or to Chertkov (the first entry expresses dissatisfaction with the former, the second with the latter: "Chertkov has drawn me into a struggle, and that struggle is very heavy and unappealing to me"), it was hardly written "for himself alone." In this sense it can be seen as a prelude to what was to come, for if the *ukhod* was also an attempt to define himself outside the context of his family and followers, it would also serve to better define his place in the "great world."

This was not the first of Tolstoy's attempts at this uncompromised space. In 1909 he wrote Sofia Andreevna a letter "from the grave" which was to be given to her after his death: "They will give you this letter when I am gone. I am writing you from the grave to tell you that which for your own good I wanted to tell you so many times, for so many years, but could not tell you while I was alive."[53] Tolstoy apparently felt that knowing she would read the letter only after his death would allow him to speak to her more freely. Later, however, in his diary, he wrote that he had abandoned this scheme because he had realized that he was not writing "before God for the sake of love."[54] God was the ideal addressee—an antipode to the public, before whom Tolstoy felt himself perpetually encouraged to "perform" his moral acts.

Still another attempt of this sort is found in a long, programmatic letter to Sofia Andreevna, dated July 14, 1910. The letter is something of a contract, in which Tolstoy outlined the conditions under which their continued coexistence might be possible, concluding with a warning that he would leave her if his conditions were not met.[55] He began the letter, however, with a long passage in which he clarified his feelings for her, with the explicit purpose of providing her with a statement to counter anything she might suspect was written in his diaries. This private clarification, written in a very public, evidentiary voice, is offered as a testament to her in the hope that it might calm her fears and enable her to accept the changes he proposed.

The letter did not, however, produce its desired effect. The furor over the will followed shortly thereafter, and Sofia Andreevna would write in her diary that at her daughter's house everyone was kindhearted, not "spiteful and secretive, like in our family hell."[56] They were, as Tolstoy might say it, unhappy in their own, particular way, and they continued in that way until the end. The strange mixture of love, fear, and paranoia which Sofia Andreevna felt on the eve of Tolstoy's departure was revealed in an incident of October 3 of that year. Tolstoy fell seriously ill, losing consciousness and breaking into convulsions; it was feared that he might not live, and Sofia Andreevna became overwrought, telling everyone that it was her fault, and that she would never forgive herself if he died.[57] So great was her anxiety over Tolstoy's papers, however, that she could not restrain herself even in this remorseful moment from going to his room and taking some papers from his desk.[58] Her children retrieved the papers from her, and her oldest son Sergei told her that if she could not gain control of herself it would be necessary to summon a family council, call in doctors, take over her property, and oblige her to separate from Tolstoy.[59]

It was Tolstoy who ultimately negotiated this separation. His parting letter to Sofia Andreevna reads much like the one he had written in 1897 and was no more successful in calming her than any of his previous written explanations. She did not resign herself to her new situation, as he requested, but threw the letter aside and ran purposefully out the door toward the large pond nearby. The letter illustrated for Sofia Andreevna once again how her personal life had been subsumed by her husband's public-mindedness: she complained in her diary that he had written the letter not to her, but "for the whole world."

Departure and Death

Sofia Andreevna's struggle to distinguish a place for herself within this "whole world" continued to motivate her actions after Tolstoy's departure. Her behavior has been alternately described as manipulative theater and pure desperation, and was probably both—a desperation that she felt needed to be amplified theatrically. Valentin Bulgakov, who rescued her from one of her suicide attempts, believed that she was sincerely trying to kill herself.[60] The consensus among the family, however, was that Sofia Andreevna's suicide attempts were calculated efforts to induce Tolstoy's return. When she announced that, since she had been prevented from drowning herself, she would starve herself to death, the children kept her under constant supervision and removed a vial of opium, a penknife, and all heavy objects from her room to prevent her from doing herself "unintentional harm."[61] Sofia Andreevna herself came close to admitting that her actions were contrived: when Sergei L'vovich told her that Lev Nikolaevich needed to see that she had gained control of herself, she answered that the only thing that would move her husband was pity. Acting on this belief, she forged a telegram in Aleksandra's name insisting that he return immediately, asked for a priest to receive her final confession, and sent for Chertkov so that she could make peace with him before she died. These efforts were undermined at every turn by loyalty to Tolstoy.[62] She asked Bulgakov to go with her to search for her husband, but he declined, based on Tolstoy's letter, and the children decided that she should not be allowed to search for their father. The children also decided that it was pointless to search for him themselves—for, as Andrei L'vovich surmised, the press and police would prove far more efficient—and decided instead to each write him a letter.[63]

Sofia Andreevna was writing to Tolstoy as well, by turns endearing ("Lyo-vochka, dovey, come back home, darling"), reproachful ("you do have to save me, for indeed it says in the Gospels that one should never *for any reason* abandon one's wife"), promising ("I began my treatment in earnest yester-day: I am to sit in a hot bath with cold compresses on my head twice a day and lie down almost the whole day"),[64] and pathetic ("I sleep in your room, i.e., I lie and sit at night and pour out tears over your pillow, and pray to God and you to forgive me, to return you to me).[65] She reminded him that their lives were already inextricably intertwined, and that they would have to answer as husband and wife before God, who mercifully had spared them both from such a sin as her suicide. She spoke of the children's support for her, evidently hoping to entice him back home by creating a tender picture of the family bonding in a moment of crisis: "All my children, taking pity on me, have come and are nursing and comforting me. Tanichka looks so thin. She is going to come again at the beginning of November for a month with her husband and little girl. Won't you come then too? Misha and Ilya, when they saw me, cried bitterly, embracing me and looking at my pathetic appear-ance. Serezha did too." Contrary to what he had written in his parting letter, she argued that it was unnatural for a man of his age to have abandoned the source of such love and support: "Old peasant men live out their last days on the hearth, in the circle of their family and grandchildren, just as in a gentry or any other way of life."[66]

In her first interview after Tolstoy's departure, she appeared in a "hastily thrown on" housecoat, supported by her son and accompanied by a doctor, who repeatedly insisted that she break off the interview. The story she told affirmed her position as a faithful and unjustly abandoned wife: in the habit of rising every two or three hours to check on her husband, she had done so twice on the night of his departure (only to meet with reproachful mutter-ing that she was meddling in his papers) but had then slept through the rest of the night.[67] She spoke of her "undying love" for her husband and told a story of how touchingly Tolstoy had greeted her that summer on her return from several days in Tula.[68] Sofia Andreevna presented herself as the protec-tress of her husband but also of her family, her concern for which had been the main cause of her dispute with her husband. Her defense of these inter-ests was undermined by an outsider—a friend of Tolstoy who had "interfered in our private life." This family nemesis did not need to be named, as readers would know that she referred to Vladimir Chertkov.

The difficulty for Sofia Andreevna came in negotiating a balance of this representation with a number of others: those that her "enemies" were mak-ing, those that she felt obligated to make to protect Lev Nikolaevich's image, and those that would be suggested by certain unflattering facts that were bound to be produced as counter-evidence. In addition, she was playing to multiple audiences and attempting to win sympathies that were often conflicting. Sofia Andreevna clearly sensed that many strangers were prepared to judge her harshly for driving her aging husband from his home. Equally troubling to her was the perspective of those who viewed Tolstoy's last days as a spiritual triumph over everyday, earthly concerns. She had her own story to tell, and she made that story every bit as dramatic as her husband's. She too had been driven to despair by the conflict in her family home, from which she had attempted her own dramatic exits: she spoke openly of her suicide attempts and of her regret that they had been unsuccessful.[69]

Many, however, were eager to view Tolstoy's estrangement from his family as the great finale to his illustrious life. As L. Grossman wrote for an Odessa newspaper: "And no matter how great the despair of the family, and no matter how deeply we respect the grief of his loved ones, the departure of Tolstoy 'into the world' is such an important event for us that on learning of it we involuntarily experience great joy and boundless satisfaction."[70] At a ceremony to honor the writer Boborykin on the evening of October 30—the first day when news of Tolstoy's departure had become widely known—the audience was asked to stand in commemoration of Tolstoy's departure. Though still uncertain as to what the act meant, or to what it would lead, the crowd of literati wished to immediately mark it as momentous. Tolstoy had gone off by himself "to settle some great accounts," wrote the author of a piece called "The Final Chord."[71]

The Tolstoyans, as might be expected, reacted with utmost seriousness to Tolstoy's departure, which they justified as a correct and long-awaited answer to the call of Christ.[72] A Tolstoyan in Ekaterinoslav told a newspaper that the contradiction between Tolstoy's lifestyle and his ideas had been the "Achilles' heel" of their movement, but that now they were holding their heads high.[73] Gorbunov-Posadov, a leader of the movement in Moscow, tried to separate the personal tragedy that the event signified for the family from its larger meaning: "People will feel sorry for Lev Nikolaevich's family and pour out tears over the grief of Sofia Andreevna. And there are no words, of course; it is a great pity for her, the poor wife, but it could not have been any other way—the man eventually had to break free of his fetters." Gorbunov-Posadov insisted "categorically" that there had been nothing catastrophic to induce Tolstoy to leave so suddenly, but that it had been a much-deliberated decision that came as no surprise to those close to him.[74]

The search for less partisan information led to the interviewing of family friends and other "insiders."[75] V. F. Lazurskii, at one time a tutor for the Tolstoy children and the author of an article on "Tolstoy and His Family," was interviewed in Odessa as an expert and told the press that Tolstoy would not have left because of a family argument.[76] D. D. Obolenskii took advantage of his position as a relative of the Tolstoy family to become a "special correspondent" of *Novoe vremia*. He arrived at Yasnaya Polyana on the evening of October 29, telling the Tolstoys that all Tula was talking about Lev Nikolaevich's disappearance, and then proceded to relate, to the surprise of the family, a good deal of what had happened at the estate. He reassured them that he had not come as a "correspondent" but as a friend of the family, then several minutes later asked if he could make a report to the newspapers.[77] Valentin Bulgakov expressed his concern in his diary that night that Obolenskii's announcement to the newspapers would send out a signal to the media and direct unwanted attention to Tolstoy, then noted his dismay that Sofia Andreevna provided Obolenskii with the text of Tolstoy's parting letter. Obolenskii justified his intrusion by reminding the family that Tolstoy had always been "more than frank" with him, but a suspicious Bulgakov recorded in his diary that Tolstoy had in fact hidden his true feelings from Obolenskii, whom he [Tolstoy] regarded as "completely alien." In fact, Bulgakov's and Tolstoy's intuitions proved correct, as Obolenskii was later the source of a premature report of Tolstoy's death on November 3.[78] Family loyalties and agendas would continue to prove surprisingly heterogeneous and conflicting in the months to come.[79]

When Tolstoy's parting letter to Sofia Andreevna was published, then his letter to Mikhail Novikov, a picture began to emerge of a Tolstoy searching for respite not only from the conflicts of Yasnaya Polyana but from the moral and psychological tensions inherent to the way of life that Yasnaya Polyana represented for him.[80] In fact, when Tolstoy spoke of his destination early on in his journey, he wanted to avoid any place that was in any way familiar, saying that he wished to go "not to a [Tolstoyan] commune and not to acquaintances but simply to live in a hut."[81] When Astapovo proved to be Tolstoy's ultimate destination, the desire to honor the dying man's last wishes compelled those surrounding him, including the family and the watching public, to replicate for him as best they could the solitude that he had sought. He was sheltered from the tumultuous scene being played out outside his room, where family, church, media, and state pursued their various agendas.

His desire to "simply live in a hut," however, was contravened by notions of what was befitting not only a dying man but also a national hero. The furniture in his room at Astapovo was rearranged to copy the arrangement in his room at Yasnaya, and furnishings from his home began to reappear: Aleksandra L'vovna brought some bedside things with her, then Tatiana L'vovna brought his pillow. Finally a special bed was ordered to be brought from Moscow. Though Tolstoy had left his family home, they nonetheless felt that his needs could be best met by surrounding him with familiar comforts. The stationmaster Ivan Ozolin became a national hero for his generous accommodations, displacing his own family to make room for his honored guest.[82]

The family struggled to determine their place in this makeshift family death scene, as they maintained for Tolstoy's sake the illusion that they were not there but played the role of intimates for the public, which took its place at the scene by a sort of eminent domain. Aleksandra L'vovna's situation was especially delicate, for she had been placed in a privileged position at her father's side but also felt herself beholden to represent the rest of her family's interests and concerns.[83] Unlike her father, she was aware of the scene outside his room—that the family was gathered in awkward remove, themselves part of the spectacle the public watched in its own vigil at Tolstoy's bedside.

As the family attempted to sort out their priorities, they ultimately deferred to the will of Tolstoy, who was still the family patriarch, no matter how unwilling he may have been to play that role. Their most difficult decision was whether or not Sofia Andreevna should be allowed access to her husband's deathbed. She was telling the world that she wanted to be at his side at this moment of crisis, although Tolstoy had emphatically expressed his opposition to such a meeting. Ultimately the children sided with their father, whose wishes were supported by the advice of his doctors (who warned against placing such a stress on his weakened heart).[84] The public, meanwhile, was also actively discussing what was best for the patient, chiming in with their own remedies and expressing concern that the strange situation in which he found himself would accelerate his demise. Differing theories were offered as to how he had fallen ill, but all of them seemed to confirm that his illness was caused by his departure from the care and comfort of his family home. Perhaps it had happened when he had lost his hat in the dark on his way to alert the stable master that he was leaving Yasnaya, or on the coach ride that followed, when he had not dressed warmly enough, or on the subsequent train ride, when he had ridden between cars because the third-class coach was too crowded and smoky, or at Shamordino, when he had sat writing under an open window in spite of Aleksandra L'vovna's and Makovitskii's pleading that he close it; perhaps Aleksei Sergeenko was to blame for appearing at Shamordino when Tolstoy thought no one knew where he was, spurring him into another hurried, late-night departure.

Many were concerned that Sergeenko and Chertkov were protecting their own interests at the expense of Tolstoy's.[85] Vasilii Rozanov wrote a piece appearing in *Novoe vremia* on November 6 in which he blamed Tolstoy's followers for disturbing the peace that he so needed during his illness: "The [bustle] *around* the house is no doubt communicated to him, increasing his pulse and disturbing his sleep. Now, when all Russia is thinking about Tolstoy, his 'friends' and relations should know that Russia cannot help but judge them, and that they are a far cry from fulfilling Tolstoy's request for peace and solitude."[86] Rozanov saw what he called the *venenum Chertkowi* as especially injurious and promised that Russia would judge Chertkov harshly for his role in precipitating Tolstoy's demise. In the same edition of *Novoe vremia* a piece entitled "Tolstoy for Rent" decried Sergeenko's control of access to the dying writer.[87] Chertkov and company, these writers argued, were holding "their" Tolstoy hostage and "producing" his death according to their own designs on his legacy.[88]

The right wing's morbid interest in the Tolstoy story focused not only on the dying writer but also on the demise of his family relations. The family, and in particular Sofia Andreevna, became a cause célèbre for the conservative press, which described their exclusion as an injustice and opened a spirited campaign against the Tolstoyans, whom they held responsible for the situation. A *Novoe vremia* piece asked readers to imagine Sofia Andreevna's horror as she awakened to find her husband gone, then learned that he was ill, but was not allowed to see him—"Only Sofia Andreevna is not allowed! Only her presence is considered extraneous, and she is condemned to wander under the windows: 'she walks around the home where L. N. lies and beats, like a bird wanting to fly into the nest where her loved one is, but the doctors don't allow this meeting.' It's scandalous!"[89] The Black Hundreds newspaper *Kolokol* created a particularly bleak picture:

> Count Tolstoy is dying not in his ancestral home, in the circle of his loving family, but at some wayside station, surrounded by strangers, but his wife, who lived a whole long life with him, surrounding him with concern, care, and tender love, and his children, grandchildren, and great-grandchildren—they must give way to these outsiders, are not even allowed to go to the bed where their husband, father, grandfather may be succumbing in the final struggle with his approaching death.[90]

The contrast between the desolate image of Tolstoy at Astapovo and that of the "ancestral home" he had abandoned, between the "outsiders" and the loving, caring family they displaced, was meant to be instructive. For the right-wing press, Tolstoy's death was the tragic finale of a tale of subversion of the family, to which many dramatic details would soon be added.

The Dispute over the Will

Throughout late 1910 and early 1911, a steady flow of new facts, falsehoods, rumors, and accusations emerged from behind the wall of privacy that had shielded the origins of Tolstoy's final drama from public view. Although for a brief period immediately after Tolstoy's death a mournful silence reigned, it did not take long for insinuations about the causes of his departure to flare up again; without the quieting influence of Tolstoy's presence, they became still more rancorous. The result was nothing less than a family argument carried out in the editorial pages of the nation's leading newspapers. This discord reached a new pitch once the family began to contest the secret will. The public was fascinated by the dispute but also questioned whether it was proper to tarnish the name of a national treasure by bringing such arguments into the open. Many commentators expressed their dismay that the family chose to do precisely this, while others insisted on their right to know.

The first person to disrupt the familial quiet around the grave was Lev L'vovich. He had written a letter to *Novoe vremia* from Paris on October 31, countering rumors that his father had left over a family argument and insisting that his father had been moved by his desire to find "solitude in God." There was, according to Lev L'vovich, no need for discussion of any other motives. He quickly changed his story, however.[91] On November 16 a new letter by Lev L'vovich appeared in *Novoe vremia* stating quite the opposite view. He now felt obliged to inform the public that he had material evidence that Chertkov had meddled in the family's private affairs and instigated the final struggle that precipitated Tolstoy's departure.[92] He apologized for making these claims in a public forum, but he argued that he felt the need to defend his family's rights and closed by expressing his certainty that "all good, upright, honorable people" would understand his "pure intentions."

This moral high ground turned out to be more treacherous than he had imagined. *Gazeta kopeika* responded by expressing its confidence in quite the opposite outcome: "All honorable people, reading this unfortunate raving, will come to the conclusion that this junior Lev Tolstoy should take a drink of water and be quiet."[93] The next day the newspaper supported this claim by reporting, under the heading "The Scandal of Lev L'vovich Tolstoy's Letter," that the letter was being unanimously discounted as tactless, even in the halls of the Duma. As Chertkov's friends and colleagues rushed to defend him, they found the best strategy was to express indignation at Lev L'vovich's indiscretion at bringing such a private matter into the public's view.[94]

This view found support among moderate and left-leaning newspapers, which also took the opportunity to heap self-righteous scorn on *Novoe vremia* and *Golos Moskvy* for publishing Lev L'vovich's letter and for supporting his views in their editorials. Even Meshcherskii, the editor of the reactionary *Grazhdanin*, wrote that he could not imagine dragging such private matters into the arena of the press; he would have refused to print the letter out of respect for both Tolstoy and the "sanctity of family life."[95] Worse still, members of Lev L'vovich's own family spoke out against him. Ilya L'vovich answered first with a short letter and then a longer piece, printed in *Russkoe slovo* and reprinted in other papers, in which he argued that Lev L'vovich's measure of Chertkov's significance in the matter only belittled the image of their father.[96] Similar statements came from Sergei L'vovich and from his sisters, Tatiana and Aleksandra L'vovna. Chertkov himself declined to respond in print to Lev L'vovich's accusations but was reported to have commented that Lev L'vovich had only hurt himself with his letter.[97]

None of these objections prevented the conservative press from picking up the story and even adding some dubious details of its own.[98] The right-wing newspapers were particularly keen on playing up certain contrasts that Lev L'vovich had drawn in his letter, in which he had identified himself as the "proud son" of his father and his selfless mother and the descendant of a noble Russian family, whereas Chertkov was small-minded and self-centered and the "most evil enemy" of the entire civilized world, albeit "unintentionally," perhaps.[99] This view of Chertkov set the tone for others voicing anti-Tolstoyan views; Tolstoy himself, they suggested, had fallen under the baleful influence of his sycophantic admirers. A flowery description of Chertkov's headquarters at Teliatniki appearing in *Utro Rossii* prompted *Novoe vremia* to contrast "sectarian affectation, which inhibits simple and sincere feeling" to the more natural atmosphere of a family home.[100]

From this point of view Lev L'vovich became the patriotic defender of all that was noble, while Chertkov and his ilk represented social decay and corruption.[101] For Lev L'vovich's supporters, Chertkov was at best another Father Matvei, the spiritual adviser who had hastened Gogol's death, but at worst an enemy of the state, destroying one of Russia's national treasures in order to foment his own brand of anarchy.[102] Lev L'vovich used this latter charge (as well as one of his father's tropes) to defend his announcements to the media: "Can I remain silent about this when according to all the evidence I have Father was prepared to make peace with his loved ones and perhaps, who knows, from his pen would be pouring forth his very best works, full of peace and love, in the spirit of reconciliation with those around him?"[103] Chertkov had denied Tolstoy this imagined golden age through his selfish pursuit of Tolstoy's publishing rights, with which he could achieve wider distribution of the later works that espoused Chertkov's own cherished ideals.[104]

Lev L'vovich's letter met with more criticism than approval, however. In response, he sent a letter to *Russkoe slovo* apologizing if his actions were upsetting but nonetheless defending them.[105] A. Stolypin also admitted in *Novoe vremia* that Lev L'vovich's letter had produced an "unprecedented scandal," but described the public reaction as rather more ambiguous than had been suggested in other papers. He defended his paper's editorial ethics, arguing that the fact that the family in question was Tolstoy's justified what otherwise would have been reprehensible.[106] *Rech'* responded with an editorial entitled

"Shameful" in its November 19 issue, accusing *Novoe vremia* of fomenting a campaign of defamation against Tolstoy.

This war of words continued over the next two months, but reached a new peak in late January 1911. Sofia Andreevna refused to release some of Tolstoy's manuscripts to Aleksandra L'vovna, claiming that they were not subject to his will because he had given them to her before his death. On January 24 letters of protest from Aleksandra L'vovna and Chertkov appeared in the papers. Aleksandra L'vovna alluded to reasons that she did not feel comfortable relating (due to their "intimate character") for Lev Nikolaevich wanting her to have access to original manuscripts. Her insistence on acquiring these papers, she explained, stemmed from her sense of responsibility to her father and to the public:

> I understand very well that the heritage entrusted me by my father is not my own personal property to dispense with as I please, without answering to anyone else. I am firmly aware and try to remember at each step that I am about to take that I have a tremendous responsibility to not only my own conscience but also to other people. In view of this, I do not consider it possible to split my father's instructions to me into separate parts so that I can fulfill those which are advantageous to my mother and all our family, while allowing her not to fulfill those parts that are in the interest of all humanity.[107]

As Aleksandra L'vovna privileged the interests of all humanity, she dodged the family question, leaving it for Chertkov, who addressed it in his adjoining letter (which she had asked him to write). Chertkov claimed that Tolstoy had in fact never "given" the manuscripts to Sofia Andreevna but had allowed her to place them in the Historical Museum in Moscow for safekeeping—a measure that she had also occasionally undertaken against her husband's will. While making these clarifications, he also couched his response to Sofia Andreevna's claims in the language of respect for family privacy:

> In general we, as the closest executors of Lev Nikolaevich's will, are put in a very difficult position. The natural feeling of delicacy toward the widow of L. N. deprives us of the possibility of revealing *all* the known facts and circumstances that would immediately refute the charges of our antagonists. The latter, showing no such restraint, do not stop at backbiting, invention, shameful insinuations, and even slander in their attacks on us and take advantage of the fact that our hands are tied.

Chertkov's strategy in this letter, contrasting his own "natural delicacy" to the shamelessness of his accusers, was used throughout the dispute over Tolstoy's legacy. Both the family and the Tolstoyans used discretion to demonstrate that they were unwilling to stake Tolstoy's honor on scandalous revelations, each claiming to have trump cards that they could not play because "their hands were tied." When they could not speak openly about the private circumstances surrounding the will, both sides relied on innuendos, imputing ill will or avarice to the opposition. In a letter appearing in *Novoe vremia* on January 28, 1911, Sofia Andreevna's nephew, A. A. Bers, made the scandalous claim that Tolstoy had not written the contested will himself, as anyone who read it could plainly see ("Such a precise and incontestable document could not have been written by a philosopher and artist such as Lev Nikolaevich, who lived without any sort of ownership"). Chertkov himself, Bers claimed, had composed the will, and he was surprised that Chertkov could be so bold as to support his arguments by reference to a will that he himself had authored. Chertkov and Aleksandra L'vovna, who had been commissioned with the "enviable and respectable task" of assisting with the writing of Tolstoy's will, had not approached their task with the proper sensitivity and had therefore caused this family crisis. They were taking advantage of the tact of Sofia Andreevna, who had been a selfless preserver of Tolstoy's manuscripts, collecting them even in her own kitchen, where she saved them from a cook who wanted to use them to wrap pirozhki.[108] Recognizing that he himself was treading on thin ice, Bers included his own justification for speaking out about these family matters: "I confess that I write about the family of the deceased Lev Nikolaevich with considerable temerity. I visited Yasnaya Polyana from childhood and my view of this family does not allow the possibility that someone should dare to dig into it with dirty hands and threaten with some sort of revelations the friendly and loving family that lived in complete harmony for forty-eight years."[109]

These justifications were not enough to ward off the inevitable criticism, however. The three witnesses to the signing of the will—Gol'denveizer, Aleksei Sergeenko, and Anatolii Radynskii—sent a joint letter to the newspapers explaining that the will's officious tone was the handiwork not of Chertkov but of a lawyer hired by Tolstoy. They went on to express their surprise that Bers should have made such accusations on the basis of thirdhand evidence, and that, moreover, he had voiced his unfounded suspicions through the press.[110] The left-wing press joined in with rebukes as well. *Sovremennoe slovo* expressed indignation that Bers should portray Tolstoy as "a decrepit old man, practically a paralytic." The procedural complaints regarding the signing of the will revealed his personal interest in its outcome. Such slander, meanwhile, could come only from the pen of someone immune to the moral influence of his upbringing, education, or closeness to Tolstoy. The name of a great genius, the article concluded, should not be connected in this way to "petty people with their petty interests and foibles."[111]

Tolstoy's heritage was, on the contrary, considered national property.[112] A facsimile of the handwritten will was printed in *Rech'* on November 19;

and from the beginning, the public was invited to participate in determining the legitimacy of its own inheritance. This perspective was supported by the will itself (in which the public was the primary benefactor), as well as by the symbolic stature of Tolstoy as a national father figure. Maksimilian Voloshin wrote at the time that many people looked on Tolstoy's death as the loss of someone close to them, a notion confirmed by accounts such as the following (from Astapovo): "When the countess, sitting at the head of the bed, pulled back the sheet and I saw the dear features, which death had left in all their stately beauty, only softening their severeness, then through my tears I didn't see anything for a long time. I wanted to fall on my knees and weep as a son weeps when his dear father and friend has died."[113] Gorky, in a letter to A.V. Amfiteatrov, wrote that he felt himself "orphaned," and this trope was common among the eulogies for Tolstoy. The funeral reinforced this idea: Tolstoy's sons carried his coffin at first, but then it was borne by the local peasants, who accompanied the procession with a sign identifying themselves as the "orphaned peasants of Yasnaya Polyana." Merezhkovskii had written that Tolstoy's home was not Yasnaya Polyana but instead all of Russia, a notion that was echoed in a *Rech'* eulogy: "When there is a deceased person in a home a reverent, prayerful quiet governs the house. Right now we have a deceased person in Russia."[114] A writer for *Saratovskii vestnik* criticized Sofia Andreevna for telling a Tolstoyan that he could not take one of Tolstoy's hairs that was resting on his chest when he died: "The countess was not right. That which belongs to the people, that is a national relic, cannot belong to blood relations."[115]

As the family balanced its personal interests and property rights with those of the public, it learned that the public did not wish to observe the spectacle of splitting hairs that this compromise entailed. Although no one objected to the family's refusal of a request from a Moscow research institute for Tolstoy's brain, the contentious process of dividing up the more assessable portions of Tolstoy's patrimony elicited a great deal of emphatic criticism and disappointment.[116] When news of the civil procedure regarding Tolstoy's papers became public, *Sovremennoe slovo* complained: "That which seemed a poorly contrived rumor, which so strongly resembled slander, on further checking turned out, to our great dismay, to be the most genuine truth."[117] The next day the newspaper continued to decry this "bazaar of life's vanity," arguing that resolution of the dispute over the manuscripts through a judicial process would be a dishonor to Tolstoy's name, which the public conscience would not accept.[118] While the public had displayed a voracious appetite for details about Tolstoy's private life, now people complained that they were seeing too much: "It would be good to lower the curtain on this whole story, from which Tolstoy's name is suffering more than anything else." Though there was no consensus as to who was the wronged party in this dispute, dismay over its conspicuous nature was universal. *Novoe vremia,* which clearly supported the family's position, asked for "an immediate end to the unheard-of quarrel over Tolstoy's grave and works."[119]

Sofia Andreevna, meanwhile, worked to preserve her place in the history of her husband's life as his loving helpmate. She solicited the sympathy that was a widow's due, reminding the public that she had lived through indescribable trials. In an interview appearing in *Russkoe slovo,* she reported that she would set to work on the letters Tolstoy had written to her throughout his life, which, she assured her interviewer, would present a true picture of their relationship.[120] The publication of these letters would demonstrate her privileged intimacy with her husband and would outweigh other evidence that had been mounted against her. This intimacy had always been deeply epistolary: "There was a rumor recently that I was reading his papers, and that this was unpleasant to him. ... But really from the first day of our marriage we had an agreement—which was never broken—that we would read everything of each other's: letters, notes, manuscripts, diaries—everything."[121] In a January interview she attempted to confirm what certain factions of the media had suggested—that Tolstoy had perished prematurely because he had been denied her devoted attentions. As evidence, she reported that she had noticed that he was not well even before he left (effectively dodging blame for his illness, which some were saying was caused by his flight from her). Her heightened concern for his well-being had made her particularly vigilant, behavior that might have played a part, she surmised, in motivating Tolstoy to leave. The interviewer paraphrased her argument, "If S. A. had been with him, she would have been able to preserve his life: she was so familiar with even the slightest changes in his health."[122]

She was also pleased to report that Tolstoy maintained a similar concern for *her* well-being, even on the deathbed that she had been prohibited from attending. A letter to a *Novoe vremia* correspondent related how Tolstoy had told Tatiana L'vovna that nothing could be more important to him than news about Sofia Andreevna.[123] *Novoe vremia* was in general very willing to help Sofia Andreevna improve her image—it not only printed the letter but directed its readers to it with a front-page announcement promising that it would "dispel the cloud of slander covering Astapovo and Yasnaya Polyana." *Novoe vremia* also sponsored the work of Al. Ksiunin, whose long pro-Sofia Andreevna article of December 9 was later published as a book. Ksiunin painted an idealized picture of Tolstoy's life at Yasnaya Polyana, colored with homey diminutives and a piteous description of the betrayal of Sofia Andreevna's selfless concern for her husband: "'I always opened the door into the corridor—she says—and heard his every breath. I would look in on him, cover him up and kiss him like a child, then go back to my room and listen again. But that night I had been reading proofs until three in the morning, and then went to bed not feeling well at all and fell into a deep sleep."[124] Ksiunin added to this a heartrending picture of Sofia Andreevna as a lonely widow who, as her children returned to their own lives, would be left alone with her memories and with the commotion around her husband's grave. To those critical of Sofia Andreevna's behavior in the months preceding Tolstoy's departure, Ksiunin offered Sofia Andreevna's explanation that she had not been well in the summer: she was overcome with work and had too many responsibilities to be able to get away for a time, even when others told her she needed to do so. Ksiunin's Sofia Andreevna was a faithful wife, who had not only selflessly fulfilled her domestic duties but had also been a "spiritual participant" in her husband's work—only to find herself displaced by the nefarious "outside person," who appropriated what for her was her "light and air."[125]

The Right delighted in pointing to the apparent unworthiness of these outsiders to uphold the legacy of the great writer, which Sofia Andreevna had apparently done with such care while Tolstoy was alive. When a collection of Tolstoy's letters appeared just days after his death, the conservative press deplored the apparent exploitative timeliness of the publication by its Tolstoyan editors.[126] Better still, they found that several of Tolstoy's letters to his aunt A. A. Tolstaya were printed without proper approval.[127] Then in early January came rumors (which turned out to be false) that pages from Tolstoy's diaries had gone missing at Teliatniki. This raised concerns from all sides that Tolstoy's works would not be properly preserved. P. Nikolin, in *Sovremennoe slovo*, bemoaned the danger "to Russian literature, to Russia, and to the whole cultural world" that control of Tolstoy's works had fallen into private hands, which could be found untrustworthy on a number of counts. Most ominous of all was a report that Chertkov was bequeathed the right to decide which of Tolstoy's works to publish. While raising no question of Chertkov's loyalty to Tolstoy, the author felt that it was Chertkov's "moral obligation" to the whole world to declare that he would publish everything, without the exception of "even one letter."[128] Nikolin proposed that copyright should be given over to an impartial literary organization to prevent Tolstoy's heritage from being compromised by a "domestic dispute." Similar sentiments were expressed in *Novoe vremia*, though with somewhat more sensational questions as to what Chertkov might do with the manuscripts (he could burn them or send them to England, the reporter pointed out).[129]

The "outsider" (*postoronnii chelovek*), introduced by Sofia Andreevna in her first interviews after her husband's departure, became a stock figure in the Tolstoy tragedy as told by her supporters. They reminded their readers that an outsider like Chertkov could disturb a family's internal balance and interfere with the natural exchange of affection among its members.[130]

Chertkov reversed this stratagem when describing the event that had provoked Tolstoy's departure: he had awakened to the sound of "someone close to him" going through his papers.[131] From this perspective, the trouble was with interiority: Sofia Andreevna was *too* close, stifling Tolstoy with her meddling and prying. The mutual self-righteous indignation with which Chertkov and Sofia Andreevna regarded each other described a conflict over notions of intimacy: did it come from the spiritual affinity of friendship or from the conjugal familiarity of marriage? The public was itself divided on this issue, sending scores of letters of condolence to Sofia Andreevna and her family but also to Chertkov. The conservative press would complain that by rights this sympathy belonged only to the family, but this distinction was not so clear to others.[132] The trope of "the proud son," with which Lev L'vovich referred to himself in his public letter, became an object of derision for the left-wing press, who applied it with tongue-in-cheek to Sofia Andreevna's "proud nephew" A. A. Bers.

Anti-Chertkov reports referred to the love of the Tolstoys for the head of their family and suggested that rumors of domestic conflict were the slanderous inventions of Chertkov and his cohorts to legitimize their claim to Tolstoy's heritage. Lev L'vovich was seen as a patriotic defendant not only of familial rights but of the national cultural heritage as well.

Chertkov supporters, on the other hand, offered evidence of splendid Tolstoyan domestic order at Chertkov's quarters in Teliatniki.[133] *Gazeta kopeika* reported that the house was furnished as modestly as possible, and that everyone, including the hired help, shared meals equally. Chertkov served as the spiritual elder in a monastic Tolstoyan community, where reverence for Tolstoy was sovereign. Whereas Tolstoy's children had impugned the integrity of Chertkov's editorial intentions, here everyone was piously devoted to the preservation of Tolstoy's words. In contrast to the reported interference of Chertkov in the Tolstoy family's affairs, he confided that he had not attended the funeral in deference to Sofia Andreevna's feelings.[134] Chertkov impressed a correspondent for *Rannee utro* as an irreproachable custodian of Tolstoy's legacy by recording their interview about Astapovo on a phonograph record.[135]

Whether what Chertkov so demonstratively sought to preserve was actually the truth was another matter. The histrionic tenor of the struggle over Tolstoy's papers led the public to harken to less militant participants in the conflict. These efforts often did not prove any more productive, however. *Gazeta kopeika* reported that the more moderate Ilya L'vovich was writing a long article on his father's last days, which would bring to light interesting and intimate details. When Ilya's article appeared, however, it was qualified by a disappointing confession: whereas in his last letter to his father Ilya had acknowledged that he knew only half of what had been going on at Yasnaya, he now felt that he knew much less than half.[136] His disclaimer confirmed what was already clear from other evidence—that the boundaries of intimacy were indistinct, and were by no means clearly defined by the family.

Family Conflict Or Social Crisis?

Some observers were not so concerned with the intimate sphere but sought the reasons for Tolstoy's family crisis within Russian society. Nikolai Iordanskii, writing in the November issue of the left-leaning *Sovremennyi mir,* criticized the tendency of conservatives to connect the *ukhod* to Tolstoy's individual psychology rather than to the social conditions under which he lived.[137] Iordanskii blamed not the family but the larger social milieu that they represented. Tolstoy's family represented the ruling class, against which Tolstoy had struggled all his life (or, "to the death," as Iordanskii put it).[138] By choosing to leave his estate and find a new place in the world among the common people, Tolstoy had adopted a more grandly paternal role, for he was leading by example toward a higher moral truth. He was not so much abandoning his own family as he was adopting a greater one—a universal, human family, to which his wife and children also belonged, of course.

More "transcendental" observers provided florid accounts of a tired, wise old man heading off into the woods, turning a deaf ear to the voices of his family and of society and heeding only an inner voice telling him that it was his time to die. From this perspective, Tolstoy was superior to the family squabbles that might have precipitated his departure and to the social turmoil that had followed it. A writer for *Russkoe slovo* claimed that neither Chertkov nor anyone else could have had any ultimate influence on Tolstoy, who had instead been moved by the powers of "his own great soul."[139] For Petr Struve, Tolstoy's *ukhod* signaled a departure not from Yasnaya Polyana itself but rather from the mundane plane of existence that it represented.[140] When the story of the departure first broke, *Birzhevye vedomosti* called it "the drama of a powerful soul subjected to the ordinary, a mighty lion in the cage of a household pet."[141] A Kiev writer worried that Tolstoy would be found and returned to his "cage," an end that would be sadly prosaic.[142] A newspaper in Vienna commented that Tolstoy's family had not been able to keep up with him, and that he did not belong to them, or to any party, but instead to the whole world, to whom he had given a great model of a virtuous life.[143] By viewing the *ukhod* as a final gesture of moral inquiry, sparked by an intuition of death, these interpreters held Tolstoy aloft, above the squabbles that had arisen around his graveside.

These writers suggested that Tolstoy and life at Yasnaya Polyana were incongruous: the Tolstoy marriage was tragic, for it tried to bind the extraordinary to everyday reality. "A loving, devoted family—the most agreeable, from an outside perspective—imposes such fetters that the one who invisibly wears them may justifiably wish to throw them off. These fetters are not suspected by us, under our social conventions, according to which one doesn't carry a quarrel outside the hut."[144] The notion of a long-suffering Tolstoy, carrying the cross of his family life until the very end, became a stock trope. As *Vestnik Evropy* described it: "Only ten days before his death did Tolstoy lay down his cross. And Tolstoy died at peace with himself—in 'the world,' in the home of a railway stationmaster, surrounded by the care and love of 'the world.'"[145]

Those who sought to preserve the Tolstoy family, whether for personal or philosophical reasons, wanted Tolstoy to bear this burden, even if it meant a great self-sacrifice. Andrei L'vovich, in his last letter to his father, asked whether it would not have been better if he had carried this cross to the end. Remaining at Yasnaya Polyana in spite of his beliefs, Tolstoy had—albeit unhappily, reproachfully, and disapprovingly—preserved the sacrosanct space of marriage and family. From this perspective, marriage as Calvary was better than no marriage at all. But it was the public nature of this act, after all, that made it most threatening to the institution of the nuclear family. Tolstoy had suffered his family on a promontory that all of Russian society could see; at the time of his passion, however, he had abandoned that cross, suggesting to the world that responsibility to the family was ultimately secondary to the moral vision he pursued.

The Self at the Center

All this attention to Tolstoy's family was ultimately focused on the place of the individual. Tolstoy himself described his departure as an attempt to save himself—"not Lev Nikolaevich, but that something of which there is sometimes a spark in me." Everyone, it seemed, shared this concern, though they perhaps did not agree on what that something was in Tolstoy that should be saved. Lev L'vovich's letter charged that Chertkov did not understand his obligations to Tolstoy as "a living person." *Khar'kovskie vedomosti* reported that Tolstoy was surrounded by people concerned only with their own personal interests in him, quoting a recent letter of Tolstoy in which he had complained: "You cannot imagine to what extent I am alone, to what extent my real 'I' is scorned by everyone around me."[146]

Some interpreted Tolstoy's departure as reclamation of this "I." One journalist described it as an act of self-creation (*zhiznetvorchestvo*); while it awakened feelings of "an almost holy terror at its tragism and inevitability," it also represented "some sort of radiant victory, some sort of new dawn."[147] Tolstoy had provided a valuable lesson but one that had troubling implications for the family:

> There is something terrible not only for Sofia Andreevna in this "family trial." It is not a literary trial but a life trial—not of the Tolstoy family but of the authority of the family, of that structure in which psychological disharmony relentlessly and tormentingly (and under the very best intentions, the greatest mutual responsibility, the commitment to endure and accept everything) leads to bankruptcy. To create life in the sense of "base perpetuity," in the words of Vladimir Solov'ev, to create new individuals—that is the matter of the "family." But to create life, to create its forms—for that the family is not cut out.[148]

Tolstoy, this reporter wrote, revealed the antagonism between the family and life-creation.[149]

Vasilii Rozanov, two weeks after Tolstoy's death, published a piece in *Novoe vremia* making roughly the same argument. In his article on "The Rights of the Family in Marriage," Rozanov complained that the spiritual life of the country, in all its expressions in the arts and sciences, had become "unmarried phenomena."[150] "The family, as it were, has lost its luster, its spirit: it has become a *fact,* on one hand, of the individual, opposed to its creative work; creative work, on the contrary, grows out of the other, unmarried aspect. All civilization has in its essence become 'unmarried.'" In another *Novoe vremia* piece appearing a few days later Rozanov argued that Russian society had become too self-centered: "We are so decidedly anarchical because we live too individually."[151] Men'shikov used the Tolstoy story as a warning against the self-creative impulse in a November 5 editorial titled "A Lesson for the Young": Tolstoy's glorious life had been "poisoned by self-betrayal" as he pursued an ascetic life that went against his own true nature.[152]

Tolstoy stood in a contradictory position in relation to this crisis. On one hand, his social concerns strike an obvious contrast to the self-centered literary mien of the fin de siècle. In a year-end review *Novoe vremia* despaired of the possibility of replacing Tolstoy in literature because of the "overabundance of individualism" among the younger generation of writers.[153] On the other hand, his final gesture was widely interpreted as a triumph of the individual over society. The November issue of *Sovremennyi mir* carried a translation of a piece by Yves Scantrel, in which he announced with revelatory joy that in his final gesture Tolstoy had become "like unto himself."[154] Scantrel drew the same sentimental picture of the abandoned Sofia Andreevna as had others; however, here his goal was not to defend her but instead to highlight the weight of Tolstoy's decision to leave her:

> You left your wife sleeping, because she could not keep her vigil in anticipation of the dangerous hour; she was your friend for fifty years; she breathed serenely, her head lowered to the pillow in the nest of her wrinkles and gray hair. And you didn't even cast a glance at her, beloved old man, because you needed at last to turn your gaze upon yourself; you needed to heed the call of love, leaving your native blood, wife, children and setting off so far ahead. Truth is with you, holding you by your right hand. Purity precedes you, pointing to your old heart, from which the seal has fallen away, and behind you is death, but it is no more than a shadow."[155]

This "real" Tolstoy had cast off the falsehood of everyday life to be alone with God and was now radiant with "superhuman joy."[156]

This self-actualization balanced self-denial and self-awareness. In late November 1910, newspapers in Kiev printed a letter from a student, B. S. Mandzhos, which had been sent to Lev Tolstoy that year, presenting him with the following challenge: "Why haven't you, a teacher and example to us, renounced yourself? Why haven't you realized your great ideas in flesh and blood? Renounce your estate, divide your property among your kin and the poor, leave nothing for yourself and wander from town to town without a penny. Deny yourself, if you can't deny your loved ones in the native circle of your family." Mandzhos was deeply convinced that a period of neo-Christianity, in which good, honest, idealistic people would once again be born, would surely follow.[157] Like Christ, Tolstoy could usher in an age of spiritual enlightenment through an individual act of self-renunciation. But such exemplariness brought with it a sort of obverse "anxiety of influence": authenticity and integrity were potentially undermined by the desire to instruct and produce effects. Tolstoy answered Mandzhos that though there was not a day in which he did not consider doing what had been suggested, such things could not be done in order to affect others (which was not in anyone's power to do) or in response to any but an internal prompting: "when it will be unavoidable not for intended external goals, but for the satisfaction of the internal demands of the spirit...when it becomes as morally impossible to stay in the present position as it is physically impossible not to cough when you cannot breathe."

Tolstoy's reply—in which he told Mandzhos that his letter had made a deep impression on him but asked that no one be told of their correspondence—reflects this agenda. Moved by this external voice, Tolstoy sought to internalize it as best he could, and in general we find him during his last years struggling to distinguish his own voice among the countless voices giving him advice or questioning his behavior. When four of his children wrote him letters after his departure explaining their views on his actions, Tolstoy singled out those of Sergei and Tatiana, which explicitly refrained from giving any advice, as being particularly understanding of his position. While at Astapovo, he clearly stated that he did not want to know what was being written about him in the newspapers. The decision to leave his family had to find its authorization in this internal voice, which, as he had written to Mandzhos, was a visceral force. This voice had spoken to Tolstoy on the morning he left, when he heard the sound of Sofia Andreevna in his study: "The disgust and indignation grow; I gasp for breath, take my pulse: 97. I can't lie down and suddenly make the final decision to leave."[158] He had been waiting for this voice to speak for a long time: in his earlier farewell letter to Sofia Andreevna, from 1897, Tolstoy had written that he was not leaving for himself but because he could not do otherwise.[159]

The public similarly tried to discriminate between these external and internal voices. The letter from Mandzhos and Tolstoy's reply, which were widely printed in the papers shortly after Tolstoy died, provided evidence as to how inscrutable this distinction could be. As Tolstoy searched for this authentic voice, he undertook a complex negotiation between public and private, self and other. This was the paradox of the "departure from the world into the world." As Tolstoy secretly abandoned his private home to enter the world in search of solitude, he embarked on an equally obscure journey across the boundaries between the self and its public persona.

The Home-Museum

No small part of this paradox is the extent to which the everyday life that Tolstoy left behind has remained so large a figure in his cult. In spite of Tolstoy's ultimate rejection of its comforts, Yasnaya Polyana still stubbornly insists on defining the essence of Tolstoy. Meshcherskii referred to Yasnaya Polyana as a charmed "Zion," and it has continued to play this role in the years since. Yasnaya Polyana is the most popular of the nineteenth-century Russian country estates to have been preserved to this day; people come from all over the world to see the habitat, and therein learn something of the spirit, of Tolstoy. No other homestead in Russia is so closely associated with an author.

The creation of a national Tolstoy museum at Yasnaya began immediately after his departure. Sofia Andreevna's sister, T. A. Kuzminskaia, came to Yasnaya Polyana the day after Tolstoy left and took care to preserve everything as it was, including a burned candle and two apples in his study. A copy of Tolstoy's *Circle of Reading* and *For Every Day* were placed on display, open to their November 7 entries.[160] A cottage industry developed around tourism at the estate, as the village peasants began offering their lodgings and their services as local guides. Within the Tolstoy house, Sofia Andreevna, Valentin Bulgakov, and the servants gave tours of Lev Nikolaevich's quarters.[161] It was also common to visit Chertkov's quarters at Aleksandra L'vovna's nearby estate, where one could view six hundred photographs of Tolstoy and visit his favorite horse "Delir" and his dog "Belka."[162] Reports on the loyalty, grief, and fond memories of the Yasnaya Polyana peasants reinforced the image of Tolstoy as the benevolent patriarch of his estate.[163] A report that an American syndicate wanted to buy Yasnaya Polyana and set up an exhibition of American farm machinery elicited concern: "It would be shameful if the sacred and very best place in Russia were to be turned into an obscene marketplace, a bazaar of worldly bustle and vulgarity."[164]

So, too, has the Tolstoy marriage had its lasting legacy. Over the course of the twentieth century a series of books appeared describing the genre "Lev Nikolaevich or Sofia Andreevna?" Vladimir Chertkov, Aleksandr Gol'denveizer, Dushan Makovitskii, Valentin Bulgakov, and five of the Tolstoy children published memoirs, while countless others have joined in describing the troubled relationship of Sofia Andreevna and Lev Nikolaevich. These studies of the Tolstoy marriage might someday themselves be the subject of a study in changing twentieth-century views on the family, gender, and sexuality, but they attest primarily to the abiding fascination of the public with the private life of Lev Tolstoy and his family.

In patriarchal cultures the death of the father has tremendous consequences for the family.[165] Tolstoy's death was certainly typical in this regard, but it also played a singular role in provoking the Russian people to reassess their patriarchal traditions. As they discussed what Tolstoy's passing meant for Russia, they always considered this question in the context of what it had meant for his family. Even as he abdicated his traditional role as head of the family, he nonetheless symbolically remained in a position that was accorded great reverence in Russian society. Thus the children, like Sofia Andreevna, needed always to maintain a deferential stance toward him; when they did not, their position could be immediately undermined with reference to family honor. In the contest over the will, arguments were consistently made in deference to this honor, which was viewed as the contestants' only legitimate motivation. Even Andrei L'vovich told the press after Tolstoy's departure that the children did not consider it within their rights to interfere with their father's actions, as his will was "sacred" to them. Though fiercely loyal to his mother, he felt it necessary to proclaim the family's ultimate allegiance to the father. It was understood that the representation of loyalties would play a pivotal role in forming the public opinions that had become so important in the private matters of the Tolstoy family. Loyalty to father and family became a steadying standard against which unprecedented actions and arguments were measured. Ilya L'vovich's memoirs of Astapovo contrast his uncertainty as to how the deathbed scene should have been managed with a keen understanding of his mother's sacrifice in accepting what had been deemed best for her husband.[166]

Family life was also a test for Tolstoy, as some dismissed the morality motivating his departure because it had caused pain for his family.[167] He had in essence abandoned his own family to take on a larger role as a national father figure; his last days, even as he sought privacy, would be a public testament of his values. The spiritual legacy he had bestowed could not, however, be detached from the everyday dramas that had shaped it. Those who defended more traditional family values cast doubt on Tolstoy's fitness to play this larger "father" role if he could not be a proper father to his own family. Tolstoy's life at Yasnaya Polyana was seen as a representation of his personal integrity but also of the inherent moral value of the belief systems that were in contest there.[168] I. Leonov, writing in *Saratovskii vestnik* on November 14, justified the media's insistence on removing "the veil of family privacy." "Tolstoy belongs to the whole world, to all humanity," he insisted, "and it is important for everyone to know why he couldn't make himself a peaceful abode in his own home."[169]

A *Moskovskie novosti* editorial admitted that it was awkward to pry into a family's private affairs but offered that the family would do well to clarify publicly the circumstances surrounding Tolstoy's "incomprehensible" last days, which appeared to them to represent some "fight for the soul" of the old man.[170] This "fight" was largely waged with weapons of representation: Tolstoy working to create a model of moral rectitude, which the Tolstoyans projected as an icon and Sofia Andreevna sought to expose as artifice. The dispute that followed Tolstoy's death provoked the public to question these representations and to seek less compromised evidence in the realm of the private. They found that perpetual scrutiny had left little of this privacy intact, even in the realm of Tolstoy's papers. Tolstoy's earlier parting letter to Sofia Andreevna, from 1897, was produced in *Rech'* as "the most important document" to explain what had happened at Yasnaya Polyana; much was made of the fact that he had never given the letter to her but had left it for her to read only after his death.[171] This letter was thus supposed to represent a more authentic private space—one that had not been invaded by another reader during his lifetime. Sofia Andreevna also understood this approach: her own parting letter, addressed to the newspapers, was a kind of anti-announcement—one that would be read after the fact and would gain credibility by the restraint she had exercised in maintaining the privacy of the feelings it expressed. Her "press release" turns this space inside out, demonstrating plainly that her "privacy" is dominated by the presence of the reader, whether in the present or the future. She sees the diaries as a last line of defense—records that will shape her memory long after she is gone.

Lev L'vovich likewise understood this dynamic, pronouncing that he had documentary evidence of Chertkov's treachery that could not be produced in public; he had thrown open the doors of Yasnaya Polyana too widely, however, and the public was inclined to dismiss his incriminations because of his indiscretion.[172] Though Sofia Andreevna refrained from the scandalizing methods of her son, she had no less trouble negotiating the boundaries between public and private. As she created media events, orchestrated public appearances, and openly worked to correct public opinion in her letters, diaries, and interviews, her artifice undermined her at every step. Her designs were thoroughly documented by others, who revealed them to the public in their own diaries and memoirs. She was, in her defense, speaking in a language that was just forming—one that would develop over the course of the twentieth century into a rhetoric for negotiation of privacy in the public sphere. It was one that was used no more effectively, perhaps, by Chertkov and the Sergeenkos, who were accused of manufacturing Tolstoy's death. Tolstoy himself proved most skilled in this delicate art—he had somehow intuited, perhaps aesthetically, that reticence was the final refuge. He made no public pronouncements during his last days but spoke only through the private documents that proved so authoritative in the public sphere.

However, his own fugitive identity, his "Nikolaev," reminds us that even this last attempt at secrecy was also informed by the expectations of the future reader. Presumably he hoped that his new name might obscure his identity in a telegraph office or might also protect his secrets at home (though neither would likely have been the case). In fact, the name is oddly revealing, as if necessary to the inevitable narrative of his departure: the nobleman turned peasant, adopting a patronymic surname appropriate to his new identity. Beneath this surface, however, we find another Tolstoy: "not Lev Nikolaevich, but that something of which there is sometimes a spark in me." Tolstoy left in search of a self that could not be named; and it was this person, so full of narrative and moral potential, to whom he sought to give greater scope.

This departure was invoked by Christ ("leave thy family") and the Tolstoyans ("renounce yourself") but also by the public, who for their own reasons demanded that the great writer relinquish himself. There was much to be done with his legend. Thus the anticipated "Tolstoyan" story would be told, but in the context of others, replete with that strange mixture of overabundant revelation and evasion that makes a modern public scandal of private life. These alternate stories obscured the integrity sought by Tolstoy and his admirers but tell much about the history of private life and celebrity in Russia. The economy of information that shaped the story—the relentless intrusion into the private sphere—essentially authenticated the searching of the spiritual wanderer. The Russian "nomadic messiah" described by Berdiaev was left at large, pointing to growing anxieties about domestic life in Russian society. How could one's higher moral destiny be reached in the confines of the home, a space so compromised by the demands of everyday life? Tolstoy's rejection of the family and departure in search of a new life anticipated changes that Russian society had long contemplated and would be asked to accept en masse just a few years later. 1917 would usher in an age in which private property, traditional family values, and the comforts of the hearth would be rejected in the name of collective good. Tolstoy's departure offered a view of this new world, brave and vulnerable at once; it is no wonder that the Russian public looked upon it with such profound curiosity.

Фот. В. Черткова.

Всѣ существа неразрывно связаны между собою.
Не думай, чтобы могло быть благо отдѣльнаго существа или чтобы зло отдѣльнаго существа не было бы
зломъ всего міра и не отразилось бы на тебѣ.

Левъ Толстой.

7. "All beings are inseparably connected one to another. Do not think that there could be some good existing of a separate being, or that the evil of some other being is not the evil of all the world and has not had some effect on you."

2

Narrative Transfigurations of Tolstoy's Final Journey

From Petersburg, 4–11:46 a.m.
Astapovo St. Ryaz. Ur. RR to Count Lev Nikolaevich Tolstoy
From the very first moment of your break with the Church I have prayed and do pray unceasingly that the Lord will return you to the Church. It may be that He will soon call you to His judgment, and I beseech you now (as you are sick) to make your peace with the Church and with the Orthodox Russian people. May the Lord bless and keep you.
    —METROPOLITAN ANTHONY

On the evening of November 4, 1910, in a state of delirium as his condition worsened, Tolstoy began to make motions on his blanket with his hands. Though he was only semiconscious at the time, those at his bedside interpreted the movements as an attempt to write—the "great writer of the Russian land" was reflexively repeating the motions that had filled so much of his life, setting forth the meditations that issued from his approaching death. This moment epitomizes the narrative dynamic of Tolstoy's last days, when his every movement was recorded and vigorously interpreted in the Russian media. When he left his home in the middle of the night and set out on his final journey, it was assumed that he was composing a conclusion to his life, and that he had something decisive to communicate to his audience. When he fell ill and could no longer complete this work, his readers gave their own, sometimes quite contradictory, directions to his movements. The reactionary Orthodox newspaper *Kolokol*, for instance, had another interpretation of Tolstoy's gesture on his covers: his hand, they agreed, spoke of what was going on in his heart but was making the sign of the cross rather than the pen.[1] The dying Tolstoy was repenting and remembering his faith, for at this deepest, unconscious level, he was not a writer but an Orthodox Christian.

Perhaps no one watched Tolstoy's last movements with greater anticipation than the two groups described above—one building the cult of the writer, the other defending the cult of Christ. During his last thirty years Tolstoy had repeatedly challenged the moral authority of the Orthodox faith and had himself grown into the role of a secular patriarch to the Russian people. He had essentially defined his own confessional space, and his followers seized on the events of his last days to persuade the public of its integrity; custodians of the Orthodox Church, on the other hand, would argue that the Tolstoyan faith had not sustained him in his last "desperate" moments and had ultimately been abandoned. The intensive coverage of the event by the media heightened the stakes, as did the sympathy of the public toward what was widely identified as Tolstoy's "pilgrimage." Church officials initially endorsed this interpretation when Tolstoy made his initial stop at Optina monastery, but ultimately they did their utmost to subvert the perception of the journey as a religious event.

If this pilgrimage was not Orthodox, however, it proved to be deeply Russian. Tolstoy's farewell note explaining that he was doing what was "usually" done by men of his age, who "[leave] worldly life to spend their last days in peace and solitude," situated his departure in the ancient traditions of Russian folk Christianity. He was following in the footsteps of Alexander Nevsky and Alexander I, who, according to popular legend, had abandoned the Russian throne to take monastic vows.[2] Such a descent appealed to the Russian popular imagination, and the public was quick to identify with an aristocrat rejecting his wealth and comfort to live among the people. But it was also a proto-Christian gesture—an imitation of Christ retreating to the desert and to Gethsemane.[3] When it was performed by someone who had been excommunicated from the Church, the Orthodox hierarchy was confronted with a defining moment of heterodoxy. If Tolstoy's pilgrimage would lead him to peasant huts rather than holy shrines, and if he wished to pray in the forests of St. Sergius to a God that had been known to Buddha as well as Christ, then how could the custodians of the "true faith" condone it? The Church's hopes for the return of a "prodigal son" were frustrated, and its clerics found themselves describing as a "spiritual tragedy" that which the public was inclined to view as a moral victory.[4]

The hope of Archbishop Arsenii of Novgorod that Tolstoy would "reject his faith in humanity and return to that pure Christian faith, according to which millions of Russians live," quantified the significance that was assigned to Tolstoy's example. Arsenii's belief in the reversibility of Tolstoy's views, and in the potential for the Church to suddenly reap benefit from its greatest enemy, explains many of the Church's actions in Tolstoy's last days. Clerics argued that Tolstoy had abandoned his former views and wished to return to the Church, and that he had ended his life a spiritual fugitive, rather than a seeker, in flight *from* his own spiritual demons, rather than in journey *toward* his own Jerusalem. They countered the popular teleology of Tolstoyan triumph with their own view of the author's theology as a dead end. The Church understood that this tale of apostasy would not be as appealing as one of apotheosis and did all that it could to bring about the story it really wanted to tell—of a repentant Tolstoy affirming the authority of the national church. It sent emissaries to Tolstoy's bedside in the hope of attaining a last-minute repentance, exploiting every angle to make this possible.

When these efforts failed, the Church intended to show that it was the best interpreter of a narrative of which the Orthodox God, and not Tolstoy, had been the provident author. In this, too, it failed, as Astapovo was fashioned in the popular press into a modern Assumption. Church officials then watched as Tolstoy was given a national funeral without their participation or sanction. Their sacred burial rites were incorporated into these ceremonies, which became public demonstrations of rebellion against church authority.[5] Tolstoy's death proved a defining moment not only for him but for Russian society as well; as people argued over what had happened at Astapovo and how their beloved writer should be buried, they set forth new cultural paradigms. The pages that follow describe the failure of the Church to pass final judgment on Tolstoy; the public instead made its own judgments, referring to its own "Book of Life," a text for which Tolstoy had written many drafts, but which was given final shape by the newspapers that set it into print in November 1910.

Tolstoy's Challenge to Orthodoxy

Tolstoy's confrontation with the Orthodox Church began in the period following his "spiritual crisis" in the late 1870s, after the completion of *Anna Karenina*.[6] Tolstoy began a study of Christian spirituality, became convinced that Orthodox theology had distorted Christ's principles, and took it on himself to correct this problem in a series of critical studies and polemical works.[7] He studied the original Greek texts of the Gospels, as well as the work of historians, in an effort to restore the original meaning of the texts. The result of these labors, which Tolstoy would later call his most difficult and rewarding, was a series of retellings of the Gospels: *Union and Translation of the Gospels, A Short Summary of the Gospels, The Teachings of the Twelve Apostles,* and *The Teaching of Christ, Summarized for Children*.[8] These works portrayed Christ as a man rather than a divinity and systematically stripped away the healings, resurrections, and other miracles that, Tolstoy argued, had been written into the text by the builders of the Christian cult. For Tolstoy the gospels were the foundation not for a mystery religion but for a system of practical ethics; they described a life that was not preternatural or inimitable but was instead an illustration of the moral potential of every individual to live according to the precepts that had guided Christ. Tolstoy viewed this argument not as blasphemy but as a return to the first principles of Christianity.[9]

In his later literary works spiritual rebirth was often predicated on rejection of the most sacred rituals of Orthodoxy. *Father Sergius* describes a revered Orthodox monk whose spiritual strength diminishes as his tremendous cult following grows; though Sergius leads an ascetic life and is ascribed the ability to heal, he is motivated by vanity and begins to lead a Tolstoyan moral life only when divested of his fame. Sergius abandons his monastic cave to pursue a true Tolstoyan askesis by tending a garden and teaching peasant children in an obscure Siberian village. In "Two Old Men," one pilgrim travels to Jerusalem on a highly ritualized tour of the shrines, only to understand on his return the moral superiority of his fellow traveler, who had stayed behind to help a destitute village recover from a failed harvest. For Tolstoy "the greatest story ever told" was one of humility and service; ritual and superstition only interfered with ethical practice. The same held true for Christ himself, who in Tolstoy's view held greater meaning as a human moral example than as a divine moral authority.

The Church had little tolerance for the notion that Christ might have been a common man. Konstantin Pobedonostsev's complaint to Tolstoy described this essential difference: "After reading your letter, I saw that your faith is one thing, and that mine and that of the Church is another, and that our Christ is not your Christ. Mine I know as a man of strength, healing the weak; but in yours I thought I detected the features of one who is feeble and himself needs to be cured." Pobedonostev's grim view of Tolstoy's Christ underscores a key element in Tolstoy's debate with the Church; for all his belief in God Tolstoy nonetheless joined in the modern deconstruction of Christian metaphysics. When he argued that "The Kingdom of God Is Within You" he described a Protestant sense of personal ethical responsibility but also a different relationship to God. He had resolved an existential crisis by finding faith in a mortal Christ who had offered redemption to humanity not by dying on the cross but by living a moral life.

Tolstoy's critique of the Church was widely considered the most significant challenge that the Russian Orthodox faith faced in the late nineteenth and early twentieth centuries.[10] The Church found itself redefining Christ for the masses because Tolstoy had redefined him.[11] They watched grimly as Tolstoy became a national conscience, an ethical thorn in the side of the Russian church and state. He held the government accountable to the tenets of the faith it espoused and challenged the principles of Orthodoxy when they were used to legitimate abuses of human rights.[12] Nonviolence, vegetarianism, and celibacy were brought into the mainstream of ethical discourse by his passionate arguments in their defense and were practiced by schools of his followers across Russia. Tolstoyan communes were organized in Russia and abroad, while his religious writings were printed in inexpensive editions and distributed by his followers with missionary zeal.

Pobedonostsev, as chief procurator of the Holy Synod, joined a host of church leaders seeking to circumscribe Tolstoy's moral influence.[13] The activities of Tolstoy and his followers were closely monitored by the Church and were often curtailed by criminal proceedings and imprisonment.[14] Threats of eternal damnation were also used, particularly where the impression could be most effective. When Tolstoyans began distributing literature to participants in the Kursk-Korennyi procession of the Cross, a church along the route displayed an icon of the Last Judgment that depicted Tolstoy burning prominently in Satan's inferno.[15] Peasants were warned that he was a demonic incarnation who would lead them into the fires of hell. In 1891–1892, when Tolstoy organized a widespread famine relief program in the Ryazan region, local clergy countered Tolstoy's philanthropy by telling peasants that he was the Anti-Christ, and that the bread he was giving away was of the devil. Stories circulated that Tolstoy was branding peasants on the forehead with the sign of the devil or buying their souls for eight rubles apiece.[16]

Local parishes throughout the country joined this campaign, and a number of prominent clergymen used the Orthodox cathedral as a bully pulpit for attacks on Tolstoy. The leading Orthodox charismatic of the day, Ioann of Kronstadt, made the struggle with Tolstoy a personal obsession, publishing a series of pamphlets that described him as the most dangerous of heretics, a companion to Judas, and a pagan "lion/Leo" feasting on Christians.[17] Archbishop Nikanor of Kherson and Odessa was another leading opponent, whose collection of sermons against Tolstoy's teachings went through a number of editions. Though more philosophical than Ioann, he was not immune to infernal flourishes, concluding one oration with a passage from Matthew suggesting that "every tree that does not bring forth good fruit" should be cut down and thrown into the fire.[18] References to such "cutting down" or "cutting off" are abundant in the Church's anti-Tolstoyan literature, invoking both divine retribution and the need to cut off, or excommunicate, Tolstoy from the Orthodox Church.[19]

Rumors of such an act had begun circulating in the late 1880s, and they reached a peak in 1892 during the famine relief campaign in Ryazan. The relief program disturbed the Church on several counts, not only drawing widespread attention to Tolstoy's charity but also offering a public workshop on his ideas. Peasants were served vegetarian meals by enthusiastic

8. (8a) A daily wall calendar from 1902, the year after Tolstoy was excommunicated from the Church. (8b) A bookcase designed by I. P. Ropet as an altar to Tolstoy.

Tolstoyans, who outpaced the Church in exercising the most practical of ethics. Church officials were deeply disturbed by the popular appeal Tolstoy gained through the campaign and began searching for a pretext for decisive action against him.[20] A scandal surrounding the publication of an article in the London *Daily Telegraph* about the famine (in which Tolstoy assigned responsibility for the peasants' hunger to the Russian aristocracy) seemed to provide the necessary justification. In fact, a recommendation was made at the time to sequester Tolstoy in the infamous Spaso-Efimevskii monastery in Suzdal, which had served as a "church prison" for over 150 years.[21] This measure was not taken at the time due to Alexander III's determination not to make a martyr of him. With Alexander's death, however, the campaign for excommunication was revived—in 1896 Konstantin Pobedonostsev wrote to S. A. Rachinskii, concluding a diatribe against Tolstoy with a prediction that the question of his excommunication would be taken up after the coronation of Nicholas II.[22]

It was not, however, until 1899, when *Resurrection* began appearing in the journal *Niva,* that the campaign achieved decisive momentum. The work that ultimately provoked the Church to act was not a political or religious tract but instead Tolstoy's last novel. Popular history has maintained that it was in fact Tolstoy's caricature of Pobedonostsev in the novel that galvanized the Church's resolve. Whether or not this was the case, Pobedonostsev was hardly the sole instigator.[23] Archbishop Amvrosii of Kharkov, scheming with the Kiev Metropolitan Ioannikii, sent a letter to the Synod urging excommunication and authored a protocol of the official pronouncement.[24] Tolstoy became seriously ill later that year, and in 1900 Ioannikii circulated on behalf of the Synod a secret letter instructing local church officials that, in the event of Tolstoy's death, no offices should be performed unless Tolstoy had repented beforehand.[25] In effect, this was a preliminary excommunication, and its language clarifies the extent to which the act was intended to defend both creed and crown: the turn of the century was a time of popular unrest in Russia, and the letter warned that services for Tolstoy, an outspoken critic of both church and state, might serve as opportunities for political demonstrations. In 1901, as this spirit of dissent spread throughout the country, Amvrosii again proposed excommunication, and this time the Synod agreed.

V. M. Skvortsov, the publisher of *Missionerskoe obozrenie,* an influential ally of the Synod, and a vocal anti-Tolstoyan, was given an urgent commission on February 5, 1901, to outline the principles of Tolstoy's beliefs for the use of the Synod. This evidence was needed for a decree that was being prepared by the Synod to protect the Orthodox faithful from Tolstoy's influence by clarifying how he had betrayed his faith.[26] The *Poslanie* they eventually issued was, in fact, not a formal "excommunication" in that it did not conclude with the traditional litany of anathemas. Accounts of the preparation of the document indicate that the Synod worked to soften its language, to construe the gesture as a benevolent effort to point out the error of Tolstoy's ways, and to leave open the possibility that he might return to the Church. Metropolitan Antonii stated this intention in a note to Pobedonostsev regarding the semantic strategy for the edict: "not a judgment on the dead, as they say of the secret protocol, and not an indictment without a hearing, but a 'warning to the living.'"[27] As powerful as its antipathy to Tolstoy might be, the Church found it expedient to take a position that was clearly mediated by Tolstoy's popularity.

Despite their efforts, however, Tolstoy and the public perceived the proclamation as an excommunication. Intended to stigmatize Tolstoy and dissipate his moral authority, the act of the Holy Synod instead magnified his support and drew attention to his heretical beliefs. Indeed, Tolstoy's popularity and authority only grew as a result of the excommunication. Demand for his writings increased, particularly for those that had stimulated the Church's act (many of which had been published only outside Russia). Tolstoy received a flood of letters of support and found crowds of supporters gathering at the entrance to his Moscow home. If the Church believed that it could topple Tolstoy from his lofty pedestal in the eyes of the public, it found instead that the writer's support was often more stable than its own. The *Poslanie* missed its mark, and its backfire only added insult to the injury of Tolstoy's "heresy."[28]

When the sympathies aroused by the excommunication rose to yet another peak during Tolstoy's illness in 1901–1902, the prospect of striking the heretic without injuring national pride over his many accomplishments, and without wounding the feelings of his many admirers, became still more dubious. As Tolstoy's struggles with malaria, typhoid fever, and lung, liver, and heart ailments brought him close to death, the public warmly reiterated the affection and support they had shown at the time of the excommunication. Yasnaya Polyana was flooded with letters from well-wishers, and when it was decided that Tolstoy needed the warmer climate of the south, his train was met with large demonstrations at stations along his route. A crowd of three thousand gathered at the station in Kharkov, sending him off with shouts of support and best wishes for his recovery.[29]

The Church sought a position less antagonistic to these sentiments, which only heightened as Tolstoy's illness progressed. When his condition finally became critical, the Church issued a secret circular (as it would in 1910) forbidding performance of church services; but it also undertook a desperate scheme, instructing a local priest to enter the house if Tolstoy was dying

and to emerge immediately after his death and announce that he had renounced his heretical beliefs.[30] This plan was discovered, leading Tolstoy's
family and friends to devise a plan to cover up his death until accurate accounts of his passing had been dispatched to reliable sources. Tolstoy finally
recovered, but the incident set the stage for his eventual death in 1910, when
access to his quarters would be strictly controlled.[31]

The national celebration of Tolstoy's eightieth birthday in 1908 was another dark moment for the Church. Tolstoy confessed his own embarrassment over the fanfare, which included such tributes as the following hymn,
found in a handbook on celebrating the event in schools:

Hymn to Lev Nikolaevich Tolstoy[32]
in 3 children's or women's parts

Our wise and gentle teacher
Turn to us your sensitive ear
The Almighty extended
Over you a mighty spirit.

With wise and humble word
You prevail over the universe
Under God's protection
From those heights of peace and quiet.

Draw us little ones to you
Let us look upon your face
In the light of scarlet mountain dawns
Show us the bright path!

We gather grasses from the hills
We gather flowers too
Singing out in hymns of praise
We make wreaths in your honor

Shield our grasses and flowers
with your pure gaze
Give a greeting answer
To our boisterous songs

We will nimbly weave all the rays
of your eyes into wreaths
We will collect the grain
of your blessed speech in baskets

The light of love will catch fire
In the universe from those rays
The light of love, holy and imperishable
You, call us to you!

9. This folksy drawing of "Tolstoy with the children of Yasnaya Polyana" is based on a famous photograph. It has been flavored with a Dickensian touch.

> We will spread the seed
> Of your words in a benevolent ring
> And love for everyone, a great wonder,
> Will flower anew in the fields
>
> You are a teacher, wise in life
> A friend to the meek and a father.
> Pride and glory of all the fatherland,
> You are a wondrous crown of the world.

Admirers of Tolstoy throughout the world were in fact being urged to join this chorus to sing his praises. A Los Angeles monthly titled *Fellowship*, devoted to "religion without superstition," compared Tolstoy to St. Paul, St. Francis of Assisi, and Buddha and cited his anniversary as the first time in human history that the world would unite in celebrating the birthday of one man. "The celebration of Tolstoy's eightieth birthday, by artists and literary men, by reformers and statesmen, and by men of the world, has a greater significance, and holds a greater promise for the future progress of humanity, than the sailing of any fleet, the outcome of any local election, or the triumph or decline of any church, because it is the race's tribute to a man of principle; and men of principle are the world's ultimate redeemers."[33]

The Church again tried to limit these attentions, instructing clergy to discourage their parishioners from participating in the anniversary celebrations and issuing a statement urging Orthodox believers to boycott the event. Again articles and pamphlets were produced to counter the widespread publicity in favor of Tolstoy.[34] Anxiety over Tolstoy's influence was so high that a local censor seized an issue of the conservative Kharkov weekly *Drug naroda* because it reprinted a *Kolokol* attack on Tolstoy in which his beliefs were elaborated too extensively.[35] In another misstep, a scandal arose over reports that Ioann of Kronshtadt (evidently feeling that eighty birthdays were enough for Tolstoy) had composed a prayer asking the Heavenly Father to rid the earth of the Yasnaya Polyana heretic and his followers.[36]

The Church also made benevolent gestures of "paternal" concern for Tolstoy throughout the period of their estrangement; emissaries were often sent to the Moscow and Yasnaya Polyana homes of the "wayward son" with undisguised agendas. Dmitrii Troitskii, a priest in the Tula prison, visited Yasnaya Polyana in 1897 and thereafter took it upon himself, with the blessing of the Tula Bishop Pitirim, to serve as Tolstoy's spiritual adviser. These missionary efforts continued to the end of Tolstoy's life, but two sets of letters between Troitskii and Tolstoy from October 1910 show little evidence of progress. Tolstoy's second answer to Troitskii, written just five days before he left home, included a passionate resistance to these overtures.[37] The previous year, after a visit by the above-mentioned Parfenii, Tolstoy indicated in his diary a particular sensitivity to at least one of the purposes of these visits:

It is especially unpleasant that he asked to be informed when I was dying. If only they don't think up something along the lines of persuading people that I "repented" before dying. And for this reason I pronounce, and, it seems, I am repeating, that *to return to the Church, to receive communion before dying I cannot do, just the same as I cannot before dying speak obscene words or look at obscene pictures, and thus everything that will be said about my deathbed repentance and confession is a lie.*

I say this because there are people for whom, according to their religious understanding, confession is some sort of religious act, i.e., a striving toward God; for me any such outward activity, like confession, would be a renunciation of the spirit, of goodness, of the teaching of Christ, and of God.[38]

Tolstoy had clarified these feelings before. He had said in 1901 that there could be no discussion of his "reconciliation" with the Church, the very legitimacy of which he did not recognize.[39] Sergei L'vovich recalls his father suggesting that they ask him in his last moments whether he considered his faith to be true; if he could no longer answer with words, he would nod his head.[40] This disposition is corroborated by Ivan Nazhivin, who writes that a month before his death Tolstoy told him: "I would sooner give the bodies of my children and loved ones to be ravaged by hungry dogs than to summon some sort of special people to perform a religious ritual over their bodies."[41]

The Events of 1910

In spite of such statements, when Tolstoy left his home and appeared at the monasteries of Optina and Shamordino in the fall of 1910, the Church found renewed hope for reconciliation. When Tolstoy's stay at the two monasteries ended abruptly after less than three days, the Church endeavored to prove that he had wanted to stay longer but had been hurried away by enemies of the faith. Reports from the monasteries offered some support for this effort: Archimandrite Ksenofont of Optina reported that on his arrival Tolstoy had asked if it wasn't unpleasant to the caretaker of the monastery's lodgings to admit one who had been excommunicated from the Church. Later Tolstoy had inquired about the elders, asking if the elder Iosif was receiving visitors. The next day a mysterious young man had arrived and had spent a long time with Tolstoy writing something in his cell. (This latter figure was P. A. Sergeenko, whose appearance at this juncture would prove a key piece of evidence in the Church's version of events—he would be portrayed as an agent of Chertkov, sent to roust Tolstoy from the enemy camp.) The Abbess Ekaterina of Shamordino reported on Tolstoy's interest in renting a nearby hut and on his sudden departure, apparently under the influence of letters brought by his daughter Aleksandra L'vovna.[42]

These reports were forwarded to the Synod in Petersburg, which used them to organize its subsequent maneuvers around Tolstoy's deathbed. Metropolitan Antonii instructed Bishop Veniamin to send Father Iosif to Astapovo "to offer the count a spiritual meeting and religious consolation with the goal of his reconciliation with the Church."[43] Tolstoy had expressed interest in visiting Iosif at Optina, and the two of them had in fact previously discussed spiritual matters. When it was learned that Iosif was unable to make the journey, another monk, Varsonofii, was sent in his place.[44] Varsonofii was given instructions to exploit every possibility to meet with Tolstoy and bring about his reconciliation with the Church. This plot was abetted by the Ministry of the Interior, as Petr Stolypin sent a special agent with orders to facilitate this process, telling him that the tsar himself very much wanted Tolstoy to die at peace with the Church.[45]

Varsonofii arrived at the station with another monk, Panteleimon, only to find that Tolstoy's quarters were off-limits to them. Aleksandra L'vovna refused to inform her father of their arrival or to meet with Varsonofii herself.[46] He appealed to one of the doctors, Nikitin, who told him that the physicians had decided unanimously that no outsiders should be allowed into Tolstoy's quarters, as any disturbance might critically worsen his condition. The best Varsonofii could do was to elicit a promise from Andrei L'vovich, the best ally of the Church among the Tolstoy children, to help him receive an audience. As Varsonofii explained in his report, he remained at the station, "twenty steps" from Tolstoy's quarters, ready to come to him at any moment.

He was never given this opportunity however, nor were Bishop Kiril of Tambov, who was given a special train to Astapovo and arrived on November 5, or Bishop Parfenii of Tula, who like Varsonofii was commissioned by Antonii and the Synod but arrived only on November 7, several hours after Tolstoy's death. When Varsonofii was refused access, the Synod pinned its hopes on Parfenii, who was himself one of their members and who had reported two years earlier that Tolstoy appeared to be undergoing a spiritual transition that was bringing him closer to the Church. When he learned that he had arrived too late, Parfenii fulfilled his other commission—to learn if there were any indications of repentance that might allow the Church to give Tolstoy a Christian burial. He met with Andrei L'vovich, who had introduced himself to Parfenii two years earlier as the only Orthodox believer in the family, and who was seen as the most likely to provide the sort of information the Synod wanted.[47] Andrei reported, however, that there were no signs that his father had wanted to reconcile with the Church, and that the family had decided against an Orthodox funeral. The latter came as a surprise to Parfenii, who had information suggesting that Sofia Andreevna and the Tolstoy sons were sympathetic to the Church's designs. In his long report to the Synod he related how Sofia Andreevna had recently asked the local priest, Tikhon Kudriavtsev, to bless the house and sprinkle it with holy water to rid it of the spirit of Tolstoy's disciple, Chertkov.[48] Before leaving Astapovo, Parfenii declined to perform services for Tolstoy at the local church—the first enactment of what would be a ritual refusal across Russia.

Back in Petersburg, officials had been poised to accept any sign whatsoever of contrition as sufficient to reinstate Tolstoy in the national church. *Russkie vedomosti* reported on November 6 that Stolypin was pushing for retraction of the excommunication and that the Synod was doing everything it could to make this possible. But though they had fashioned a collection of evidence that Tolstoy was changing his orientation toward Orthodoxy, none of it proved substantial enough for their purposes. They met for three hours on the evening of November 7. Although some members were in favor of re-communication, as were the Council of Ministers and Synod head S. M. Luk'ianov, this group stood in the minority.[49] Though they wished to make some gesture of reconciliation, the Synod found no basis for this in the actions of the deceased or the will of the family and finally decided to prohibit all services for Tolstoy.[50]

The Church thus relinquished its authority over Tolstoy's burial rites in what was to be a highly symbolic funeral. They were able to exercise only a negative authority—in the prohibition of services, censorship of public pronouncements, and isolation of the deceased heretic from the public. On these counts the government again offered its services: Tolstoy's body was transported in a freight car on a heavily guarded train, and transportation to the funeral, held at Yasnaya Polyana just two days after his death, was limited to a few trains coming from Moscow. Other public commemorations of the event were strictly prohibited, not only by the Church but by the state police as well. The Ministry of the Interior ordered that announcements of religious services in papers should receive police clearance to assure that they were not used as a ruse for "anti-government demonstrations."[51]

The Church, meanwhile, continued to fashion its own story of Tolstoy's last days based on detailed accounts of his visit to Optina and Shamordino and the report of Bishop Parfenii from Astapovo.[52] While the full extent of these efforts was only revealed during the Soviet era, the Church intentionally made public some its efforts at the time. The newspapers were informed of the deliberations of the Council of Ministers and the Holy Synod, and they reported on telegrams sent to Astapovo from the bishop of Ryazan and Princess Kurakina urging Tolstoy to repent.[53] The newspapers also carried Metropolitan Antonii's dramatic appeal to Tolstoy at Astapovo (see p. 55) and reported that he cried when he learned of Tolstoy's passing.[54]

Although these stories may have been leaked to the press to soften the image of the Church, they fit into a larger pattern of ambivalence. Newspaper interviews with Orthodox clergy reveal a great deal of confusion and uncertainty. Some clerics had hastened to welcome a repenting Tolstoy, whose return could bring, as Archbishop Arsenii of Novogorod admitted in an interview with a Moscow reporter, tremendous benefit to the Church.[55] Most took more cautious positions. One priest commented that if Tolstoy was indeed returning to the Church, then it was a joy for Orthodox faithful to see this "great, wondrous work" performed by a merciful God; if, however, Tolstoy was simply fleeing his family situation, then these circumstances proved that the famous writer had lost his reason, which would explain his "abnormal, rash outbursts toward everything sacred."[56]

It happened that the Church's vision of a "great, wondrous work" was not being carried out. The mourning of Tolstoy became another un-Orthodox spectacle, as the traditional rites of the Church were appropriated and given new meaning. First was the viewing of the body in the home of Ozolin, who, as a Lutheran, had no traditional Orthodox icons or candles.[57] Orations were performed not by priests but by young students, who led crowds all over Russia in singing "Eternal Memory," a song from the Orthodox funeral ceremony that was strictly prohibited for nonbelievers. "Civil *panikhidi*" were held in theaters and movie houses, where crowds stood in demonstration of their respect for the deceased and demanded cancellation of performances. When the Church refused to perform services for its great enemy, the public simply improvised their own, demonstrating that their claim on these sacred rites transcended their faith in Orthodoxy.

During these transformations, the Church was recast not as an agent of God's mercy upon the dead but instead as a vengeful, earthly body, administering sacred rites according to its own political will. Thus in many of the Tolstoy ceremonies the Synod's decision to obstruct the process of mourning became a focal point for antichurch sentiment. At a Petersburg University gathering on November 8 one speaker referred to the "holy fathers" who had excommunicated Tolstoy with "bloodstained hands."[58] The next day, defiant students packed the Armenian Church, which had agreed to perform services for Tolstoy, and later that day demonstrators gathered in the Alexander Garden, across from the offices of the Synod. While the right-wing press attributed these sympathies solely to disenchanted students and political activists in the cities, Kornei Chukovskii described conversations with peasants at Tolstoy's funeral who had told him that Tolstoy would end up in heaven regardless of whether or not Orthodox services were performed.

The public insistently assigned to Tolstoy sacred space that the Church had denied him and thus, in essence, had itself abandoned. After the funeral, this process continued as the small mound in the woods of Yasnaya Polyana became a national shrine. The papers reported on daily gatherings at the grave, which were punctuated by practices traditional to Christian relic veneration. University students gathered at the grave singing "Eternal Memory" and reading from Tolstoy's *Circle of Reading* (a spiritual anthology that here stood in the place of traditional Orthodox prayer books). A Greek pilgrim gathered some soil and asked the estate steward to give him a stamp verifying that the earth was from Tolstoy's grave.[59] Newspapers also reported rumors that the grave was harboring supernatural forces: a tall bearded man had appeared suddenly from the dark and fallen to his knees at the grave, weeping and praying for a long time; on another night a small, wrinkled old woman flew down, and when a watchman shot at her, she just laughed and flew away.[60]

The convergence of witch and pilgrim upon the grave in the woods of Yasnaya Polyana suggests the blend of Christian and folk belief that played

Въ Ясной Полянѣ послѣ кончины Л. Н. ТОЛСТОГО.

Фот. А. И. Савельева.

Пилигримы на могилѣ великаго писателя.

10. "At Yasnaya Polyana after the Death of L. N. Tolstoy." The smaller caption reads "Pilgrims to the grave of the great writer." The majority of these visitors are wearing student uniforms.

on the popular imagination surrounding Tolstoy's death. The grave itself, a simple mound at the end of a wooded alley with no cross or other marker, stimulated this imagination. It is situated where, Tolstoy's brother had told him as a child, a magical green stick was buried; if found, the stick would bring human happiness. Even as his burial eschewed Christian practice, the folkloric utopia that inspired it betokened a vision of human redemption to which the Church still wished to lay claim. The lone grave is suggestive of the enigma that is buried there—a writer estranged from his national church but close to his people and his native land.

Novoe vremia, meanwhile, reported on another strange event, this one involving not peasants at Yasnaya Polyana but the likes of Dmitrii Merezhkovskii, Petr Struve, Semyon Frank, Viacheslav Ivanov, and Dmitrii Filosofov. This was the November 16 gathering of the Religious Philosophical Society in Petersburg, which featured some of the leading Russian intellectuals of the day. In a report laced with undisguised sarcasm, *Novoe vremia* viewed the mystical extravagance of the event as "something nightmarish." Struve told the crowd that his 1905 visit to Yasnaya Polyana had revealed to him that even then Tolstoy had undergone a "religious transfiguration" and was "where the majority of people go only after their deaths"—with God.[61] Frank explained that faith and reason were synthesized in Tolstoy, whose death should become a "point of departure for a new widespread religious movement." If this did not happen, Frank argued, history would show that Tolstoy's contemporaries were not worthy of him. A. V. Kartashev suggested that if the Church was going to excommunicate Tolstoy, then it should have established a special status, corresponding to his great holiness, according to which Tolstoy could be buried.

Describing the way each new speaker exceeded his predecessor in scaling the heights of encomium, the reporter found particular ironic delight in the performances of the Symbolists in attendance. Claiming that it was impossible to speak about Tolstoy, but also impossible not to speak about him, Vyacheslav Ivanov somehow struck this incoherent balance: "illustrating his position, he was neither silent nor did he speak, but with a low, sing-song voice let forth such nonsense that people in the audience were rolling their eyes. 'Tolstoy is an individual who was completed in the forms of perfection.'" Dmitrii Merezhkovskii described the mystical spiritualization that was taking over the entire country, rich and poor alike, proclaiming: "In the death of Tolstoy is our common resurrection. The green stick is his testament. It is the cross of our emancipation. We pray beneath this cross that the resurrection of our motherland might soon be realized; we pray for the whole earth, which the deceased so loved." At this point, the Old Believer Father Mikhail complied with this request, offering a prayer to Tolstoy that was full of mystical pathos—"a strange adulteration of 'Our Father.'" The prayer at times became unintelligible, prompting a member of the audience to call for an end to the "comedy." It was followed by a signal from Filosofov, whereupon those assembled on stage began singing "Blessed Are the Meek in Spirit," a version that scarcely resembled the original, its tempo accelerating to a point that the reporter could imagine the participants breaking into Dionysian dance.[62]

The reporter for the relatively conservative *Novoe vremia* clearly sought to belittle this gathering and probably exaggerated its rhetorical excesses. The January issue of *Russkaia mysl'*, however, carried pieces by several of the speakers at the memorial evening, which gives us an unbiased account of their ideas.[63] Petr Struve's article, "The Meaning of Tolstoy's Death," argued that Tolstoy's departure from Yasnaya Polyana was motivated not by his family situation or any political or religious aspirations—he was beyond these concerns and was "going to God." Struve saw "not the physical death of Tolstoy, not a natural physiological fact, but a religious transfiguration. I saw with my own eyes and felt with trembling how Tolstoy stood outside of 'life.' . . . Here was the greatest triumph—of man over death." This sort of personal journey "to God," without the intermediacy of the Church, was in turn projected onto the Russian public in an editorial entitled "We and Tolstoy."[64] The author suggested that confusion as to the meaning of Tolstoy's legacy indicated that his death had stimulated "some sort of deep internal work on the consciousness of our intelligentsia." What was striking about the response to this death was not the mass movements of the public in the streets but instead the way that each individual in these crowds had been affected personally. It had "awakened the *religious* self" of the country.[65] This view, of course, inverted that of the Church, which portrayed public demonstrations of sympathy for Tolstoy as soulless emanations of his internal spiritual disorder. Describing Tolstoy's departure as "purely religious," the author did not feel it necessary to identify with that religion but instead to acknowledge a different connection to Tolstoy: he had made people recognize the superiority of the internal over the external and the "religious basis for personal and social life." He had thus awakened hope for a "deep spiritual enlightenment of the individual."[66]

Dmitrii Merezhkovskii's panegyrics also appeared in *Rech'* on November 9: "Who is he? An artist, a teacher, a prophet? No, more. His face is the face of humanity. If the inhabitants of other worlds asked our world: who are you?—humanity could answer, pointing to Tolstoy, here I am."[67] Calling Tolstoy the son of man, Merezhkovskii complained to the Church that excommunicating him was excommunicating all of humankind, and damning him was damning the whole world. He then explicitly stated what the Church seemed to fear most: "If you cannot pray with us, then go away, don't bother us. We will pray for him alone." He ended with a request to the heavenly Tolstoy for intercession, so that the kingdom of God might at last come to the earth.

The sublimation of Tolstoy's death by Russia's leading religious philosophers reminds us that cultic veneration of Tolstoy was occurring at many levels of Russian society. The Dionysian memorial meeting of the Religious Philosophical Society was ridiculed in the pages of *Novoe vremia*, but it represented a larger trend that was no laughing matter to the Church. Its solemn participants were the counterparts of students defiantly singing Orthodox hymns in the streets and of peasants acknowledging that Tolstoy might have bypassed the traditional Orthodox rite of passage to heaven—all of whom were transforming the symbolic language of the Church, subverting its authority over not only the Tolstoy narrative but the Christian narrative as well.

The Church itself, moreover, demonstrated a degree of "dual-faith" regarding Tolstoy. On the day of Tolstoy's funeral, the newspaper *Rech'* carried a series of articles showing that Christian sympathies were in fact divided. One interview with a high-ranking informant revealed that some in the Church felt that it had been a mistake to excommunicate Tolstoy, who was rightly called the conscience of the world. Church leaders had dealt too formally with Tolstoy, who deserved the same sort of liberal understanding that had been accorded St. Francis of Assisi in his time.[68] An Orthodox priest wrote a letter to the editors urging the Church to forgive Tolstoy, just as Christ had been forgiving toward his tormentors.[69] A longer article also appeared by the Old Believer Bishop Mikhail, who presented an exalted description of Tolstoy's struggle to renew the Christian faith and argued that Tolstoy was guilty of nothing except, perhaps, being blinded by love. The Church, Mikhail argued, needed dissent in order to grow and develop, and Tolstoy had relegitimized the faith for people who could not believe in the traditional manner.[70] Even in Kharkov, whose Archbishop Amvrosii had been a primary instigator in the excommunication, a priest argued in a local newspaper that Tolstoy was not expelled from the Church (because he was not anathematized) but had instead left of his own volition; refusal to pray for him was the result of a political agenda and revealed a lack of true understanding of the relation of the Church to "the fallen."[71]

As details of Tolstoy's final days emerged, the meaning of his visits to Optina and Shamordino became a key point of contention in the press. The Tolstoyans were adamant that Tolstoy had gone to the monasteries only to visit his sister, and that if he did intend to spend time there it was not so that he could take monastic vows. Even the anarchist Petr Kropotkin, far away in England, could discern this and wrote a letter to the London *Times* to clarify reports that Tolstoy had considered renting a hut near Optina; he explained the Russian tradition of secular communities surrounding monasteries and offered his opinion that it was impossible that Tolstoy would so suddenly and radically renounce beliefs he had held for thirty years.[72]

The renunciation that was so improbable for Kropotkin nonetheless figured repeatedly in the narratives of the Church, which are equal in variety and interpretive energy to those of the Tolstoyans. This was particularly true of the reactionary wing of the Church, which told dramatic tales featuring Tolstoy as a spiritual fugitive who failed in his "escape" and attempted return to the Church. On November 4, *Kolokol* carried a story titled "Thou Hast Conquered, Galilean!" describing Tolstoy as a godforsaken apostate unable to find refuge for his troubled soul. According to that account, Tolstoy was spooked from Yasnaya Polyana by a dream and fled to Optina, seeking comfort under the wing of the church that he had so vainly profaned. Tolstoy was not prepared, however, for the wanderer's life, as his much-publicized ascetic tendencies in his later years had been empty affectations ("simply the amusements of a rich landowner"). Thus after traveling just a short distance in the rain he had already fallen mortally ill and would end like Julian the Apostate, vanquished by Christ. Another *Kolokol* piece ("From Whom Was He Running?"), its author claiming to "see through" the current publicity, described Tolstoy in "flight" from the "demonic influence" and "spiritual captivity" of the Tolstoyans, who wished to prevent his return to the Church.[73] A similar story in the Black Hundreds newspaper *Russkaia zemlia* titled "What Was He Running From?" claimed that reports of Tolstoy's calm death were not true, as an eyewitness from Astapovo had informed the reporter that many who visited Tolstoy's body as it lay in state at Astapovo had been troubled by the look of horror and suffering in his face. Decrying the lack of Christian rituals that might have assuaged this suffering, the author tendentiously concluded, "God preserve anyone from dying like that," a plea that offered less sympathy than judgment.[74]

One can detect a certain pleasure in these accounts of Tolstoy's "cruel end," for they confirm the authority of Christianity over the Tolstoyan life narrative. I. K. Surskii describes how Ioann of Kronshtadt predicted such a demise for Tolstoy and offers a fantastic version of the manner in which this vision had proven prophetic. Writing in emigration and thereby relying on secondhand information, Surskii (perhaps unintentionally) muddles the facts a great deal, while adding his own spurious details: hounded by visions of demons, a contrite Tolstoy comes to Optina monastery, intending to spend his last days there, only to be "caught" by his daughter and the family doctor, who succeed in drugging him and whisking him away by night. Worse still, the dose of tranquilizer is too strong for the declining Tolstoy and induces his fatal illness. Around this time a monk on Valaam Island reports seeing a vision of Tolstoy running toward one of the churches there, being chased by a pack of devils who hound him into a chasm in the surrounding cliffs.[75]

Surskii's remarkable tale, though perhaps not typical of the Church's Tolstoy lore, expresses in a rather naked metaphor what many Orthodox clerics worked to do in the wake of Tolstoy's death. They wished to show his death as a downfall, a horrid spectacle from which Christians would avert their eyes. Works like the 1911 anthology *The True Face of Lev Tolstoy* suggested an unmasking that would reveal the horror beneath what, by popular account, was a story of triumph.[76] Contributors to the collection blamed the "pagan-anarchist" Tolstoy for the suffering of his followers, who had been imprisoned, lashed with knouts, hanged, and exiled. A Ioann of Kronstadt piece warned: "This is a roaring Leo [*lion*], looking for someone to devour." The concluding piece, "The True Representation of the Death of Tolstoy," drew explicit attention to the "horror" of Astapovo, which some of Tolstoy's admirers had dared call his Calvary. The author was willing to allow the "treacherous" Jews to place Tolstoy on Golgotha but not upon the central cross: "Look, you insane Jews, at our contemporary rational world Golgotha and the human disgrace that surrounds it and, as much as you are able, look more honestly: maybe you will see that your idol the Judas Tolstoy endured a great deal of suffering and torment in his last week and died as it turns out on the left side of Christ the Savior and His Holy Church."[77]

This "world Golgotha," such arguments suggested, was simply a repercussion of the spiritual violence that Tolstoy visited on his readers.[78] A 1911 tract published by Skvortsov and *Kolokol* depicted Tolstoy as a prideful, inveterate man who dropped out of school to lead a dissolute life of gambling and carousing, then got married and came to his senses a bit, only to turn in his later years against everything sacred in the Christian and social orders. The outcome of this spiritual anarchy was predictable: in his last days, overcome with hatred for his family and surroundings, Tolstoy ran from his home "as if he wanted to repent, but God gave him over into the hands of the very people he had corrupted, and they didn't allow him to repent, and the 'impudent profaner' died a refugee under a stranger's roof, like the hateful Cain, after the murder of Abel, having run from his own land and people."[79] That Tolstoy's ideas were inherently alien to the Russian people was illustrated by his own estrangement from his home and heritage.[80]

The propaganda issued by leading institutions of the Church was often no less strident and took up the same themes of flight and alienation. The revered Trinity monastery of Sergiev Posad issued a book on Tolstoy's death by Bishop Nikon, who was known for his venomous contributions to *Kolokol* and *Russkaia znamia*.[81] Nikon directed colorful invectives toward various enemies in the Tolstoy camp, from Prince Meshcherskii (who was sharply critical of Nikon's treatment of Tolstoy) to the smokers at Tolstoy's funeral: "A cinematographer immortalized the smoke of the people smoking cigarettes at the grave of the deceased—how wonderful is prayer, the singing of 'Eternal Memory,' with cigarettes in your lips!" It was good, Nikon continued, that the Church had closed its doors to the likes of these.[82] A pamphlet published and "blessed" by the Kievan Caves monastery titled "Who Was Lev Tolstoy?" offered scarcely more Christian charity, concluding that Tolstoy was "the most evil enemy of the Church of Christ, a shameless blasphemer, an enemy of Christ our Savior and a lying infidel."[83] As they defined where Tolstoy "was really going," who he "really was," and what was "really the truth," the shrill voice of the Church often stood in stark contrast to that of the secular press, which answered with such benign publications as the Moscow collection *Who Was Tolstoy (according to the Best Opinions in the Russian Press).*[84]

At times the Church itself took a more moderate tone. A Ryazan pamphlet titled *Where Is the Truth? (On the Current Question of L. N. Tolstoy)* set forth the basic reconciliation story but produced more substantial evidence and offered a more forgiving conclusion. Lamenting that Russia's great genius was isolated from his church, the authors suggested that Tolstoy was something of a victim of the troubled times that he had helped create.[85] In a November 22 lecture on Tolstoy, Metropolitan Antonii adopted a similar strategy. Antonii viewed Tolstoy as a "Russian national philosophical writer" whose "theoretical cosmopolitanism contradicted the national spirit of his philosophical sensibility."[86] Antonii argued that the very foundations of Tolstoy's thinking were essentially alien to the Russian people. Though he had attracted a following in his native land, Tolstoy was in essence a false prophet, and the national crisis provoked by his death was the result of the contradictory nature of his legacy. Plagued by spiritual pride, Tolstoy could not resolve these contradictions; this was why he lacked moral tranquillity and spiritual calm, and why he could lead his literary heroes (such as Levin and Nekhliudov) *toward,* but not *to* moral rebirth. Nor could Tolstoy achieve that goal: "Tolstoy himself, standing at death's door, stood only at the doors of the teachers of the repentance of the holy Bible but could not go in and died without making peace with God."[87] This unresolved spiritual crisis explained too the scenes following Tolstoy's death—the funeral demonstrations that confused mourning with militancy and were based on misunderstanding of his teachings.[88] Quoting Tolstoy himself, who said that only two of every hundred readers of his novels had read his philosophical works, Antonii argued that Tolstoy's last narrative was being read by people ill-equipped to interpret it.

The Church, in contrast, was quite prepared to take "proper" measure of Tolstoy on his day of reckoning. The January 1911 issue of *Missionerskoe obozrenie* took up this agenda explicitly in Nikolai Chepurin's "The Life and Deeds of Count Lev Nikolaevich Tolstoy Judged according to His Teachings." Chepurin gave a long account of the contradictions in Tolstoy's teachings and practice and suggested that writers should not urge others to do things that they themselves could not, or did not, do.[89] From this perspective Tolstoyanism was spiritually unviable, and its legacy was a two-fold mortality: the excommunicated Tolstoy would be denied eternal salvation, and his teaching would prove equally perishable. *Missionerskoe obozrenie* continued to drive this message home in the months following Tolstoy's death. A report on sectarianism observed that Tolstoy's followers had not shown any special activity in the wake of his death, which was attributed to the same contradictions and to doubts raised by Tolstoy's flight to the monasteries and subsequent "tragic" death.[90] Tolstoy's lack of faith in an afterlife, the journal argued, undermined his appeal, for belief in life beyond the grave was the most important article of faith for the people. In the April issue a piece by an anonymous priest was entitled "Where Did He Arrive?" a question that was answered by a pathetic description of Tolstoy's homely, lonely grave.[91] Tolstoy, the author argued, had finally understood the emptiness of his life and the illegitimacy of his ideas, only to be denied refuge in Optina by his own followers.

Aftermath: Inverting the Sacred and the Profane

As the Church worked to educe the profane in the Tolstoyan sacred, it found itself wielding a fragile rhetorical authority that was repeatedly undermined by its own maledictions. *Russkoe slovo* reported that Bishop Germogen of Saratov was handing out thousands of leaflets containing phrases such as: "All the Jews and vile pagans are calling Russia to the dismal grave of the eternal thief, the Russian Judas-Tolstoy, crucified on Golgotha on the left-hand side." The January 1911 issue of *Vestnik Evropy* picked up on the story and remarked that such behavior on the part of a high official of the Church only had a negative effect on the popular attitude toward the Church.[92] The liberal press in fact made every effort to publicize the Church's excesses, at times bemoaning them, at other times ridiculing them.

Rech' was particularly active in following these excesses. On November 6 it reported that Germogen had sent Skvortsov a telegram warning against the campaign of the left-wing press to stir up interest in Tolstoy's ideas by generating publicity around his illness and reminding him of the predictions of Amvrosii and Ioann of Kronshtadt that Tolstoy would die a "cruel death." On November 11 it reported that the Petersburg Ecclesiastical Academy had threatened to expel anyone initiating a campaign to send a telegram of condolences to Sofia Andreevna. On November 19 it derisively commented on a "thrice-secret" telegram prohibiting administration of services for Tolstoy—issued at the time when this widely known prohibition had caused a national scandal. *Rech'* also reprinted stories from other newspapers: *Viatskaia rech'* had reported that Bishop Filaret had instructed the local clergy to heighten vigilance for monuments erected with the name Lev—and to prohibit them if they were dedicated to Tolstoy. On November 21, *Rech'* reprinted a passage from *Kolokol* blaming Tolstoy for Russia's loss in the Russo-Japanese war.

The standard-bearer for such mudslinging was the monk Iliodor, whose reputation for immoderation in defending the faith preceded Tolstoy's death. *Rech'* reprinted a piece from a Tsaritsyn paper in which Iliodor compared "the holy archangel F. Ioann of Kronshtadt" to the "archangel of Satan, the great sinner and godless one, Lev Tolstoy."[93] Now, Iliodor wrote, when Tolstoy would go to hell, "from all sides will be heard the loud shouts of thousands of lost souls, who will cry out loudly 'There goes our ruiner and corruptor. Oh, woe, woe unto us!'...Let the godless, the blasphemers, the Jews, the newspaper vermin and other servants of Satan cry, for their teacher and leader has died. But we, the Orthodox Russian people, will rejoice because this godless one has died." Even *Novoe vremia* ridiculed Iliodor for a piece appearing in *Kolokol*, in which he claimed to be able to study the morality of Tolstoy by reading the writings of his "followers"—in this case 497 letters written to him in response to his attacks on Tolstoy. These letters, of which he cited the following as an example, convinced him of Tolstoy's inability to inspire love and brotherhood:

> Listen, you scoundrel Iliodor! First, I congratulate you on your name day (November 19), and second I wish that you would kick the bucket this very day. You, blackguard, said something about setting a dog on Tolstoy's grave, but on yours, fool, we...! Oh, you vermin! They need to put you in prison, cursed with anathema. From my soul I wish that you would contract cholera.
>   Your well-wisher.[94]

Iliodor's tactics embarrassed the Church and led to his relocation away from the capitol, but this did not prevent him from continuing his anti-Tolstoyan campaign.[95] In September 1911 he sent a five-hundred-word telegram to Moscow Mayor N. I. Guchkov, complaining that the proposed purchase by the "ancient city" of Tolstoy's Moscow home would be a disgrace.

Reporting on this story in its newly formed journal, the Tolstoy Museum hastened to add that Iliodor's letter was replete with grammatical errors and censurable expressions.[96] As the two sides engaged in this mutual defamation, pointing to the rhetorical excesses of their opponents as evidence of inferior spiritual development, it was hard to recognize the moral high ground that was being contested. Even the more subtle recriminations of both sides were in effect based on the same strategy. In trying to keep one another from laying claim to Calvary, they engaged in a clumsy game of king of the hill, as both sides continually pushed too hard and found themselves tumbling gracelessly downward.

Ioann of Kronshtadt had often been seen as the Church's main contender for this crown. He and Tolstoy were considered contending moral authorities, and Iliodor was not alone in contrasting the two at the time of Tolstoy's death.[97] It was probably not mere coincidence that a book describing the *Last Days and Blessed Ending* of Father Ioann should have appeared in 1911, some three years after his death. It contained lavish illustrations of Ioann's state funeral, which had included an elaborate procession from Kronshtadt through the crowd-lined streets of the capital, presided over by the metropolitan and a large retinue of ecclesiastical elite. This ceremoniously traditional procession could be easily contrasted with Tolstoy's recent funeral, which had been ceremoniously new and obscure.[98] N. L. Lazarev made this comparison explicit in a book entitled *Living Thought of the Twentieth Century (1905–1912)*. In contrast to Ioann's funeral, wrote Lazarev, at Tolstoy's the religious sentiments were not "real": "We see a multiracial and multifaith public, whereas a real religious-moral group that would have practiced the same faith with him was not there at all."[99]

Men'shikov likewise juxtaposed the two in his Tolstoy eulogy in *Novoe vremia* on November 9, following on a line of comparison he had begun in his December 1908 eulogy for Ioann (not long after the public celebration of Tolstoy's eightieth birthday).[100] In the 1908 article Men'shikov wrote that Tolstoy represented the best of that aristocratic intelligentsia that had separated itself from the people, while Ioann had risen up from among the people, coming, like Lomonosov, from the frozen north of "Holy Russia," where he had learned the oldest traditions of the national faith. Ioann wore the mantle of the Caves monastery, Sergius Radonezhskii, and Serafim Sarovskii: "Flesh of the most noble native flesh, bone of its bones, the Kronshtadt elder did not only dream about holy Rus, like Tolstoy, but was himself holy Rus, and himself carried it in his heart! This is what was made him so dear to the people. This is why the people immediately recognized him as their own, as everyone immediately sees a lamp at the top of a hill."[101] Another *Novoe vremia* writer drew a similar comparison in an article called "Mystical Power": "with his simple and childish spirit Father Ioann was closer to the people than the great sage Lev Tolstoy. The ascetic and supplicant is more understandable to the everyday Russian crowd than the worldwide genius."[102] Ioann had only one gift, the writer continued—the gift of sincere and passionate prayer—and that gift was more valuable to the people (who were by their very nature mystical) than any artistic talent or rationalist worldview.[103] This explained the striking ineffectiveness of the wise men and book people (read "Tolstoy") before the simple folk.

Tolstoy's estrangement from the national church could thus be construed as alienation from the common people for whom he was said to have so much love. *Missionerskoe obozrenie* went so far as to describe Tolstoy's scorn for the Church as elitist—he grew up among the gentry class, which treated local priests like peasants, and could never respect the low-born clergy representing the Church.[104] Concern that Tolstoy could transcend this class difference explains the publication in Petersburg of *The Complete Unmasking of the Yasnaya Polyana Heretic Tolstoy. The Voice of the Common Folk* by "the peasant A. Golubtsev."[105] To show that he was an authentic peasant, the editors of the text preserved Golubtsev's numerous grammatical errors, explained with the following note: "This somewhat coarse but truthful voice of the son of a wet nurse in our village gives a clear idea of the view of the Russian muzhik on the one infected by contemporary 'cibilization,' the worldwide 'varmint' Tolstoy and his vile creations."[106] Addressing Tolstoy as "Your Excellency," the peasant disowned the Yasnaya Polyana heretic who made such a show of leading a plowman's life: "What—has a wolf really eaten the muzhik's reason? Doesn't the muzhik see that you are in a peasant's skin just for show, like a clown in a farce?"[107] Golubtsev ended by turning the tables on Tolstoy—just as in *War and Peace* Bezukhov had deciphered the devil's number in Napoleon's name, so now did one of Tolstoy's beloved peasants perform a like-minded calculation on his own name, "fully unmasking the Yasnaya Polyana heretic," as his title promised, as the Anti-Christ incarnate.

By means of a complicated calculation, using the numerative values of Russian letters, Golubtsev comes up with the following:

L/30	N/50	T/300	V/2
e/5	i /8	o/70	o/70
v/2	k /20	l/30	l/30
———	o /70	s/200	n/50
37	l /30	t/300	o/70
	a /1	o/70	d/4
	i /8	j/10	u/400
	ch/90	———	m/40
	———	980	———
	277		666

As usual with such calculations, to achieve the desired result requires some creative reckoning. As Tolstoy has been excommunicated from the Church, he thus loses his Christian names: subtracting the values from his first name and patronymic from his last name produces the requisite 666, although only with the patronymic misspelled (according to its common phonetic pronunciation—the sort of mistake a peasant like Golubtsev would make honestly).

As he performed this decodification, Golubtsev laid bare the device that was persistently being applied to the name and legacy of Tolstoy. Whether as Anti-Christ or Anti-Ioann, he was being turned inside out, always with the suggestion that some invidious secret was obscured in the deep folds of his life story. Shepherds of the Orthodox faith exploited the peasants' long-standing antipathies toward the gentry and fear of eternal perdition to insinuate that Tolstoy was a "lion" in sheep's clothing.

The War Continues: 1911–1913

In the years that followed, the Church continued its campaign to limit the growth of Tolstoy's cult. Vladimir Sabler, Pobednostsev's successor as Chief Procurator of the Synod, protested plans for the government purchase of Yasnaya Polyana in October 1911, arguing that government purchase of the estate of someone who had been excommunicated from the national church would send a dangerous message to the Russian faithful. To soften this position, Sabler offered Tolstoy forgiveness on an individual level: "To forgive enemies in one's personal, private life, is praiseworthy, of course, but to glorify enemies and enrich their children at the government's expense is unacceptable."[108] This tactical mercy was an appealing stratagem for confronting Tolstoy's popularity, and it was used on other occasions as well. In an article for *Vera i razum* in 1912, for instance, Father Nikolai Lipskii explained that the Church did not prohibit individual members from praying, as the emperor had, for Tolstoy. (In his public statement after Tolstoy's death, Nicholas had expressed his sententious wish that God would have mercy on Tolstoy's soul.) The title of the article, "When Did the Great Tolstoy Die?" alludes to another strategy that the emperor had used upon Tolstoy's death—mourning the loss only of the "great Tolstoy," the author of great literary works. Tolstoy's turn from literature after *Anna Karenina* was a greater loss to the nation than was his death in 1910, Lipskii argued, and represented his suicide as an author.[109]

The difference between individual and national mourning for Tolstoy was made abundantly clear to a priest who took it on himself to perform services at Tolstoy's grave in late 1912. When he subsequently wrote a letter to the editors of *Russkoe slovo,* a scandal erupted once again over the issue.

A commentator for *Russkoe slovo* questioned the authenticity of the priest, whereupon Sofia Andreevna sent a letter attesting that the priest had presented his official papers to her, had indeed performed services, and had told her: "Now Lev Nikolaevich is not a heretic; I absolved him of his sin."[110] The priest also defended his actions in the newspapers. In an anonymous letter, signed "The priest who prayed for the sinful soul of Lev, the servant of God," he explained that he had had no personal goal in performing the service, nor sympathy with Tolstoy's views, but that he had prayed for Tolstoy as one sinner prays for another, and that it had been a comfort to Sofia Andreevna.

The services, together with the priest's letter, brought another round of denunciations from defenders of the faith. Trinity monastery published Nikolai Kuznetsov's *On the Question of Prayer for Count L. N. Tolstoy,* in which the author chastised the "still-hiding" priest for stirring up the emotions and confusion over Tolstoy's burial once again.[111] Emphasizing the importance of church canon, Kuznetsov reviewed the history of the Church's rulings on the matter of burying the non-Orthodox and concluded that no exception could be made for Tolstoy—the collective identity of the Church depended on the equality of its members and strict observance of its rules. Admitting that the Synod was losing its authority, he insisted that the priest could offer his own prayers at Tolstoy's grave but could not perform church rites.[112] N. Ya. Varzhanskii also responded to the story. In *Missionerskoe obozrenie* he railed against the humanistic pride of Tolstoy but also against the priest, who, like Tolstoy, had committed a "sin unto death." It was entirely senseless to perform the service for Tolstoy, who neither wanted nor deserved it. Varzhanskii's conclusion, much like Kuznetsov's, decried a larger crisis, of which the incident at Tolstoy's grave was only a symptom: "Ours is a distressing, dissolute time, a time of banality and cynicism."[113]

But the grave could also be construed as a dismal focal point for these forces, as was done with evident glee later that year. The author of a *Vera i razum* piece, derisively titled "The 'Great Grave,'" reminded his readers how Tolstoy's grave was supposed to become a new Mecca, an eighth wonder of the world, and then proceeded to detail a series of abuses of the shrine. People had been having drunken picnics there, writing their names and foolish sayings on the fence, until Sofia Andreevna had finally declared that admittance to the estate would be allowed only on Thursdays between 10:00 and 12:00. The author recounted his own experience observing a group of students in Tula playfully inviting others to accompany them to Tolstoy's grave: "So what need is there for Tolstoy here? What need for his 'great grave'? Indeed, this is simply an amusing sidetrip for some young people, flirting with one another out of idleness. It's unpleasant that for this they need the pretense of visiting a grave, even if it is the forest grave of Lev Tolstoy."[114] He belittled the numbers of visitors to Tolstoy's grave in comparison to those at St. Sergius Radonezhskii's and delineated the features of an authentic Russian shrine:

> We have real saints. There is no tumult surrounding their names, no newspaper correspondence, no shameless bragging. Around their graves there is not this ugliness that reigns at the "great grave" and in which all the spiritual poverty of our intelligentsia was revealed....The "great graves" will not eclipse the graves of our dear saints, which don't stand alone and in obscure sadness but shine with grandeur in God's temples in hallowed monastic cloisters. Our dear graves will stand for centuries, but yours, gentlemen of the intelligentsia, are already defiled by you yourselves in their first year.

Again Tolstoy's triumph was construed as tragedy—his grave desecrated by his own admirers in an unwitting travesty of "real" relic cults. The title of the article attests, however, that in the popular mythology of the day there was indeed a small mound in the woods of Yasnaya Polyana that was known as the "great grave." That the author felt it necessary, three years after Tolstoy's death, to impugn this mythology further attests that the "great Tolstoy" still lived, and that ridding him from the public consciousness was not so simple a task as burying an epithet in quotation marks.

The Church's campaign to tell Tolstoy's story as a Christian object lesson has continued to our day. In 1960, the fifty-year anniversary of his death, several books appeared that made it seem as if those years had hardly passed. In Munich, I. M. Kontsevich's *Istoki dushevnoi katastrofi L'va Tolstogo* was published, containing a chapter on Tolstoy's visits to Optina and Shamordino and reminding readers that what followed his sudden departure from those cloisters was a spiritual "catastrophe." In the United States, the Holy Trinity monastery chimed in with *On the Fifty-Year Anniversary of the Death of Tolstoy* (the title of one of the pieces, "A Dark Jubilee" conveys the spirit), and *Father Ioann of Kronshtadt and Count Lev Tolstoy*, which feature selections from Ioann's voluminous attacks on his great enemy. Most recently, the Trinity monastery in Russia has rejoined the battle with *The Spiritual Tragedy of Lev Tolstoy*, another collection of reprints from the time of Tolstoy's death.[115] As it entered the new millennium, the Orthodox Church was still working to paint Tolstoy into a spiritual corner and to steer its followers away from this impasse.

As new volleys continue to be fired, it becomes clear that this rhetorical battle over Tolstoy's legacy was never conclusively decided. It is now only a minor skirmish in the hinterlands of public consciousness, but it nonetheless reveals what is really at the heart of our discussion—that the story of Astapovo, full of intriguing gaps and loose ends, compelled its readers to render some decisive conclusion to the spiritual journey it described.

As they equated Tolstoy's death with his ideas, Orthodox interpreters joined their secular counterparts in investing it with parabolic meaning. Even as they worked to deconstruct the notion of Tolstoyan apotheosis, they effectively helped shape the story of Tolstoy's death into a national narrative. For the Orthodox, Tolstoy found no salvation: his grave was a dead end, where he and his ideas would be forgotten. A vast outpouring of elegiac remembrance showed, however, that much of the public had no interest in such a renunciation of Tolstoy's talents. They saw more value in a narrative of triumph, and even if it was not clear what Tolstoy had taken with him as he left this life, they did not wish to divest that obscure legacy of some great meaning. For those sympathetic to Tolstoy's morality, his death itself could provide this meaning: it could be seen as a moment of truth, toward which he walked with stoic and knowing grace. Astapovo was a destination reached, his death the closure that was sought as he left his home. For the Church, the last episode in Tolstoy's life could only be incorporated into less compelling narratives—of unreformed and damnable godlessness or of a repentant sinner denied his chance to reconcile with God. Although some indeed chose the former alternative, most found that the second was more compatible to public sympathies and set about, with self-interested imagination enlivened by their subject's enigmatic visits to its monasteries, to show that Tolstoy's final journey was a return to the Church. Tolstoy's pilgrimage became flight, and its terminus a sudden, irrevocable descent. In some cases it was imagined that this descent was mediated by prayers of repentance, but often it was set forth in all its imaginable horror. While Tolstoy supporters spoke of the universality of his ideas and referred to him as an "Everyman," the Church worked to singularize and isolate him and to limit the scope of collective mourning. They rendered him as an orphan in death—not belonging to the family of the Church, not ritually joined to their number, but instead carried aloft at his funeral by a confused mass of political ne'er-do-wells and social misfits stimulated by his writing to view the event as a political opportunity.

An advantage to this story was that it placed Tolstoy in the role of victim, so that the Church could liminally join in the national mourning. Many who counted themselves among the Orthodox faithful were kindly disposed toward Tolstoy the man, regardless of what they thought of his religious ideas. A. Stolypin, writing in *Novoe vremia* two days after the funeral, described the desire to resolve the tension between these impulses: "I have witnessed how much people are seeking a way out, how unanimous they are in doing any little thing that might lead to a reconciliation of their conscience, which is torn between obedience to the Church and love for Tolstoy's soul."[116] Sergei Bulgakov wrote of a spiritual enlightenment transcending the differences that Tolstoy had with the Church, with which he was united by "invisible, subterranean ties."[117] As public rituals marking Tolstoy's death transcended these differences, it was evident that the writer and his readers were connected by similar bonds. What the Church construed as heterodoxy were in fact powerfully binding cultural paradigms, structuring ideas and symbols over which its authority was diminishing. Tolstoy's death illustrated that spiritual narratives did not need to be Orthodox to resonate deeply with Russian society. The Church resisted this appropriation of its symbolic language but could do little to wrest it from the hands of its "enemies," many of whom would some few years later adapt it to the needs of the Revolution. This explains why church officials wanted so desperately to be able to tell the story of Tolstoy's return that would affirm their place in Russian society.

But what, in the end, might Tolstoy have been unconsciously writing on his blanket? A. P. Sergeenko has argued that Tolstoy traveled to Optina and Shamordino neither to take up residence nearby, nor to confide in his sister, but instead to gather material for literary projects. Four days before he left home he had written in his diary an idea for a story about a priest who was "converted" by someone whom he was trying to convert. The idea was inspired by Troitskii, the local priest who had been working so hard to bring Tolstoy back into the fold and with whom Tolstoy was corresponding at the time. Two days later he had a dream about a romance between Dostoevsky's Grushenka (from *The Brothers Karamazov*, which he was reading) and the critic Nikolai Strakhov; he wrote Chertkov the next day about his intention to develop the dream into a story; and on the first night after his departure, already at Optina, he again wrote of this project.[118] Sergeenko appeared there the next morning to bring news of what had transpired at Yasnaya Polyana after Tolstoy's departure. Sergeenko's report upset Tolstoy greatly, and he went for a walk, from which he returned still in a gloomy mood. When Sergeenko came to Tolstoy's room a bit later, he found Tolstoy writing down notes on a piece of paper, which Sergeenko later read. On the paper was written a list of things to be brought from home, and a list of four subjects for fictional works.

Included in the list were the Grushenka-Strakhov romance and the Troitskii story—"The Priest, Converted by the One Who Was to Be Converted."[119] Thus Tolstoy, as he wandered the environs of Optina, was as convinced of the changeability of his antagonists as the Church was of its great opponent. He also still believed in the power of narrative to perform this action by aesthetic, rather than polemical, means. So too did the last episode of his life carry on its work by aesthetic example; as zealous Orthodox interpreters tried to make the "un-converter" into the reconverted, they found that their story had less appeal than its Tolstoyan variant. The reverence with which Sergeenko recalls looking at the list of literary themes reveals the tremendous charisma of Tolstoy as a narrative authority: what tremendous life force must still exist in

Tolstoy, Sergeenko remembers thinking, if Tolstoy could be concerned with literary work in the midst of such spiritual turmoil. In the story of Tolstoy's last days, that life force, and the narratives that it engendered but did not finish, compelled others to join in the collective project of writing a story that celebrated not God but man. Even as they thought themselves to be waging war over the Russian faith, the Tolstoyan and Orthodox faithful who told and retold the Tolstoyan story were themselves, perhaps not even unknowingly, undergoing this conversion.

Фот. В. Черткова.

Ходилъ купаться. Чудное осеннее утро, тихо, тепло, зелень, запахъ листа. И люди вмѣсто этой чудесной природы съ полями, лѣсами, водой, птицами, звѣрями, устраиваютъ себѣ въ городахъ другую искусственную природу съ заводскими трубами, дворцами, локомобилями, фонографами.

Левъ Толстой.

11. "I went for a swim. A beautiful fall morning, quiet, warm, green, the smell of the leaves. And in place of this beautiful nature with its fields, forests, water, birds, and animals, people build themselves a different, artificial nature in cities with smokestacks, palaces, locomobiles, and phonographs."

3

The Media at Astapovo
and the Creation
of a Modern Pastoral

Instantly the telegraph carried the sad news across the whole world. The
damp morning found Astapovo already on its feet. In a lone window a
lamp shone.
   —Correspondent's report

If newspapers had existed when Moses went to die on the mountain or Jesus
ascended into heaven, then the divine legends would not have come to us in
the form of legends. In their place would have been bulletins.
   —M. Artsybashev

The first reports of Tolstoy's departure from Yasnaya Polyana
appeared in newspapers throughout Russia on October 30,
1910: "A messenger sent from Yasnaya Polyana said that yesterday, October 28,
at 5:00 in the morning, Lev Nikolaevich Tolstoy left his home with Doctor Makovitskii; his whereabouts have for two days been unknown."[1] This
news, first appearing as a small item, by the next day had become a national
sensation; already a tremendous media celebrity, Tolstoy had given the press
a story brimming with drama and mystery. Russia's most famous person, at
the age of eighty-two, had secretly left his home in the middle of the night,
setting off for an unknown destination. The story captured the imagination
of the Russian public and combined with the power of new technologies to
become a media event in a surprisingly modern sense. The press required
new installations of telegraphic equipment to keep pace with the wires being
dispatched to their anxious editors; photographers and film crews arrived,
extra supplies were sent, all served by the essential vehicle of modernity—the
railroad.

Tolstoy was by many years the last survivor of the generation of writers
that put Russian literature on the world map, having outlived even younger
contemporaries such as Anton Chekhov. No one appeared ready to take his
place. The eulogies that were to appear not long after his departure from

12. A montage of journal covers marking Tolstoy's eightieth birthday in 1908.

Yasnaya Polyana referred to him as the "Last of the Mohicans" of Russian literature, or, more commonly, using Turgenev's famous epithet from his deathbed letter to Tolstoy, "the great writer of the Russian land." In his later years he played the role of a venerated father figure, his authority legitimated by his tablet-breaking morality. The grief that Russians felt in parting with this patriarch was imbued with a good deal of nostalgia; amid the social turmoil at the beginning of the twentieth century, Tolstoy seemed the last vestige of a more stable and storied past. His hoary sensibility was captured in his farewell letter to Sofia Andreevna explaining that leaving worldly life was what men of his age normally did.

By the time this letter was conveyed to the press and then widely publicized in the papers, the possibility for Tolstoy to abandon "worldly life" was in considerable doubt. Media coverage of the story only intensified as Tolstoy became fatally ill and halted his journey in the remote railway station of Astapovo. Reporters set up a media center at the station, even as Tolstoy prohibited reports to the press on his condition or his movements and refused to hear what was being written about him. The newspaper dutifully reported Tolstoy's wishes in the papers but continued to undermine them. The result was a singular moment in the advent of modern media, as the rustic, pastoral image of the dying Tolstoy was mass produced for the public in the daily newspapers. By the end of the weeklong ordeal at Astapovo, Tolstoy and the telegraph had become inextricably wed: "As soon as Tolstoy died, Gol'denveizer announced through the window: Tolstoy has died. In an instant the telegraph carried this sad news from this small station to the world."[2]

The focus in this dispatch to an editorial office is not the announcement of Tolstoy's death itself, which had been relayed earlier, but the fact that the transmission had been instantaneous and worldwide. This itself is newsworthy, and in the reporter's view implies a certain gravity of its own. But if the medium is the message, it is one that Russian readers found troubling and confusing. They feared that the sensational tone the journalists adopted and the tremendous volume of reportage they generated would distort their record of a defining national event. The reforms of 1905 had created a highly competitive newspaper trade, a free market of information in which Tolstoy's story would be used to sell papers. It would be colored by the overt political orientations of the newspapers and in the kopeck press would be aimed at the lowest common denominator. Would the story survive its rough handling, bandied about in clumsy headlines, rushed to press to meet daily deadlines? Would the newspapers sustain the heroic action that many believed had occurred at Astapovo, or would it be rendered into "pulp" by the mechanisms of modernity? Readers feared that they would not get the real story of Astapovo but some sort of journalistic phantasm.

We know of these anxieties because they were reported by that same media, which self-reflexively critiqued its own behaviors and standards. As the journalists crushed into the small railway station—sleeping in boxcars, hounding for information and elbowing for access to tired telegraph operators called to the scene on their behalf—they made an unmistakable physical impression. But they also interposed themselves rhetorically, intruding on the narrative itself. They painted themselves into the picture, and just as in Velasquez's *Las Meninas* or Courbet's *Atelier* the result is a striking moment of public introspection. Tolstoy was represented in this work as a modern subject, a painting within a painting, while those creating his image found themselves in the middle of the canvas, occupying a space that they could no longer pretend belonged only to Tolstoy.

The Panopticon in the Pasture

The media frenzy is a commonplace in our time, but in the Russia of 1910 it was considerably more alien to the public consciousness and, perhaps, less conscionable. When Tolstoy left the train at Astapovo, he was being tailed not only by a government agent but also by a reporter, who was soon joined by a large contingent of the local and national press. Almost instantaneously he became, as one contemporary commentator noted, "a person standing naked under the open surveillance of the highest police—the world press."[3] The public also participated in this stakeout: the peasants at Yasnaya Polyana described Tolstoy's actions in the days before his departure; the coachman told of the early-morning escape; monks and nuns from Shamordino and Optina detailed his every move at the monasteries; a fellow passenger described Tolstoy's train ride from Kozelsk to Astapovo in great detail.[4] Anyone who had any contact with Tolstoy was recruited by a battalion of correspondents eager to add some new detail to the story: "The newspapers are full of conjectures as to his whereabouts; vying with one another, they scurry to show off how well-informed they are and have sent off all their 'special correspondents.' And you can imagine how happy the reporter will be who manages to find Tolstoy before everyone else, and to shout to all Russia: 'There he is! Stop him! Get him! Get him!'"[5]

This honor fell to Konstantin Orlov, a reporter for *Russkoe slovo,* which proved to be the most energetic and enterprising of the papers. Orlov had been commissioned to follow Tolstoy wherever he went and to "constantly send the most detailed telegrams." He was the first of the reporters on the scene at Astapovo, and the first to send news to Yasnaya Polyana of Tolstoy's whereabouts.[6] The press then continued to overstep traditional boundaries of family privacy. The Petersburg Telegraph Agency asked Mikhail Tolstoy to wire the "slightest details" of his father's condition, as it was necessary that they be announced worldwide.[7] Sergei Tolstoy, once he had come to his father's bedside at Astapovo, wrote to his wife that he wouldn't send her information about what was going on there because she could learn everything in more detail from the newspapers.[8] The newspapers pressed anyone close to the scene for news, opinions, hints, and conjectures. The Moscow physician A. P. Semenovskii, called to Astapovo to treat Tolstoy, recalled the scene: "At the station we met a whole crowd of reporters, who had arrived from everywhere on the morning trains. They are very curious and ask about everything."[9] Dushan Makovitskii described the pressure on the stationmaster Ivan Ozolin, in whose apartment Tolstoy was staying:

> A correspondent came. I asked him, and Aleksandra L'vovna another, not to come, and not to bother us. L. N. doesn't wish for the newspapers to make any announcements about him—but they received information all the same from the Ozolins. Ozolin received four telegrams that day from *Russkoe slovo*, begging for information (by telegraph) and sending him 100 rubles, which he did not accept, having learned from us that L. N. did not want any announcements about himself to be published. He, the poor man, did not know what to do. These telegrams puzzled, troubled, and upset him. Instead of concentrating on helping out . . . [Makovitskii's ellipsis][10]

The extent to which Tolstoy "belonged to the world" confused the boundaries of family privacy even for those with closer relationships to the Tolstoy family. Prince Dmitrii Obolenskii, a longtime family friend, played an active role in breaking the initial story of Tolstoy's departure from Yasnaya Polyana, feeling a responsibility to keep the media abreast of the "true story" of Tolstoy's departure. "Being close to the family," Obolenskii reported, "I hurried to take a troika to Yasnaya Polyana to find out what had really happened. Before leaving I informed *Novoe vremia* of the rumors circulating in Tula."[11] These dubious priorities—one might have expected Obolenskii to verify first, then inform—backfired a few days later when Obolenskii was the source for *Novoe vremia* of a premature report of Tolstoy's demise on November 3, which did much to alienate the family from the press, and from *Novoe vremia* in particular.[12]

Other newspapers played their hands more shrewdly. *Russkoe slovo* couldn't have presented a more disarming calling card to Sofia Andreevna than its long laudatory article by V. Doroshevich of October 31. Expressing sympathy for Sofia Andreevna for her trying experience as the wife of a genius, Doroshevich "kissed the hand" that had tirelessly and thanklessly copied out the greatest novels of Russian literature. *Russkoe slovo* subsequently procured an interview with Sofia Andreevna at a time when her doors were closed to correspondents from other papers.[13] Gaining such an audience at this juncture placed *Russkoe slovo* in an enviable position, for Sofia Andreevna's role in the drama of Tolstoy's last days offered that personal dimension that made the story so compelling to newspaper readers. Her suicide attempts on learning of her husband's departure had already been widely reported in the papers, and the reporter did not neglect to highlight her disheveled appearance in the prefatory remarks to his interview (she leaned on her son's arm, apparently unable to stand on her own, and appeared in a housecoat, evidently having just gotten up). Though Sofia Andreevna was so distraught that she could not proceed logically through the interview, she persisted (despite her doctor's objections) and gave *Russkoe slovo* the scoop they were looking for, blaming "a friend" of Tolstoy (obviously Vladimir Chertkov) for having pushed her husband to leave the family home.[14]

The pathetic mien of Sofia Andreevna became a central element to the iconography of Astapovo, where her daughter Aleksandra and the Tolstoyans excluded her from Tolstoy's bedside just as resolutely as they did the reporters. Her willingness to display her despair at this decisive moment in her family life allowed the media to develop a sensational subplot to the story. She, like the press, was living in an extra passenger car at the railway station, waiting every bit as anxiously for the doctors' bulletins.[15] Sofia Andreevna's alienation from her husband at this critical juncture turned her personal grief inside out, exposing a most intimate scene to public view. Her visits to Ozolin's apartment, captured in a well-known film sequence by Joseph Meyer, were described by a reporter: "She walks beside the house where Lev Nikolaevich is lying and pecks like a bird wanting to fly into the nest where her most beloved being lies."[16] A traditional family ritual was supplanted by a much more public one, as the Tolstoys' gathered around a table in the station cafeteria reading the daily papers to learn what was going on and what was being said about them.[17]

The only key participant in the events at Astapovo who was paying no attention to the media was Tolstoy himself. When he felt well enough on November 3 to ask for a reading of the daily papers, he declined to hear anything that was being written about himself, a request which, in the case of most newspapers, would have generated an unusually brief reading. As *Russkoe slovo* had pronounced, "Right now the only thing people are talking about in Russia is the departure of Lev Nikolaevich Tolstoy from Yasnaya Polyana."[18] The newspapers filled multiple pages with regular columns detailing the latest developments of the story under such headlines as "The Latest on Tolstoy," "Tolstoy's Departure from the World into the World," and "From Astapovo."

Tolstoy's Most Popular Story: "He Left!"

At a time when the "kopeck papers" were generating readership by printing serialized boulevard novels, it was quickly discovered that the daily stream of dramatic developments at Astapovo could be used in the same way. The Kopeck Library of Sensational Novels, published by the most popular of the kopeck papers, *Gazeta kopeika,* offered tales from Russian life, often connected to elements from the news. The boundary between news and fiction was indistinct in the papers as well; as Jeffrey Brooks notes, the editors of the kopeck newspapers "made their newspapers inexpensive, displayed serial fiction prominently, and paid lavish attention to crime, scandal, and human-interest stories."[19] These popular novelizations often won the attention of readers whom Tolstoy had himself worked laboriously to attract. The Posrednik publishing house, run by his followers, published inexpensive editions of "edifying" works by Tolstoy and other authors as a means of inculcating morals among the people. The kopeck papers, however, found that pulp fiction was more attractive to their readers than Tolstoyan preaching. One serialized story, concerning a benevolent bandit named Anton Krechet, ran from 1909 to 1916; when factory workers were asked why they read the paper, they answered—because of Anton Krechet.[20] As part of the agenda of the kopeck papers was to foster readership among 'the people', they worked to popularize the classical nineteenth-century Russian writers. The Astapovo story, featuring the last of these fabled writers, was thus doubly appropriate to their needs.

Gazeta kopeika placed the Tolstoy story on its front page and offered extensive coverage as a daily feature through the end of November.[21] Tolstoy's mysterious disappearance, followed by Sofia Andreevna's two suicide attempts and the scandalous finger-pointing between Tolstoy's family and followers, provided plenty of fodder for the readers *Kopeika* had targeted. (One writer expressed surprise that a famous Moscow police dog Tref, who had proven himself "a real Sherlock Holmes," hadn't been called in on the case.)[22] V. A. Anzimirov, a publisher of the paper who also wrote serialized novels for its Moscow edition, actually contributed a number of pieces putting fictional twists on the story of Astapovo, which were then later included in an inexpensive anthology printed in book form.[23]

In the aftermath of Tolstoy's death, one newspaper commented that the world hadn't lost Tolstoy—he had merely passed "from real life to legend." This process had begun before his death, and was persistently fueled by the work of editors of newspapers like *Gazeta kopeika*. If anyone was unaware of the tremendous significance of this narrative, the newspapers were there to remind them: "For isn't it a fairy tale, isn't it a scene from the deepest, biblical antiquity—the departure of this rich man and aristocrat first from the luxury and vanity of the life into which he was born, then from everything that we ourselves deplore in our lives but which has so thoroughly entangled us from all sides that we can't even imagine freeing ourselves from it?"[24] It would not be easy, however, to disentangle this legend from the trappings of modern life that Tolstoy seemed to have escaped. Already on October 31 *Novoe vremia*

13. (13a) The cover of the kopeck newspaper *Gazeta kopeika* from November 3 with an image based on a drawing by Leonid Pasternak. (13b) On the right is a drawing of the layout of the Ozolins' apartment at Astapovo. Tolstoy's room is in the middle on the bottom. To the left is the room of Chertkov and Makovitskii and then that of Aleksandra L'vovna.

was commenting: "News of L. N. Tolstoy abandoning Yasnaya Polyana had scarcely appeared before it gave birth to a whole corpus of literature."[25]

That this corpus could be produced so quickly is due in no small part to the rise in technologies, the most significant of which in this case was the telegraph. In 1910 there were over 190,000 kilometers of telegraph lines in Russia, largely laid out along railway lines, with the provincial telegraph offices usually located in railway stations.[26] Thus, in traveling by train, Tolstoy

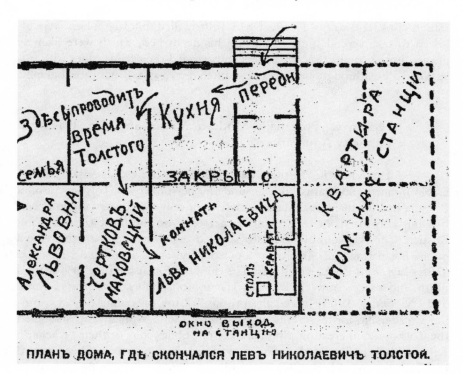

ПЛАНЪ ДОМА, ГДѢ СКОНЧАЛСЯ ЛЕВЪ НИКОЛАЕВИЧЪ ТОЛСТОЙ.

was in constant intercommunication with the telegraph; reporters and state agents were able to make reports of his movements along the way, and when he got off the train at Astapovo, he was helped to a bed that was within earshot of a telegraph station. For the press in Russia, as elsewhere, the telegraph was a tremendous boon, and it changed the very nature of the newspaper. Many papers prided themselves on access to its dispatches, and printed sections titled "The Latest Telegrams" as a daily feature. Partly as a result of the advent of the telegraph, as well as of the broadening distribution system offered by the railroad, Russian newspapers were enjoying significant growth in circulation at the turn of the century.[27] Other features, such as illustration (particularly among the more popular papers), were added to increase their attractiveness. Those following the Astapovo story, for instance, were provided with maps showing the location of the station, as well as with drawings of the Ozolins' apartment and Lev Nikolaevich's room. Photography was also used widely, and images of the scene at Astapovo played a prominent role in the daily coverage of the story. The whole world could see the principal players: a worn and worried Sofia Andreevna leaning on her son's arm, Chertkov and Gol'denveizer, the team of doctors, Ozolin, the telegraph operators, the station cook, and so on. Finally, when Tolstoy died, photographers were allowed to take several shots of him on his death bed, which were likewise printed in the papers.[28] Many papers emblazoned their front pages with images of Tolstoy throughout his last days, often drawing on familiar iconography.

"Glasnaya Polyana": Modern Media and the Tolstoyan Publicity Apparatus

These new media tools were added to what was already a considerable publicity apparatus built around the personality of Tolstoy. Yasnaya Polyana had for many years been a mecca not only for vegetarians and pacifists but also for reporters seeking to get copy on the most famous living Russian. Chertkov and other Tolstoyans had also done their part to create a public fascination with Tolstoy as a personality: P. A. Sergeenko's *How Lev Tolstoy Lives and Works,* which was in its third edition at the time of Tolstoy's death, and a series of works by Isaak Teneromo (notably *The Life and Words of L. N. Tolstoy,* 1908) placed the private Tolstoy on public display, priming a readership for the events of 1910. Like the mass media, artists joined the Tolstoyans in creating a broad array of public icons of their "teacher": Repin and Ge had painted numerous portraits; heroic busts had been carved by Ginzburg and others; Chertkov had created a carefully crafted library of photographs. Tolstoy's celebrity before Astapovo was parodied in a number of articles interpreting his flight as an escape from the constant commotion at Yasnaya. One of these, appearing in *Sankt-Peterburgskie vedomosti,* uses the report of Tolstoy's departure as an epigraph, then advances a theory of what has moved Tolstoy:

> This is how it happened:
> In the morning there arrived thirty female and twenty-six male students, Drankov with his cinematographer, five artists (a water-colorist, an oil painter, an engraver, a pointillist, and a mozaicist), four conscientious chimney sweeps, a couple of Americans, one Jewish lad, about fifteen poets, the driver of a large wagon train, a mattress maker, and a dozen very serious young men, who headed straight for the bedroom, carelessly throwing off their things on the way:
> "Don't be afraid! We're here for an interview...."
> Everyone wanted to have a talk with the great writer.[29]

This motley crowd engages in a competition to produce the most extravagant image of Tolstoy. Repin, Sergeenko, and Teneromo are ecstatic at the proposal of a pilot to take Tolstoy up in the air, but this offer is quickly superseded by the American's proposal to take Tolstoy with him on a trans-Atlantic flight in a hot-air balloon.[30] The piece ends with Tolstoy's escape, whereupon the enterprising followers set to work: Repin painting "Tolstoy in Solitude," Sergeenko writing a new volume entitled "Far from the World," and Teneromo buying twelve typewriters for a new set of memoirs.[31]

The suggestion that Tolstoy's departure could be manufactured into the ultimate publicity stunt pointed to a new anxiety—that the hero of this narrative might never be able to escape his own narratability. Some cynics suggested that Tolstoy was a willing participant in this process, and that his departure was just a "pretty pose." Most observers took Tolstoy at his word, however, and struck a medial position, generating this publicity at the same time as they questioned it.[32] They reported that a few days before leaving Tolstoy had written to the peasant Mikhail Novikov, seeking a small village hut where he could live, but then insisted on the propriety of drawing him back into the public sphere. A writer for *Sibirskaia zhizn'* declared on November 1: "Tolstoy must be found. He doesn't belong to himself, or to us—he belongs to the world."[33] The popular journalist S. G. Petrov, writing under the pseudonym Skitalets ("The Wanderer"), explained: "Lev Tolstoy went off into the world because he belongs to the world. His home is not Yasnaya Polyana, and his family is everyone in the world."[34] M. Liubimov, writing in *Golos Moskvy*, described the sensation of Tolstoy's departure as a struggle between the public and Tolstoy over the possession of his life.[35]

Many commentators at the time viewed this struggle as inevitable: "But Tolstoy won't dissolve in the motley mass of the common people; like a burning torch, he'll attract the attention of the world once again.... The world is too small for people like Tolstoy."[36] It was fascinating to consider the story from this point of view—to watch the mechanisms of modern media set loose on the trail of the most famous living person, the most hallowed son of the Russian land. From this perspective, Tolstoy's attempts to hide only made him tower ever more largely over the Russian horizon: one writer described him as the sun attempting to hide, while another asked: "Is it conceivable that Tolstoy could hide? Can a giant hide in an anthill?"[37] "They'll find Tolstoy in the Kozelsk region, or in Shamordino monastery," wrote another, "and again the 'visitors' will come with their manuscripts, the guests, and the Tolstoyans in their reverential poses, and, of course, the newspaper reporters."[38]

A third group encouraged public pity for Tolstoy, and engaged in collective browbeating over its own overzealousness. Vladimir Azov's *Rech'* editorial was critical: "Lev Nikolaevich Tolstoy has no personal life. He lives in a house with glass walls, around which reporters from every possible newspaper have set up camp. Telegraph wires extend from this glass house to all ends of the earth. Tolstoy rode his horse longer than usual this morning. Isn't that Tolstoy's personal matter? No—that's a cause for telegrams."[39] Tolstoy's tragedy superseded Buddha's, for the latter had at least been able to find solitude: "There was a desert for Buddha, but there is no desert for

Tolstoy. No matter where he goes, the telegraph, cinema, and automobile will overtake him." The media Panopticon had revealed itself to the Russian public as a mechanism with alarming potential. "The tragedy of loneliness is horrible," Azov wrote, "but the tragedy of someone who is never, under any circumstances, able to find a moment to himself, is twice as bad."

Even as they constructed the media event of Astapovo, many newspapers also questioned their disruption of the idyll they celebrated in their editorials. An editorial in *Minskii golos* described the "enterprising editor" seeing Tolstoy's departure as a means to sell papers and failing to consider the rights of Tolstoy and his family to their privacy: "they won't miss the chance to figure out right this moment at least an estimate of how they can increase their profits if only they make haste, without concern for the expense, send off their correspondents, and fill half the newspaper with their reports of the latest words, letters, and meetings of Tolstoy." Reminding readers that Tolstoy had left his home to seek peace and solitude, the author appealed to the Russian public: "Don't go looking for him, don't send off telegrams with absurd and foolish rumors, and don't fill the newspapers with sensational and vulgar headlines. Tolstoy left in search of peace. Quiet, gentlemen, quiet!"[40]

Such reprimands indicate collective anxiety as to the propriety of the media's activities but also demonstrate how that anxiety was used to dignify Tolstoy's actions. A. Lisovskii, writing in *Iuzhnaia zaria,* told the public: "Stand back and keep quiet! Here, not far from us, something solemn and holy is taking place."[41] Such commentators formed a tenuous alliance with Tolstoy's followers, who generally positioned themselves as defenders of his "peace and solitude" and issued instructions to the media toward that end. An unnamed Moscow Tolstoyan, in an interview for *Utro Rossii* which ran under the headline "Escape from a Horrible Captivity," set out guidelines for appropriate behavior by the press:

> It's necessary that the media, which will illuminate this event in the life of our dear writer, approach the matter in a serious, deeply restrained manner....It doesn't make sense to dig into all the private matters hidden behind the white walls of Yasnaya Polyana. Out of love for Lev Nikolaevich it is necessary to avoid the unworthy tone and scandalous sensation which the boulevard newspapers will no doubt create. Further, it isn't right to give fodder to the hooligan press, who on their own will find plenty of mud to sling at the precious, gray-haired head of the great old man and will breathe on his holy name and pure image with their impure breath. We have before us a heroic spiritual deed, before which it is necessary to bow with respect, leaving the personal to its own ends and taking from that deed only that which is noble and humane.[42]

Aleksandra Tolstaya's announcement on November 2 to the Associated Press also requested respectful boundaries around her father's sickbed: "the situation is most comfortable. Only the correspondents bother us. I implore them not to come."[43]

But the press did come. The small apartment in which Tolstoy spent his last days was besieged by reporters, as Aleksandra would later remember, "catching every word," and cinematographers, "minute by minute getting everything they could on film."[44] Vladimir Azov wrote at the time: "Tolstoy decided to run from the world. The world followed him, caught up with him, and again placed him in a glass jar."[45] A writer for *Mariupol'skaia zhizn'* imagined Tolstoy arriving at Optina only to find Teneromo there waiting; thinking that one interviewer is not so bad as the throng at Yasnaya, Tolstoy continues on his way, only to be ambushed by a reporter from a Moscow paper, who is then joined by a whole crowd of reporters, leading Tolstoy to retreat back to Yasnaya Polyana.[46] Had Tolstoy recovered and learned of what had transpired around him, this scenario might indeed have come true. Instead, it was only those outside his room who were witness to what *Golos Moskvy* called "the battle of wills" over Tolstoy's genius.[47] Tolstoy's close friend Aleksandr Gol'denveizer described the media frenzy at Astapovo: "They positively tear each one of us to bits... the moment we appear anywhere in the station."[48] The drinking and carousing of the reporters added to a general intemperance that was not befitting this solemn scene.[49] Gol'denveizer noted: "All of that crowd was a troubling contrast with the fateful, mysterious battle of life and death taking place just two steps away, in the stationmaster's little house."[50]

Tolstoy or Nikolaev: The Quest for Moral Agency

Tolstoy's public persona added its own dimension to this "troubling contrast." His search for solitude resonated with the quietist tendencies he had demonstrated in renouncing meat, tobacco, wine, war, wealth, copyright, Orthodoxy, and so on. His later writings followed this same ascetic impulse, as he stripped away unnecessary ornamentation, insisting that "the truth is always simple." *Father Sergius* is programmatic in this regard, ending with the narrative ellipsis of the hero's new day-by-day existence: the famous religious healer defrocks himself and goes into hiding in a peasant village, where he realizes the virtues of a simple life tending a garden, teaching children, and caring for the sick. Tolstoy's last journey was perceived as a realization of this scheme, in which he would likewise escape his fame, swallowed up in the "great world" where people had not read his novels, cared little for what he thought of the tsar's politics, and treated him as one of their own. He would find spiritual refuge in this quotidian nirvana, where he could realize the aspirations he had described in his final letter to his wife: "Life isn't a joke, and we don't have the right to throw it away according to our own will, and neither does it make sense to measure it according to the passage of time. It may be that these months which remain for us to live are more important than all the preceding ones, and we need to live them well."⁵¹ At Astapovo Tolstoy continually complained of excess concern for his comfort, as this was not "how peasants die," and in his last hours he told his son Sergei, "I will go somewhere where they won't interfere with me." Earlier that day he had suddenly sat upright in his bed and told his daughter, "I would have you remember one thing: there are countless people in the world other than Lev Tolstoy, but you concern yourselves only with Lev."

Newspaper readers learned that Tolstoy's desire to lose his distinction in the world was being undermined even by those closest to him, who were engaging in the same enterprise as the reporters outside. Besides attending to his physical needs (seven doctors would be consulted), they took meticulous care of his legacy, reporting his every word and movement to Aleksandr Sergeenko, who was in charge of keeping the record. Others were keeping their own notes as well, including Chertkov and the tireless Dushan Makovitskii.⁵² Every effort was being made to mark this moment, to distinguish Tolstoy's presence amid the great, unnumbered masses.

Seeking solitude, Tolstoy was being revealed to the world in a more richly detailed and compelling manner than ever before. The reporters played a critical role in this process. Whereas Zhukovsky fulfilled the same bedside role for Pushkin as did Chertkov, Sergeenko, and Makovitskii for Tolstoy, the presence of the media added a new, decidedly twentieth-century dimension to our record of the scene. Modern technologies increased the breadth of the renderings of Astapovo and made them more dynamic. The competitive scramble of so many different reporters to capture some side to the story that others had missed reduced the effects of individual selectivity on the record we have of Astapovo. As the author of the introduction to the 1928 publication of the collected telegrams from Astapovo asserts, the modern media allow us to know the event more intimately and more exhaustively. The collection is indescribably rich, he explains, because it pertains to

> a very large circle of people, and a very complex family situation, arising in Tolstoy's last days, and shows important and insignificant people, coincidentally brought together by events; it depicts the press, the social mood of the country. In a word, it gives the sort of vivid picture that only a precise apparatus, such as the railroad and its telegraph, can give . . . as if all the surroundings of Tolstoy and the extremely complex spiritual experiences of those around him were depicted, minute by minute, in a cinematographic film.⁵³

This passage highlights not only the wealth of documentation provided by the telegrams but also the diminished role of Tolstoy himself. The legacy of

14. Bulletin confirming Tolstoy's death signed by the doctors at Astapovo: "Today at 6 hr. 5 min. a.m. Lev Nikolaevich quietly passed away. Shchurovskii, Usov, Nikitin, Berkengeim, Makovitskii, Semenovskii." Though it is written on a telegram blank, it apparently was not sent. A note at the bottom reads: "This sheet serves as a bulletin, which was given to the correspondents."

Astapovo is of a national event, in which the telegraph and press played a conspicuously participatory role and Tolstoy a passive one. The dynamics of this interaction are illustrated in the report on the announcement of Tolstoy's death. When it had become apparent that the end was approaching, a group of reporters gathered on the porch of the house to await the news:

> 4:50 a.m. Night. Storm. Astapovo keeps vigil; correspondents hover about house all night; movement in Italian window, they approach patient with lamp, five minutes later someone wrings hands in despair. 5:00 a.m. critical weakening of heart activity; situation dangerous. Sent for family. Bulletin dictated to correspondents. Ilya L'vovich with trembling voice. Correspondents shocked, go to telegraph, not wanting to believe unavoidable end.... We experience with all our hearts the last minutes of the great teacher.[54]

Tolstoy's death quickens the narrative pulse of the story, generating tremendous energies of grief and interpretation. The massive transmission of press reports that followed his death could be described with the Russian word *perezhivaniia,* which can mean "trying experiences" but also "relivings" and "outlivings." New technology allowed the public to follow the story in a simulation of "real time." Newspapers printed the full list of the dispatches they received from Astapovo, so that readers could follow events in progression—even when earlier telegrams had been rendered obsolete. This technique gave new energy to the story, as the telegrams precisely describe the progression toward death but also the focused urgency of emotion which accompanies it. Tolstoy's death does not eliminate or resolve the drama of his life but educes and defines it; as Walter Benjamin writes, "Death is the sanction of everything the storyteller can tell."[55] The telegraph made much of this sanction, imbuing the story with an animating vividness: knowing that Tolstoy died on November 7, 1910, we still feel relief that his temperature dropped at 4:00 on November 5, and that the camphor injected on the morning of November 6 produced its desired effect.

The End of an Age

Tolstoy's rejection of these sympathies only intensified the journalistic process that excited them. The activity of the media at Astapovo made a public travesty of Tolstoy's intention to die a peasant death, but it also exalted his personal integrity. Vasilii Rozanov, in an editorial appearing in *Novoe vremia* the day after Tolstoy's death, despaired of the chaos that would emerge in a Russia without his moral example: "and around him, before him, after him—there is nothing apparent in contemporary literature except a black and hopeless emptiness. It's frightening to remain in this emptiness, especially after him and his great restraining, exhorting example, which held everyone back from the brink of disgrace."[56] It was this very disgracefulness (*bezobrazie*) which seemed to have rallied its forces at Astapovo, against which Tolstoy stood as a censoring, controlling figure.[57] It was as if the young writers often depicted receiving condescending praise from Tolstoy were to be left alone for the first time and would be unable to restrain themselves from following their own worst rhetorical inclinations.

It was more than just the standards of literary taste that were at stake, however. Aleksandr Blok, writing in 1908 on the occasion of Tolstoy's eightieth birthday, anticipated the national anxiety over his approaching death: "While Tolstoy is alive, and going along the furrows behind a plow, behind his white horse, the morning is still fresh and dewy, unthreatening, the vampires sleep, and—thank god. Here comes Tolstoy—indeed, it is the sun coming up. But

15. Tolstoy looming large among contemporary writers, including Korolenko, Chekhov, Gorky, and Andreev. The drawing commemorates Tolstoy's seventy-fifth birthday in 1903.

if the sun sets, Tolstoy dies, the last genius leaves—what then?"[58] The anxiety in Blok's essay explains, perhaps, why the press followed Tolstoy as compulsively as did Sofia Andreevna. The dying Tolstoy was a setting sun that would not rise again. Tolstoy, moreover, had chosen a particularly emotive landscape over which to set. If the media hovered over the scene of this spectacle, they did so as representatives of their readers, who wished to see it as well.

But the desire of the public to witness this spectacle was mitigated by concern that its presence as observer would obscure its beauty. Tolstoy had, after all, insisted that no one follow him. Recalling the tremendous scandal that had recently occurred when a painting was slashed in the Louvre, A. Iuzhanin warned his readers in *Voronezhskii tetrad'*: "What a beautiful picture we're tearing to bits and trampling with our feet—what harmony we're destroying with our clumsy outbursts, what a precious crown we're stripping off the head of the genius!"[59] The pastoral image of Tolstoy at Yasnaya Polyana had already been blemished long ago; in a cartoon appearing at the same time as

16. "In the Bosom of Nature: Tolstoy Ploughs," with Repin ambi-dextrously at work on two easels trying to keep pace with a host of competitors. Drawing by Re-mia.

Blok's essay describing the reassuring scene of Tolstoy behind his plow, the infiltration was abundantly clear.

Astapovo was a last chance for Tolstoy to create this scene as he wished. In November 1910 the self-satisfied posture of Tolstoy in the above cartoon had disappeared—the sense that he participated in, and perhaps encouraged, this media fascination with his persona was given little consideration at this decisive moment. An image of beleaguered authenticity was more compelling than the winking sarcasm that might have created a more self-respecting position for the media and the popular culture it represented. Instead, the press made a spectacle of itself, and in its criticism of that action expressed a collective anxiety over its disruption of this idyllic scene. While Tolstoy's death represented the passing of something old, the construction of the media circus around it suggested the birth of something new and terrible, a method of communication fascinating in its appeal to public curiosity about private events. Tolstoy's personal and family crisis, and then his death, had been turned over to the world—but people did not know how to read it, or even whether they should.

In an essay appearing after Tolstoy's death, D. Brazul wrote in *Kubanskii krai* of the hindrance of Tolstoy, including a litany of the offending implements that allowed it:

> He wanted to leave us; he obscured his path and hid the goal of his travels, but without pausing to think for a moment we let loose with everything we had to prevent him from fulfilling his plan. Special trains, automobiles, the telegraph and telephone—and all the thinking world, as one person, followed after him and knew his every step.[60]

Using this list of technologies as a mantra, Brazul asked how the public could have restrained itself from applying these forces "when something great and tremendous, the likes of which we have never seen before, was leaving us!" "We couldn't help ourselves," he explains.[61] The public seemed to lack, as Rozanov had suggested, the necessary self-restraint to honor the will of its national genius. Perhaps the trouble lay in the nature of Tolstoy's genius. One writer argued that Tolstoy was an equal of Aristotle and Leonardo da Vinci but was a negative genius who did not create his age so much as he questioned and disciplined it.[62] Another writer similarly argued that the technical advances of the day would be forgotten, but that the moral achievement of Tolstoy's rejection of the world would last: it was "a thousand times more important to us, and not only to us but to all humanity, than the much-publicized Portuguese revolution, the Chinese constitution, and even the invention of dirigibles and airplanes."[63] That Tolstoy would scorn the society of modernity, that he would seek solitude during the advent of the age of communication, suggested a check on the reckless march of progress. He was walking away from the culture that was being created through the popular press, and was challenging the minds stimulated by that press to see something more than scandal in his departure: "He is tired of you. He's tired of the world.... Solitude, concentration, and contemplation, a life outside our life—that's all he needs."[64]

This vision of Tolstoy seeking "solitude and concentration" was a balance against a disintegrating world, a world in which his readers had perhaps lost the necessary scope to fully comprehend Tolstoy. "Don't divide him!" one writer pleaded, "understand him as a single whole. Or perhaps our inferiority prevents us from understanding the whole of his greatness?"[65] The prevalence of such histrionic self-questioning indicates a fear that all the machinery of modernity was missing the mark, that the modern world, despite its advances, was ill-equipped to fathom the truth that motivated Tolstoy. "He went there, into a secret place, where we, despite our control of automobiles, special trains, and telephones, are still too small and insignificant and cannot penetrate. . . . We can't see into the depth of the future into which his memory will live."[66]

In the summer of 1910 Tolstoy alluded to his imminent departure by saying that he was going to create a Russian "Robinson," but he instead became a Russian Gulliver, encountering a Lilliputian world where no one could comprehend his thoughts or imagine his future. The giant Tolstoy had long been seen looming over the current literary and political landscape, but here he was towering over all of civilization:

17. Drawing from the cover of *Satirikon* of November 13, 1910. By A. Radakov.

The Tolstoy who dominated the Russian horizon as he departed from Yasnaya Polyana was no longer a literary, political, or religious gargantuan but was instead a mythic conscience, the parameters of which were no longer limited by current events or polemics. In a piece entitled "Our Conscience Incarnate," Tolstoy was viewed as a specifically Russian moral phenomenon but with universal, timeless significance: "he understood with titanic power, from the very depth of the Russian national conscience, the eternal questions of the soul, and with unusual directness set them before us and before all the thinking world."[67] The enigmatic, open-ended *ukhod* became a repository into which the immeasurable bounty of this conscience could be poured, against which society could commit a countless number of sins.

These sins, as it turned out, were often largely of inadequacy and ignorance, but they were seen to cause Tolstoy no end of suffering. A journalist for *Golos Moskvy* wrote, "And when we, all of us, small like worms, struggle for, create and destroy that which seems important or unimportant at the moment, when we come to know grains of truth and oceans of temptation, when we fall and get up—he, knowing the truth, stands above us, powerful and great, and lives through our suffering."[68] Lack of ethical discernment among the "little people" surrounding Tolstoy, as readers were reminded again and again, had driven Tolstoy not just away from his family but away from a public that had proven equally inadequate. An article in a Zhitomir newspaper titled "Without Love and Understanding" reproached its readers: "And we're inclined to blame Tolstoy's family for everything, accusing it of heartlessness, exploitation, and even provocation—a family of people who are guilty only in that they, like all of us, weren't able to understand or love Tolstoy."[69] There was nothing for this misunderstood genius to do but to leave not only his familial estate but the entire civilized world as well.[70] But it began to appear that there might not be an escape for Tolstoy. The clamor of the press and public following Tolstoy became a "bad dream" haunting him on his journey, with the potential to drive him back from his goal, as the writer for *Mariupol'skaia zhizn'* had imagined.[71]

There is no evidence of Tolstoy being affected by the media coverage of his journey, but these lamentations indicate concern that the press was hindering him on another level. At risk was the sublimation of Tolstoy's prophetic search for truth, the construction of a legend of the great Russian writer turned pilgrim. "The majestic, biblical, legendary image of the father-hermit," wrote a Voronezh journalist, "an image, the likes of which the world hasn't seen since the days of the prophets and apostles, will be destroyed, tarnished, and vulgarized."[72] Like the painting in the Louvre, the picture of Tolstoy setting off on his own into the "great world," this moment of pastoral sublime, was in danger of being defiled. "Be quiet!" an anonymous editorial in a Viatsk newspaper commanded, "Don't spoil the triumphant minutes. Don't touch your petty, dirty hands to the blindingly pure crown of thorns with which the great, suffering hermit of Yasnaya Polyana has crowned himself."[73] The *ukhod* was a moment of vicarious liberation: Tolstoy had shown that it was possible to leave the boulevard world where pettiness reigned. "He left!" a writer happily observed in a Saratov newspaper, "He grabbed a little bag with his favorite books, put on a work shirt and some peasant slippers, and left."[74] Whether or not this simple gesture existed as a real possibility was perhaps not as important as its resonance as an aesthetic one, an aspect that was not lost on artists at the time. As the writer Leonid Andreev said of Tolstoy's departure: "He wants to die like a great artist! How beautiful that is! How rich! Tolstoy lacked one final stroke in his life, and here he found it himself."[75] It was this defining touch, it was feared, that the public would obstruct.

But if the media and the public projected their own diminutive shapes onto the canvas of this final scene in Tolstoy's life, their presence there was perhaps less detrimental than was imagined. In a eulogy appearing in *Novoe vremia,* Vasilii Rozanov confirmed that Tolstoy had found that "final stroke" in his death, in spite of the interference and misunderstanding of the public which preceded it: There is something wonderful, exceptionally noble, and original in this death. Who else has died this strangely, wildly, and magnificently?"[76] It is clear to us now that the excesses of the media were essential to this scene, as some writers recognized even at the time. Speaking in words strikingly reminiscent of Blok's description of the "vampires" surrounding Tolstoy at his plow, an unsigned editorial in a Baku newspaper called to the crowd: "Go ahead and shout, you enemies of truth, about the whimsical old man having pulled another stunt. Circle, you black crows, around his holy, gray-haired head. Things wouldn't be right without you. Without you the simple words 'Tolstoy went off into the world' wouldn't resound in all their glory."[77] The contrast of these "simple words" with the *glasnost'* of the press, with the image of the telegraph operators slumped in exhaustion at Astapovo, is crucial to the paradoxical role played by the media at the time of Tolstoy's death. As Tolstoy turned away from society and the media, they glorified his aversion to their attentions.

Andrei Bely grasped this idea in an essay appearing in *Russkaia mysl'* in January 1911, in which he spoke of the artistic genius of Tolstoy being displaced by a moral genius that could be expressed through silence. His later teachings only revealed "one thousandth of that, for which he no longer had words."[78] While the press was making the most of dealing in these "thousandth parts" which were suited to words, Tolstoy expressed a lofty, unparceled silence full of unqualified, unspeakable potential. In granting this rhetorical position of silence to Tolstoy, the public staked a position for itself of abject prolixity. Dmitrii Merezhkovskii drew the same contrast in his response to Tolstoy's departure: "There are things, about which one should not talk. And shouldn't we keep quiet about this? We talk too much in general. We don't know the art of 'blessed silence.'"[79] For Bely this silence was more powerful than any words or actions and was the basis of Tolstoy's "magnetism" in his later years.[80] And if silence could speak more powerfully than words, so could death generate a powerful life force. In Bely's essay, Tolstoy's death is not the setting of the sun but instead the rising of a new sun over Russia—"the end turned out to be the beginning." This silence, Bely asserted, illuminated the vast open spaces of Russia; Astapovo became the center of a Russia surrounded by open fields—"*clear,* like God's day, *radiant fields.*"[81]

Not everyone reading the legend of Astapovo was as sanguine as Bely, however. If Tolstoy's escape had the potential to cleanse the landscape of Russia (and of the twentieth century), it required, as Bely suggested, open space in which it might expand and resonate. An article appearing in *Rannee utro* made the call to Russia to open up these expanses to Tolstoy: "And he went, bright and strong, to all people.... Don't stand in his way with your petty little measures.... Give way to the bright wanderer. Let him go where he wants, and let there be joy wherever he stops—and let Russia be wide open for him."[82] But if the world were to prove too close for the giant Tolstoy, if it were to wall him in, how would he ever leave it? How would this "bright and strong" pilgrim, setting out like Siddhartha, as one writer put it, show the world that it was possible to leave, that humans were not slaves but gods?[83] What were the newspapers showing, except that he could not leave? All the traces of his secret departure had been discovered, and the world had followed and closed in around him.

Thus was invited the "Golgotha" reading of Astapovo, in which redemption came only after a crucifixion of Tolstoy. "Don't hinder him," Lisovskii exhorted the readers of *Iuzhnaia zaria,* "with your clumsy and unnecessary interference, from going where his conscience calls him and where his highest reward awaits him.... For his sake give to others just a grain of that love, the cross of which he has raised now upon his aging shoulders."[84] Perhaps those taking this approach knew that a remake of the "greatest story ever told" would sell newspapers and understood that mounting their own transgressions on the aging shoulders of Tolstoy would only broaden the appeal of their story. Tolstoy would, after all, stand taller among a crowd prostrating themselves before his image. In publicizing their own vulgarity, they were building a narrative cross upon which to crucify him and seemed to take as much pleasure in masochistically contemplating their sin as they did in watching the "setting sun" before them: "We're shams! And all our life, even in our most sincere effort to live more humanly, is completely and hopelessly ensnared in lies and falsified, and we ourselves are falsified in it, with counterfeit bodies, counterfeit souls."[85] This debased, false society that was powerless to appreciate and understand its "great writer" had, in fact, a long tradition of crucifying its artists. An article by V. Obninskii appearing in *Utro Rossii* portrayed Tolstoy as the latest in a great tradition of tormented writers destroyed by the Russian public:

> How do we justify our latest crime? Indeed, wasn't it we, both executioners and condemned, dull and refined, educated and ignorant, who pushed the great old man on the eve of his death to flee his home, where everything should have been pleasing, moving and restful....We ruined Pushkin and Lermontov, deprived Gogol of his reason, drove Dostoevsky into hard labor, chased Turgenev into a foreign land, and now, at last, we piled the eighty-three-year-old Tolstoy onto the wooden bench of a remote railway station![86]

Only in death could Tolstoy achieve his escape, but even here there was a danger of betrayal—a danger that the witnesses of the event would not understand it—that Russians would not understand their own messiah. The response of the unworthy, philistine public, wrote A. Aprelev, was "not reverential contemplation of his feat but a lot of empty curiosity, superfluous and nonexistent details, hints, and often narrow-minded conjectures."[87] This inability of the public to comprehend its own artists suggested, in Obninskii's view, the gravest consequences for Russian society: "And at the same time that every other nation, from the Chinese colossus to tiny Portugual, is moving upward, bringing the best and most beautiful of its achievements to the top, our life is some sort of collective descent into a bottomless, dreary pit, in the depths of which awaits nothingness, our spiritual death."

Russia's lamentations over Tolstoy's death mourned the departure of a national writer but also a loss of rhetorical discipline and integrity. If the vampires that Blok saw being held at bay by Tolstoy emerged in full force at Astapovo, they did not prey on the dying Tolstoy so much as they consumed his readers, captivating them with stories that he would not have told them. Those who adopted these discourses were as engaged as any Tolstoyan in the building of a cult of "the great writer of the Russian land." The intersection of that cult building with the mercantile interests of newspaper publishing perhaps only reveals more candidly the ways in which cults are products of, and address the needs of, their creators. In the diffuse discourses of the media we encounter the construction of the Tolstoyan cult in its most capitalist form, where the great variety of often conflicting interests in Tolstoy meet in a public marketplace of consumers.

Tolstoy's contemporaries sought to capture him on film because it would preserve him for the ages; he would remain forever alive on celluloid, and we would forever see his peasant clothes, his wizened face, and his bemused gaze into the camera, into a future which insisted on carrying him with it, despite his resistance. This resistance provides the tension that generates narrative and thus is a critical part of the drama motivating the work of the journalists at Astapovo. Some were only too happy to back away (at least rhetorically) and leave Tolstoy at large, to grant him an unfettered, epic sweep with which he could create his own final narrative. If there were others who maintained a less respectful distance—the "philistines" who generated the boulevard novel version of Tolstoy's departure—they too made their own significant contribution. They provided the horizon over which this sun would set and helped illuminate that pastoral death far beyond the skies above the small railway station, across the broad expanses of a "great world" that had become increasingly situated within the purview of modernity and its media.

Ясная Поляна. Лѣто 1906 г.

Среди нашихъ чувствъ и убѣжденій есть такія, которыя соединяютъ насъ
со всѣми людьми, и есть такія, которыя разъединяютъ. Будемъ же утвер-
ждать себя въ первыхъ и руководствоваться ими въ жизни и, напротивъ,
сдерживаться и осторожно разбираться въ словахъ и поступкахъ, которые не
соединяютъ, а разъединяютъ людей.

Левъ Толстой.

Фот. В. Черткова. Серія V, № 6.

18. "Among our feelings and convictions are those that unite us with all people, and
those that separate us. We will strengthen ourselves in the former and be guided by
them in life, and, on the contrary, restrain ourselves and carefully discern those words
and actions that do not unite, but separate people."

4

Tolstoyan Violence upon the Funeral Rites of the State

31–7:43 p.m.
Yelets Ural. To Capt. Savitskii.
The writer Count Tolstoy passing through on train 12 has fallen ill. The
stationmaster Mr. Ozolin has taken him into his apartment.
—Private Filippov

On the morning of November 9, watching the beginning of
Tolstoy's funeral, the governor of Tula and a special agent
from Petersburg were alarmed to notice the flash of a large red cloth in the
crowd. The two had been placed in charge of overseeing the funeral and were
spying on the procession as Tolstoy's body was carried from the train station
at Zaseka to Yasnaya Polyana, to be certain that no "antigovernment" demonstrations accompanied it. An undercover officer was quickly dispatched to
determine what the offending red material was. As it turned out, it was only
a piece of cloth being used to cover a cinematographer's camera, and everyone relaxed. A short while later, a message was sent back to Interior Minister
Stolypin informing him that the ceremony had begun without incident.

Later events would prove, however, that this "red flag" had been too
quickly dismissed. Though the funeral proved to be largely free of political
content, the screening of the footage of the proceedings, which was pre-
miered in Moscow the day after the funeral, soon came to be viewed as a
political tinderbox and was banned across Russia. Presentations of the film in
theaters provided an occasion that had become politically volatile—namely,
for the public to gather in what could be perceived as commemorative gestures toward Tolstoy. These cinematic wakes were quickly prohibited, and
a Ministry of the Interior circular issued to all provincial governors and city
mayors required police clearance for announcements of religious services
(*panikhidy*) for Tolstoy in local papers. Written guarantees that priests would
actually perform these services were also required, to assure that they were

not arranged to disguise public demonstrations.[1] Ultimately the Orthodox Church decided to prohibit altogether such services for the excommunicated Tolstoy. Likewise, access to the funeral at the author's estate at Yasnaya Polyana was limited by both familial and governmental arrangements. As a result, officially sanctioned opportunities for public remembrance of Tolstoy were inadequate. The government limited these opportunities because it understood quite well that the emotions quickened by Tolstoy's death could, if not carefully managed, stimulate the political unrest that had been only tenuously managed in the years following the 1905 Revolution.

The secret police had been taking the pulse of this emotion even in the days before Tolstoy's death and had received clear warnings of what to expect. A report from Kiev concluded with the warning of a freight-yard clerk that if the government tried to interfere with public commemorations of Tolstoy's death, "then they are just making it worse for themselves, since the indistinct grumbling and dissatisfaction have been spreading among the working masses for some time and are just waiting for a push to erupt to the surface."[2] The gallows diplomacy that Stolypin had used with the revolutionaries of 1905 would not work here, for the public was organizing itself not around the red flag of revolution but around the coffin of a national hero.

The delicacy and latent energy of the situation were perhaps best captured by a moment near the end of Tolstoy's funeral. As the funeral was civil, there was no priest leading the procession or directing the crowd through the ceremony, which was largely being improvised by the participants. Security forces were concerned that such a ceremony could be hijacked by political ne'er-do-wells, but it in fact proved quite peaceful; the crowd sang quietly as they escorted the body, then filed past in silence as it lay in state in the family home, and later kneeled reverentially as the coffin was lowered into the ground. At this last juncture, however, something unusual did occur. A Moscow police officer, called to the funeral to act as a censor and positioned near Tolstoy's body throughout the proceedings, remained standing as the rest of the crowd knelt during Tolstoy's interment. As the crowd noticed the irreverent officer, they insistently corrected his behavior: "They shouted at him 'Police—on your knees!'—and he submissively dropped to his knees."[3]

The awkward position of this lone police officer is in many ways emblematic of that of the authorities in general during the days after Tolstoy's death. When it became clear that Tolstoy would not be buried according to Orthodox rites and therefore could not be given a state-sponsored funeral, willful crowds gathered, not only at his funeral but at ceremonies throughout Russia in the weeks following his death, to honor Tolstoy in rituals that excluded church and state.[4] The governing bodies of the Russian church and state found themselves facing two impolitic alternatives: forced to choose between

19. The crowd on their knees as Tolstoy's coffin is lowered into his grave, November 9, 1910. Photograph by A. I. Savel'ev.

standing apart from this crowd in an opposition that revealed their alienation from the people, and kneeling in demonstrations of sympathy with one whose views were overtly antithetical to their most basic tenets. At times they submissively joined, making gestures of reluctant obeisance; at other times, they reacted with nervous but resolute antagonism as the traditional Russian rites of burial were displaced by secular, and often overtly political, rituals.

The ambiguity of Tolstoy's final narrative was consequential to the political sphere, just as it had been to the religious one. Nowhere were alternate endings to that narrative more hotly and voluminously contested than in the political arena of late 1910. Though Tolstoy was not overtly affiliated with any particular political party or program, and was largely antagonistic to the political process itself, he was seen by authorities as a sort of revolutionary yeast that could be absorbed by any number of dubious political organizations and give rise to new hopes and demands on the part of a restless public. This concern was particularly significant at the moment of his death, when the public would have license to gather in his name and might use the opportunity to advance antigovernment agendas. This property was not unique to Tolstoy but had over the preceding half-century become characteristic of leaders of the democratic intelligentsia, the funerals of whom had repeatedly served as focal points of political turmoil and social unrest.

What followed the funeral was not so typical, however, and can be tied more specifically to Tolstoy. In his last days Tolstoy had moved to bring his life into closer accord with his ethical system—one that had destabilized the foundations of the aristocratic family, autocratic politics, and patriarchal Orthodoxy. When, in late October 1910, he set off from his family home, the narrative of emancipation which the public read into the act was, to the horror of the authorities, a compelling representation of abandonment of traditional, patriarchal values. The specific political context of Russia in the period after the 1905 Revolution is also significant. It is no accident that in his political afterlife Tolstoy continued to threaten the political status quo as a spokesman against the death penalty. Capital punishment had not been common in Russia before 1905 but came into widespread use under Stolypin in the years afterward. Tolstoy, a vocal opponent of this practice, had promised in a 1909 article to speak against it to his dying breath. His fulfillment of this promise (he completed a short piece on the question during his final journey) gave demonstrators a rallying cry with which to overtly politicize his death and sharpened the response of the authorities to the public sentiments and reactions that it elicited.

The complex behaviors of the government and public following Tolstoy's death mixed honest political emotion and belief with a great deal of posturing and dissimulation, as both Right and Left tried to turn political sympathies on the axis of Tolstoy's death. The government tried to exchange thinly disguised gestures of grief for favorable public opinion, while many who shared Tolstoy's disdain for Orthodox ritual passionately condemned the official refusal to allow church services for him. The political battle over Tolstoy's grave became a complicated chess match, in which the endgame was often obscured behind various sacrifices and exchanges, and in which seemingly incidental pieces like cinematographers' cameras acquired the potential to determine the outcome. Tolstoy's beliefs, and in particular his campaign against the death penalty, placed him in the middle of this political struggle; at the same time, his pacifism and anarchism made him politically malleable. The Right could attack those who joined the campaign against the death penalty, claiming that their defiant demonstrations made a mockery of his beliefs, while the Left could claim that in its repression the regime was symbolically desecrating Tolstoy's grave. Ironically, even as he lay most passively in his grave, Tolstoy was unable to resist this violence, which would forever be associated with his memory.

The Tradition of the Public Funeral in Russia

A police circular issued as Tolstoy was nearing death warned: "Presently all the opposition groups and students are reacting quite strongly to the illness of Count Tolstoy, and we can expect, in the case of a crisis, all manner of demonstrations."[5] Such anticipation was based on historical precedent, both in Tolstoy's life and in a disposition the Russian public had shown to project political significance on the deaths of national writers and ideological heroes. This tradition was in fact cited in the November 1910 issue of *Vestnik Evropy,* in an editorial describing the social effects of the death and funeral of the popular liberal S. A. Muromtsev, who died one month before Tolstoy. From the time of Russia's political "awakening," the article began, the funerals of those "who had risen above mediocrity and had left a trace on the national conscience" had become public events of great significance. The first of these political funerals had been for the actor Aleksandr Martynov in 1860.[6] Martynov had been immensely popular among the democratic intelligentsia, and his funeral turned into a disturbing display of populist emotion, as thousands lined Nevsky Prospect to view what became "an openly antigovernment demonstration."[7] When the police tried to restore order, the crowd responded with cries of "Down with the police!" and forced them to retreat. When large crowds again gathered the next year for Dobroliubov's funeral, it was clear that the public funeral, responding to the charisma of ideologies as much as to that of individuals, had become a feature of social life in Russia. According to the article, the funerals of Nekrasov, Dostoevsky, Turgenev, Saltykov-Shchedrin, and Shelgunov had further developed this tradition.

The autocracy sought ways to minimize the political content of these unsanctioned gatherings and to control the publicity surrounding them. When Dostoevsky died in 1881, the government announced that his widow would receive a 2,000 ruble pension, and that the state would pay for the education of the children. Though Anna Grigor'evna wrote in her memoirs that she did not accept this largesse, her refusal was not publicized, and one government official bragged at the time of the cleverness of this public relations gesture.[8] The funeral Mass itself was also largely co-opted by the government—it was a state affair, attended by Konstantin Pobedonostsev and members of the royal family, from which the author's family was nearly turned away because they did not have tickets. Some years later, however, Pobedonostsev would cite Dostoevsky's funeral (along with Turgenev's) as an example of a growing and troubling tendency on the part of the public to accompany the Orthodox funeral procession with elaborate civil ceremonies, "not without the secret intention of creating the opportunity for demonstrations."[9] Dostoevsky's funeral service had been preceded by a huge procession down Nevsky

Prospect; the coffin was accompanied by a crowd of thirty thousand, including seventy to a hundred delegations and fifteen choirs, which were in turn viewed by as many as a hundred thousand observers. Though the procession was largely peaceful, observers noted that the police had been unprepared for such a mass gathering and were unable to control the crowd.[10]

Anna Grigor'evna Dostoevskaya would later write that the most impressive aspect of the funeral was that the crowds and delegations had organized themselves so quickly. This spontaneous, organic response, exceeding and contravening the initiatives of the government, revealed the political autonomy of the Russian public and indicated to the government that it did not have the defining power to circumscribe the meaning of Dostoevsky's death. For Suvorin, the funeral was an unprecedented triumph of Russian creativity and thought, a spectacle such as had never before been seen in Russia.[11] The government, of course, would have preferred that such spectacles have a less ambiguously chauvinist content.

The longer the public had to organize its own responses, the authorities learned, the more trouble could then ensue. When Turgenev died in Paris two years later, the prolonging of the burial process as a result of the transportation of the body back to Russia provided what was, from the point of view of the authorities, a dangerous surfeit of preparatory time (several weeks). Nikolai Strakhov wrote to Tolstoy at the time that everyone was occupied with Turgenev, and that his funeral would be "something colossal. Obviously they want to make a demonstration out of it," he wrote.[12] As Turgenev had lived his last years as an expatriate, the return of his body to Russia for burial became a richly symbolic event, necessitating particular vigilance on the part of the authorities to assure that it would not acquire an improper "spin." The head of police, Viacheslav Plehve, ordered that no advance publicity about the itinerary of the train should be allowed, so as to avoid "ceremonial meetings," and efforts were made to control the public perception of the procession. One official wrote at the time of the necessity to censor the newspaper correspondents reporting back to Petersburg: "Without doubt they will telegraph Petersburg about the transport of Turgenev's body through Pskov and the meeting, and I am sure in advance that they will try to give these things as broad and triumphal a significance as they can, a significance that in essence will not be there."[13] The government learned to downplay events as much as possible and to work in advance to limit the scope of panegyric emotion of the public. The unveiling of the Pushkin monument in 1880 had provided a recent reminder of the collective energies that could be innervated by national narratives around celebrated authors (not to mention previous literary bombshells in the eulogistic mode: Lermontov on Pushkin, Turgenev on Gogol, etc.) When it was learned that Tolstoy was slated to participate in a memorial evening for Turgenev of the Society for Lovers of Russian Letters, the event was permanently "postponed," with the explanation that the speakers needed more time to prepare their addresses.[14]

By the time of Tolstoy's death, these practices, describing the struggle between the state and the larger public over the memory of the deceased, had become generically encoded. Post-event posturing and the accompanying practice of "funeral-reading" became central to the institution of national mourning. In the above-cited article in *Vestnik Evropy,* for example, the author interpreted the size and patience of the crowd at the Muromtsev procession in Moscow as a sign of ideological sympathy with Muromtsev and a "rehabilitation of the First Duma" over which he had presided. Muromtsev's metonymic association with the Duma, which Nicholas had dissolved in 1906 after only forty sessions, invested his funeral with the pathos and emotion of the frustrated aspirations of the 1905 Revolution. The author, like Dostoevsky's widow, was most impressed by the self-motivation of the crowd; this spontaneous energy revealed popular emotions and political sentiments deeply internalized within Russian society and thus could be read as a sign of the times.[15] Once funerals had begun to be interpreted this way, their representation in the public sphere (particularly in the press) came to be seen as a field of open political warfare.

A popular notion among conservatives of the time, and one that would be repeated often in the aftermath of Tolstoy's death, was that the Left could exploit such occasions to advance views that were not even shared by the deceased. L. A. Tikhomirov, the editor of the conservative *Moskovskie vedomosti,* wrote in his diary: "This death is going very well for the revolutionaries.... The Revolution marvelously exploited the remains of a person who had broken with it. The same thing will happen with the legacy of Muromtsev."[16] The experience with Muromtsev's funeral had indeed set the stage for Tolstoy's and put the authorities on their guard. In a letter to Count Benkendorf, the governor of Tambov wrote: "The death of Tolstoy, especially after the commotion surrounding Muromtsev's funeral, will encourage the Jewish/Kadet [Constitutional Democratic] intelligentsia and the press to make still more noise."[17] In light of these expectations, Benkendorf was asked to prohibit in advance political demonstrations in the form of standing salutes in various councils, and other similar precautions were taken throughout Russia.

Tolstoyan Particulars

There were, of course, particularly "Tolstoyan" reasons for these precautions as well. Popular emotion had already shown a tendency to swell into rebellious affection for Tolstoy: when he was excommunicated from the Church in 1901, he received a flood of congratulatory telegrams and was greeted as a hero everywhere he went. When he became ill later that year and traveled to the warmer climate of the south, the government found that strict secrecy regarding his movements could not forestall spontaneous public demonstrations in his honor. Three thousand people gathered to greet his train in Kharkov (having learned by word of mouth that he was passing through) and gave him a long, thunderous ovation when he appeared in the window of his compartment. Shortly thereafter, when his illness took a grave turn for the worse, both church and state set to work in anxious anticipation. The Ministry of the Interior gave notice that press reports on Tolstoy and his illness should be limited to factual information, refraining from any editorial commentary.[18] Local police worked to fulfill orders from the highest offices in Petersburg; the latter made secret arrangements for the transport of the body and even gave the local officers a precautionary rehearsal. The secret dossier on Tolstoy's illness in the Crimea includes not only stipulations as to the route by which he would be carried back to Yasnaya Polyana but also pre-prepared announcements of his death, ready to be distributed after the proper date was filled in.[19]

Tolstoy had expressed great surprise at the boisterous sympathy expressed by the crowd greeting his train in Kharkov, but he had done much to cultivate it. Earlier that year, when the government had forcibly conscripted 183 Kiev students into the army as a response to widespread student demonstrations in 1900, Tolstoy had answered with an open letter to those responsible, entitled "To the Tsar and His Advisers."[20] This sort of intercession on behalf of the Russian masses came to define his relations with both the public and the government. Tolstoy wrote a great number of such appeals in his later period, some of them public and some of them private. One that particularly alienated him from the tsar's court was a letter to Alexander III pleading clemency for the assassins of Alexander's father. That Tolstoy in his later years referred to his esteemed addressees in familiar and at times condescending terms cannot have endeared him to Nicholas or his advisers.

The last of these personal appeals to change the policies emanating from Petersburg was a series of private and public addresses regarding the death penalty, which Stolypin had used liberally in the aftermath of 1905. He wrote Stolypin a private letter—"as a brother, as a human being"—in 1907, attempting to convince him to take a more just means to gain control of the country.[21] When this approach failed, he went public with the last of his works to create a major impression on Russian society during his life— "I Cannot Remain Silent." Though it is clearly written as a public appeal, the manner of address is still personal, as Tolstoy speaks in the second person throughout: "Stop—not for yourself, not for your personal gain, not so that people will stop judging you, but for your soul, for that God who, no matter how you stifle him, lives in you."[22] Tolstoy argued that the justification of the death penalty as a matter of national security was invalid: "And do not say that you do what you do for the people: that is untrue. All the horrible things you do, you do for yourself, for your own mercenary, vainglorious, vengeful, personal reasons, so that you can live a bit longer in that state of corruption in which you live, and which seems to you a blessing."[23] His last work, which he carried with him as he left Yasnaya Polyana and completed while sick in bed at Astapovo, was yet another appeal on the issue of the death penalty—this time taking the issue to its ultimate source: the only way out of this moral abyss, Tolstoy claimed, was to bring about such a change in society that no one would be willing to perform the executioner's reprehensible duty.

The government viewed these arguments as kin to treason. Stolypin told Tatiana L'vovna in 1909 that he considered the Tolstoyans much more dangerous to the government than the revolutionaries.[24] While the latter might confront the government with occasional violence, Tolstoy and his followers worked to undermine faith in authority and respect for the government. Later that year, word was received at Yasnaya Polyana that Stolypin was not going to be so lenient with Tolstoy anymore.[25] It is doubtful that this represented a direct threat to Tolstoy: police had interfered with his work many times before,[26] but the authorities had never punished him directly, preferring instead to imprison and exile his supporters, while keeping the firm grip of censorship on his writings.[27] As a Russian general explained to a foreign visitor: "We look over his works and censor those that are dangerous to the government, but he himself we leave alone. But if any of his friends turn out to be dangerous to the government, then we send those people to Siberia."[28] Many of Tolstoy's closest followers were imprisoned or exiled at some point, including such central figures as Vladimir Chertkov, Pavel Biriukov, and Nikolai Gusev.[29] Various plots hatched against him, however, including exile abroad and sequestration in a Suzdal monastery, were thwarted by the Russian monarchs, who demurred at the possibility of making a martyr of him.[30] Suvorin's now famous observation that Russia had two tsars—Nicholas and Tolstoy—and that the former dared not attempt to disturb the throne of the latter for fear of international scandal, aphoristically characterized what was, in fact, a government policy.

During the so-called Stolypin reaction after the 1905 Revolution vigilance was intensified, though again primarily in an orbit around Tolstoy. Stolypin, in a 1908 circular regarding the observation of Tolstoy's eightieth birthday, wrote:

> Thus the most vigilant attention must be paid by government organs to the restraint of attempts by unreliable elements of the populace to use the current events for antigovernment agitation, especially as such efforts are all the more likely since the ideas propagated by L. N. Tolstoy offer the widest grounds for

such agitation. Previous directives on the general law on this subject and separate instructions relating to the periodical press and public and private meetings
give the representatives of local power the full means to act in the appropriate
circumstances according to the interests of state order and public calm.[31]

Stolypin's anxiety about dissent spreading from Tolstoy's ideas, which opened
wide possibilities for exploitation by antigovernment forces, would not change
over the next two years. Tolstoy supported many of the goals of that revolution but not the means, and he thus never belonged to, or associated himself
with, any of the current parties or ideological wings. He was, in this sense, a
loose wire dangling precariously over a highly inflammable political arena.

The State Governs Tolstoy's Death

Thus, though there was nothing overtly political about Tolstoy's
departure from his family estate, the extent to which his life had become politicized led officials in Petersburg to follow the ensuing developments with
great concern. Secret police officers had begun monitoring Tolstoy's movements as soon as it was learned that he had left his estate, and at Astapovo
they quickly moved to control the activity of the press and public.[32] A special
agent was sent by Prime Minister Stolypin to represent the government's
interests and to assist representatives of the Church in fulfilling the com-
missions of the Holy Synod.[33] Their encoded reports to their superiors are
found regularly among the wires sent from the telegraph office at Astapovo.
At the same time, they arranged with one of the telegraph operators to be
able to read all the transmissions that were received and sent at the station.[34]
They controlled the traffic in the station, deciding who was allowed to stay,
and governed the activities of the reporters and photographers. Sixty cavalry
soldiers were called to Tula on a secret mission on November 5, and two
days later additional soldiers were called in from nearby regiments.[35] In the
early hours immediately after Tolstoy's death, police approached a group of
his followers who had left for Yasnaya Polyana to prepare for the funeral, attempting to learn what arrangements they were making. When they could
not get any information from this group, they learned what they needed from
"undercover information."[36]

The arrangements, made by Tolstoy's family in accordance with his wishes,
in many respects worked in favor of the authorities, who could not but have
rejoiced on learning that the funeral was to take place just two days after Tolstoy's death, that he was to be buried on the family estate, more than a day's
journey from the capital, and that no graveside speeches were to be allowed.[37]
The family informed the police, moreover, that they would not allow the
funeral to become a political demonstration, a message that officials would
gladly pass on to the gathering crowd.[38]

Despite the advantageous conditions, elaborate precautions were taken nonetheless. The coffin was carried in an unmarked baggage car on a special train, and stations were secured or cleared in advance of its arrival. Two Moscow police officers experienced in censorship issues were called to the scene and stood near Tolstoy's body throughout the ceremonies. The objections of one of Tolstoy's sons, who found the presence of the officers in his home on the day of his father's funeral offensive, were resolutely overruled by the officer in charge, who explained to him: "there could be antigovernment or antireligious statements that could then be announced in the press as if they were public speeches."[39] Though other police officers and soldiers were less conspicuously present—they were kept hidden in the woods, out of sight of the funeral procession—their presence was nonetheless felt. Ivan Shuraev, who worked in the Tolstoy household, said at the time "the police were everywhere.... They were afraid a whole revolution would take place at Tolstoy's grave."[40] They evidently were to be perceived as not interfering but entirely prepared to interfere if necessary.

The immediate response to Tolstoy's death had given additional cause for such concern. Eight thousand students had gathered at Moscow University on the morning before the funeral for a boisterous meeting that ended with a public march—just the sort of spontaneity that the authorities had learned to fear. The two thousand who attended the funeral, however, were well-behaved. They formed a chain around the procession, and three separate choirs (totaling seven hundred members) sang in succession. Though one hundred students had signed up to speak at the grave, the family's wishes were honored, and no eulogies or other speeches were delivered. As one local peasant told a visitor from the city: "They buried him well. The students sang movingly. There was order. The students made a chain, and we made a chain—it was orderly."[41]

Stolypin had done his part to make this possible. While many were prepared to travel to Yasnaya by special train, last-minute orders from Petersburg prohibited such arrangements, with the exception of two trains for students.[42] Thousands were left waiting at the station; those with the means to do so hired automobiles (including a delegation from the Duma and the rector of Moscow University), but they managed to arrive at Yasnaya only after the funeral (some later in the evening, others not until the following day).[43] As an editorial in *Rech'* reported, "Under these circumstances the external aspect of Tolstoy's funeral could not take on the grandiose measure that it would have under more favorable conditions."[44] Those who were able to attend the ceremony were, for the most part, students from Moscow, local peasants, and friends and admirers from the surrounding area. Valerii Briusov, who came as a representative of the Moscow Study Circle for Literature and the Arts (Literaturno-khudozhestvennyi kruzhok), complained: "How few people are gathered here! Probably not more than three or four thousand. For all of

Russia, for the funeral of Tolstoy, that's a really insignificant number. But then everything possible was done to deprive Tolstoy's funeral of its national significance."[45]

It is unclear to what extent this campaign succeeded. Briusov, despite his disappointment with the size of the crowd, found something more moving in this relatively humble ceremony than he had found in larger public funerals: "Everything came off simply, but in that simplicity there was something more powerful than the emotion and sensation at other funerals. It was just as if someone had told everyone how they needed to act during those hours."[46] Behavior at the graveside was said to be very reverent—everyone sang quietly (if one voice was too loud, others hushed the singer), and the crowd kneeled and bowed their heads. The Moscow theater director L. A. Sulerzhitskii, who had taken on the role of master of ceremonies, briefly explained the choice of the burial site.[47] Many felt that Tolstoy's ceremony, stripped of the ritualized behavior that would have accompanied any Orthodox funeral, was a more sincere expression of the grief felt over his loss. The author's son commented: "At that time it was unusual, but I think that the absence of the clergy only contributed to the solemn mood of the majority of those who had come to the funeral."[48] Several people in the crowd fainted, perhaps the result of a sense, as the student A. F. Bobkov described, that something "really great and unusual" was taking place. Bobkov recalled his feelings at the day's end as he headed back for Moscow: "The whistle of a steam engine sounded. There is vanity. That's our life flowing on. . . . I walked and kept thinking about how to make my life better and simpler. . . . I live badly."[49]

For many the funeral evoked the simplicity that Tolstoy had sought in his later writings and in his life. It harmonized with his desire to "die like a peasant" and his last words, much publicized at the time of his funeral, expressing his dismay that, amid the countless people in the world, so much attention was being paid to him. His death in the most quotidian of public spaces (a railway station), and the tremendous publicity surrounding it, confirmed this democratic ideal, as did the subsequent funeral: whereas other public funerals had ended with the interment of the body in one of various national "pantheons," Tolstoy was buried in an unadorned, unmarked grave in a quiet alley. Standing back from the crowd, Bobkov commented, it was easy to imagine that it was a peasant who was being buried.[50] The Yasnaya Polyana peasants helped create this atmosphere, decorating the path of the procession with pine branches, and played a prominent role in the ceremony: they were first, after the family, to view the body, and they carried the coffin to the accompaniment of a large banner thanking Lev Nikolaevich for his kindness.

On the heels of his departure "into the world" from Yasnaya Polyana, Tolstoy's connection to his estate had been rendered less aristocratic; the funeral, too, enunciated a message of social transformation—of radical reorientation

ПОХОРОНЫ Л Н. ТОЛСТОГО.

20. (a) The procession taking Tolstoy's body from the Ozolins' apartment at Astapovo. The coffin is carried by Tolstoy's sons. (b) The funeral procession at Yasnaya Polyana.

of the traditional relations between the nobility and the peasants. For the conservative forces in society it was most unfortunate that this ceremony should take place under "un-Orthodox" circumstances. If the funeral ritual connects the deceased to society and provides an opportunity in which to shape collective identities, to what society did this heterodox ceremony bind its participants? And what if the Orthodox ritual had lost its suasive, cathartic power? That an effective, compelling ceremony worthy of a national hero such as Tolstoy could be created without the participation of the Church suggested a shifting of the charismatic center of Russian society. The ruling establishment in Petersburg desperately wanted to reclaim Tolstoy, even by means of deception, to prevent this desacralization of rituals essential to its vision of the national identity. There must have been considerable gnashing of teeth among those who had wanted Tolstoy to be buried as an Orthodox Russian at the appearance of commentary like the following: "On the grounds of Yasnaya Polyana a great ceremony took place. Among young saplings and an ancient grove a grave has been dug. 'Without church singing or incense' the country buried its priceless treasure. The people themselves accompanied the remains of the deceased. They said parting words, and sang the farewell salutation. A civil funeral for a great citizen."[51]

National Mourning

Still more troubling to the government was the repetition of this heterodox ceremony, with its appropriated rituals, throughout the country. A key part of the Tolstoy ceremony was the singing of what was in fact one of the most moving pieces of the traditional Orthodox funeral liturgy, the song "Eternal Memory." Official church canon dictated that this song should not be sung for nonbelievers. Its performance to preserve the memory of Tolstoy was thus viewed by the authorities as a sign of protest; and they made repeated, but failed, attempts to stop it.[52] The choirs at Yasnaya repeated the song all the way along the road from the train station to the estate, and then again later throughout the ceremony. Many spoke of the emotive effect of the repeated singing of the song during the procession. Briusov wrote: "Someone begins: 'Eternal Memory.' Even those who never sing join in. You want to add your voice to the general choir, to the chorus of everyone. At that moment you think that this choir is all Russia."[53]

And the singing did, in fact, spread far beyond the ceremony at Yasnaya Polyana; it had begun at Astapovo on the day of his death, had been picked up the next morning by the students meeting at Moscow University, and in the days to follow became the central ritual in civil memorial services across Russia. Worse still, the song was incorporated into student demonstrations over the next week, many of them overtly political and antichurch in nature.

The gesture proved so contagious that it spread into the very core of the Church: students at a Kishinev seminary had begun singing the song after their morning prayers on November 10 and had then demanded that the day's classes be canceled.[54] In the press and in memoirs from the time, the singing of "Eternal Memory" became a metonym for the iconoclasm of Tolstoy's funeral; sung in a new context, in manifestly un-Orthodox ceremonies, the insistent repetition of the song suggested that even the most familiar rituals were ominously mutable and only provisionally affirmed their traditional meanings.

The all-Russian choir that Briusov imagined participating in this unsanctioned ritual, joining peasants with aristocrats, inhabitants of local villages with students and dignitaries from Moscow and Petersburg, and later, demonstrators from across Russia, was a specter that horrified the government. But attempts to disorganize this gathering were indecisive, and anything more repressive would have been viewed as inappropriate. Tolstoy, as even those who did not agree with his ethical system were wont to admit in the wake of his death, was the one national figure who had done the most to bring Russia to the world's attention. Stolypin's special agent Kharlamov himself felt the need to pay his respects: "Troubled by all these thoughts, I could not deny the spiritual demand to pay my respects to the remains of the great man, forgetting for a time the orders regarding my 'incognito.'"[55] Metropolitan Antonii was reported to have cried on being informed of Tolstoy's death. Count Witte was quoted saying he had changed his opinion of Tolstoy based on his last days—while he had previously doubted Tolstoy's greatness based on the contradictions between his life and teachings, he now felt that Russia had lost a great man.[56]

Judging by Russian newspapers in November 1910, the country had lost a titan, who touched every aspect of life. Articles detailed not only Tolstoy's literary accomplishments but also his activity in the army, as a sportsman, as a teacher, with children, as a bicyclist, as the subject of films, and so on. The breadth of reports of various public commemorations testifies to a desire for national catharsis: newspapers gushed with reports of panegyric gestures as they listed countless closings of schools, universities, theaters, factories, and governmental offices and described funds collected in Tolstoy's name for libraries, schools, houses for the poor, the placing of portraits in libraries and schools, various commemorative gestures, speeches, and memorial evenings, the texts of honorary resolutions and telegrams of condolence, and discussions of the meaning of Tolstoy. Moreover, evidence was pouring in from around the globe that Tolstoy's death was an event of tremendous international significance, at times suggesting that he was better appreciated abroad than at home. (A newspaper reported the shock of a native in Helsinki on learning that a Russian expatriate was attending the theater on the day of Tolstoy's funeral.) As these practices continued, the effusive grief over Tolstoy's death seemed to define his greatness; as a group of twenty-two political exiles in Tot'ma wrote in a telegram of condolence—"We can see what he was by the immeasurable wave of grief and tears that has filled all corners of the world."[57]

The Russian government, it seemed, should respond in kind. International attention, moreover, raised the danger of national embarrassment. A Russia that was increasingly becoming part of the European and international community—a development toward which Tolstoy's status as a writer of world renown had contributed—was now self-consciously on stage: would it show the world that it could not properly appreciate its own national genius?[58] A report in *Rech'* on the November 9 session of the Duma suggested that its members were very much aware of their responsibility. As they gathered before the call to order, the writer observed, there was a heightened sense of ceremony and purpose among the crowd: "knowing that the State Duma at some point soon is going to have to express its attitude toward the event in the form of an act awaited conscientiously by all Russia has created a general mood of special solemnity, mixed with apprehension." In the State Council, as Chairman M. G. Akimov called on members to stand in honor of Tolstoy, he explained to them that Russia, as the birthplace of the writer, should feel the loss more than other countries.[59]

Tolstoy's status as Russia's most significant international personality was of no little importance. Vladimir Korolenko wrote: "Our country is poor and lawless, but it gave the world Tolstoy, whose death speaks so distinctly of eternal, undying life." It seemed, in fact, as if Tolstoy overshadowed all of Russia, becoming, for Korolenko, independently sovereign:

> The world doesn't want to judge Tolstoy, neither from the point of view of the official government, nor from the point of view of the Greek-Russian Church. The world is inclined, if you will, to the opposite: it is ready to evaluate Russia (socially and spiritually) according to its attitude toward Tolstoy. The great writer became something on the order of a great moral sovereignty, who, from many perspectives, it is advantageous to have as an ally. And if such an alliance doesn't actually exist... what then? It is best to invent one.[60]

L. A. Tikhomirov, as he watched Stolypin bow to this public pressure, saw the government carrying diplomatic negotiations with Tolstoy's legacy: "Stolypin, imagining that all Russia was behind Tolstoy, decided to 'meet public opinion halfway,' so that he could forestall any 'excesses.'"[61] Reporting that the Cabinet was pressuring the Synod to "recommunicate" Tolstoy, *Rech'* explained that this was considered necessary not only for the count himself but also for the country.[62] Sentiment for Tolstoy was divided, moreover, even among these highest circles. Members of the royal family were known to be sympathetic to Tolstoy; Izvol'skii, the chief procurator of the Synod in 1908, apologized to Tatiana L'vovna Tolstaya for the Synod's pronouncements regarding Tolstoy's eightieth birthday in 1908 and said he had taken no part in them.

Witte would later remark on the difficulty the authorities had in orchestrating their response to Tolstoy's death:

> As for the government, it didn't know which foot to start on: on one hand, to completely ignore a major event like the death of Tolstoy was impossible; to categorically abuse this great man was impossible; on the other hand, to allow the expression of special grief or manifestations of sorrow over Tolstoy's death was awkward, and so, in this case, expressing apparent sympathy over his death, at the same time on the sly they took police measures to assure that all sympathies were expressed as modestly as possible.[63]

Stolypin tried clumsily to start with both feet. He forbade the provision of extra trains to take crowds in Moscow to the funeral at Yasnaya Polyana but nearly bowed to pressure to allow the funeral procession to pass through Moscow itself.[64] Attempting to deflect criticism of the government's relations to the national hero, he encouraged State Council Chairman Akimov to propose that the Council officially honor Tolstoy by standing, and he supported a proposed government purchase of Yasnaya Polyana, only to have it fly in his face when the Duma balked at Lev L'vovich's price of two million rubles.[65]

The Duma itself was at odds over what to do with Tolstoy's legacy. At the beginning of the session on November 8, Chairman A. I. Guchkov called for the delegates to stand in honor of Tolstoy's passing and proposed that the session be closed for the same reason. Rather than stand, right-wing members either left the room or stayed and demonstratively sat in protest (Vladimir Purishkevich, a founder of the Black Hundreds organization Union of the Russian People, was said to have spread into as supine a position as possible); G. G. Zamyslovskii then spoke for the right wing in objecting to the proposal to close the session, pointing out that Tolstoy had rejected governments in general, and the Duma itself in particular—honoring him in this manner was thus a form of self-negation.[66]

Working to fulfill, yet curtail, the expectations and needs of the public, the government affected a position of noninterference and even respect for the deceased writer. The official statement of Nicholas II is a clear example of this practice—an attempt to define that Tolstoy who was worthy of national mourning in an autocratic Russia. The emperor regretted the passing of one who, "in the dawning of his artistic career had created so moving a portrait of the nation in one of its most glorious years," and tendentiously wished for God's mercy upon his soul. The conservative State Council followed the tsar's lead in its commemoration on November 10, pointing out the "errors" of Tolstoy's religious and political works" but acknowledging that his other works had justly gained worldwide fame and glory.[67]

It could be said that two very different Tolstoys were buried at Yasnaya Polyana—one defined by the tsar's eulogy, and another who had been a spokesperson for the disenfranchised and disaffected. Both Left and Right were well aware of this tendency. *Moskovskie vedomosti,* in its typically gloomy fashion, described it on November 9: "It is not difficult to foresee (and this has already begun) that the death of L. N. Tolstoy will stimulate the exploitation of the second, destructive half of his work. His remains will become a weapon in the struggle against that Russia with which the deceased amiably spent the first, happier half of his earthly journey."[68] Two days later, *Rech'* commented: "Some, working on the still live body, are cutting the great writer into two parts and most unashamedly throw one of them away."[69] In the days following Tolstoy's death, as the newspapers offered their countless eulogies and various public figures and institutions honored his passing, a battle was waged over which of these Lev Nikolaevichs was more dear to the nation.

As both sides attempted to capitalize on his death, the Tolstoy claimed by Nicholas—the aristocratic novelist—was but a part of the whole, and a part that had been rejected by Tolstoy himself. Akimov, in his comments before the State Council, cited the official statement by Nicholas and told the Council: "In Lev Tolstoy Russia has lost the most ingenious writer and the greatest artist of the Russian word." The authorities tried to prevent the Left from claiming anything more than this: when a memorial evening was permitted in Petersburg, the speakers were prohibited from speaking about Tolstoy's relations with the government, his attitude toward the death penalty, or the Synod.[70] Leonid Andreev declined to participate, decrying the measures being taken to cut the commemorated Tolstoy down to size: "There cannot be openness and truth there where the honest and more passionate love for the deceased strikes against the drawn sword of a gendarme, and the inspiration of the orators is drawn into the narrow sleeve of the eloquence allowed by the police."

For the Left, the redemption value of Tolstoy's body proved much greater. As the funeral spilled over chronologically, physically, and ideologically, during what came to be known as the "Tolstoy days," it was clear that the Russia defined by Tolstoy's death was quite different from the one evoked in *War and Peace.* Police reports show that for several days after the funeral there were large daily gatherings at the grave, where in some cases revolutionary speeches were made.[71] Meanwhile, back in the cities, in addition to the traditional literary evenings and memorial services, the most significant demonstrations since the 1905 Revolution began to take place in the name of Tolstoy. Officials estimated that on the day of the funeral one-fourth of the workers of the city of Moscow went on strike.[72] Classes and theater performances were canceled, and large gatherings of students convened at universities throughout the country, leading to defiant street demonstrations, arrests, and some injuries.

The line between public mourning and political activism began to blur as signs appeared at the demonstrations calling for an end to the death penalty.

The abolition of capital punishment, it was argued, would be a fitting way to honor the death of Tolstoy. The tradition of philanthropic commemoration was an old one in Russia. Churches were often built, for instance, in the name of deceased loved ones. In the eyes of the government, however, this campaign had a decidedly revolutionary flavor, as the question of capital punishment had come to the fore in the aftermath of 1905, when large numbers of those implicated in the insurrection had been executed. Stolypin was "in love with the gallows," as Tolstoy said. That this campaign should have attached itself to the funeral of Tolstoy was, moreover, a foreboding expression of ill-defined unrest and political willfulness. As the gathering crowds began to form this overtly political agenda, the government quickly cracked down. Gatherings of any kind in the name of Tolstoy, from memorial evenings to showings of the film footage from the funeral, were resolutely banned; and crowds gathering in the streets were forcibly dispersed.

Spin Control

Ideological wars are generally not won or lost in the streets but in the press. Conservative newspapers tried to win on this front by describing the street demonstrations as manufactured and inappropriate unrest: "The appearance on Nevsky of revolutionary flags with slogans proves that the 'eternal memory' of L. N. Tolstoy is just a pretext for disorder and demonstrations," explained a *Novoe vremia* reporter. The public at large, he claimed, was not sympathetic to these demonstrations but instead viewed them as a profanation of Tolstoy's memory.[73] The right-wing press was quick to suggest that it was not "real Russians" who were responsible. *Novoe vremia* ran a series of editorials blaming the demonstrations on Jewish and Caucasian provocation. M. Men'shikov offered the following:

> The usual Petersburg crowd is a northern crowd, with a predominance of light, soft faces. God knows where the thick dark stream of people who flowed onto Nevsky came from yesterday, all types from the far east and south—with wide noses and eyes black like cherries. Representatives of far-off races, long ago having become degenerate, greedy, and parasitical, they imbue the northern crowd with an entirely alien temperament, nervous and poisonous with organic hostility toward our life.

According to Men'shikov, these alien forces had not even read Tolstoy but opportunistically took to the streets in his name to pursue a vague anti-Russian agenda. The call for an end to the death penalty was merely a subterfuge disguising a much larger, more treasonous project of destroying the Russian government. It was striking, he concluded, "that the Jews manage our crises with such aplomb. No major event passes without their making use of it."[74] Another *Novoe vremia* editorial took to task the "Jewish newspapers," who "spit on what was sacred to Tolstoy," exploiting his memory while "speculating on an increase in social unrest" by joining in the call for Orthodox services.[75] The Orthodox and Black Hundreds press claimed that the street demonstrations were the work of the same "enemies of the Church" who had prevented Tolstoy from making his final, conciliatory confession; now they were turning Tolstoy's "spiritual disorder" to their own advantage.[76]

A series of editorials in the December issue of *Vestnik Evropy* told quite the opposite story, finding order and beauty where conservatives had seen only chaos. One commended the crowd at a memorial evening in Petersburg, which had been arranged with the proviso that there be no response from the audience to the speeches; the seventeen hundred attendees showed their respect for Tolstoy by "piously honoring" the request. "This is the sort of evidence of social education," the author claimed, "that could be envied even in other countries."[77] Reporting on the response to the death "in the provinces," another writer reversed the orientation of the *Novoe vremia* pieces, placing the government and the church in the role of malefactor. Whereas Men'shikov had written that Tolstoy's "misfortune" provided a "lesson for the young," this writer expressed the hope that the repression against those wishing to observe the death of the peace-loving Tolstoy had itself provided a valuable political lesson. Society, moreover, as it focused so singly on Tolstoy, had experienced a valuable moment of unification, which had a purifying and healing effect on social life.[78] A third review challenged the accusations that the demonstrations had been instigated by outsiders with dishonorable intentions—it was more useful, they argued, to consider how the demonstrations might have emerged from within the organism of society. The student unrest stemmed more directly from the lack of other more effective means for the opposition to voice its protest.[79] From this point of view, the demonstrations were natural emanations from a Russia that those in power did not wish to acknowledge—one that identified with Tolstoy and with the social transformations he represented.

The opposition delighted in watching as the government mishandled this delicate situation. A front-page editorial in *Rech'* on November 12 suggested that the government's misinterpretation of the demonstrations would lead to unforeseen and unintended results: "If government authorities limit themselves to looking for the 'springs' [*pruzhin*] and not the causes [*prichin*], if they want to eradicate evil by means of denunciations of a 'Kadet' professor, you can be sure that they won't succeed. On the contrary, this gives reason to fear that it will go further, will develop widely and establish deep roots."

For the liberal press, failure to understand the social forces at work in the "Tolstoy days" illustrated the illegitimacy of the ruling autocracy.

Conflict with Tolstoy's memory was also prevalent in official government circles. On November 10, newspapers gave extensive coverage to the political maneuvering that had surrounded the ceremonial honoring of Tolstoy in the State Council: the right-wing coalition had agreed not to lodge a formal protest against this gesture but had instead submitted a series of informal ones and was meeting to decide a further course of action. The conservative *Moskovskie vedomosti* ran an article reproaching Akimov for honoring Tolstoy in the State Council: the tsar had expressed his "sorrow" at Tolstoy's passing, but how did this authorize the Council to "honor" Tolstoy by asking all its members to stand ceremonially? Tolstoy had been critical of the very institution that Akimov represented and had written heretical tracts against the Church, to which the Russian state was inextricably wed; couldn't this honor be exploited by the revolutionaries who shared those attitudes? The chairman of the Council should remember, the editorial argued, that such gestures were symbolically important, for they reflected on the whole country, not only on formal government institutions such as the Council but also on the streets. "And that is why," the author concluded, "we must recognize that his statements in support of expressions of sympathy for Count Tolstoy are an extraordinary, grievous mistake that will, of course, have very harmful consequences in society and among the people."[80]

Rech' responded to such arguments with a series of front-page editorials in the week after Tolstoy's death analyzing the political endgame that had ensued. The government, it was reported on November 9, had been prepared for the event, as was witnessed by a series of reports on confiscating of newspapers, fining of editors, patrolling of streets, and forbidding of theater closures. The newspaper ironically recounted right-wing editorials justifying the government's treatment of Tolstoy and even complimenting it for its restraint. It was no surprise that the right wing was meeting in secret to discuss its orientation to the event—"the discussion is not about the expression of great sorrow but about a swift offensive against an enemy."[81]

For some, this divisiveness itself took on tragic, ominous intonations, showing some inherent illness in the Russian body politic. Other countries would have united in sorrow over such a loss, but Russia seemed unable to properly process the event in the political sphere.[82] While the Right portrayed the campaign to repeal the death penalty as a result of revolutionary provocation, the editors of *Rech'* argued that the students had come upon the idea themselves; it was, in their words, "an idea that was equally dear to both Tolstoy and the Russian youth." They repeatedly questioned why this campaign should have assumed such a sinister visage in the eyes of the authorities. "You can talk about this in the State Duma; you can write in the newspapers. Why can't the same thing be the topic of a street action, a public rally, or collective resolution?"[83] The inability of young students to find a proper outlet for their feelings and ideas was a sign of a dysfunctional society, they argued. "It's shameful and painful to think of the consequences summoned forth by this tragic death. It has inflamed, or rather, people want to use it to awaken slumbering passions, to settle old accounts, to compare strength, to demonstrate readiness and power." The air was filled with "anxiety, pressure, and a heavy and troubling uncertainty."[84]

Lenin, viewing these polemical fireworks from exile in Switzerland, was fascinated by what was transpiring. Two years earlier, in what was to become the landmark study of Tolstoy during the Soviet period, Lenin had described Tolstoy at the time of his eightieth birthday celebration as a "mirror of the Russian revolution."[85] Despite the archaic morality and political *naïveté* that he saw in Tolstoy, Lenin described the writer as an elemental voice expressing the will of that as yet politically uneducated mass—the Russian peasantry. This appropriation of Tolstoy, Lenin admitted, might seem rather unnatural: "The comparison of the name of the great writer with a revolution that he clearly did not understand, from which he clearly distanced himself, might seem strange and artificial at first glance." But the revolution in Russia, he continued, was an "extraordinarily complicated phenomenon," characterized by striking contradictions. Tolstoy expressed these contradictions in many ways: an author of genius but also a landowner and a "holy fool"; a remarkably powerful social critic who exposed the evils of capitalism yet advocated nonresistance to them; a sober realist but at the same time a purveyor of that dangerous opiate, religion.[86]

In the three articles that Lenin wrote in November 1910, many of the same themes are repeated. In his postmortem of Tolstoy, Lenin again finds "spinelessness" and decaying ideas by which he characterizes a passiveness that can only reflect, but not lead, a revolution. Tolstoy still represents a Russia that is unconscious, patriarchal, and feeble: "Tolstoy reflects their naïveté, their alienation from politics, their mysticism, their desire to leave the world, 'nonresistance to violence,' powerless condemnations of capitalism and the 'power of money.'"[87] Though Tolstoyanism is for Lenin a "historical error," it reflects the conditions that will lead to revolution—weakness that will become strength, dissatisfaction that will evolve into revolution. For Lenin the contradictions that Tolstoy represented did not stem simply from his own thinking but from those historical conditions that the coming revolution would correct.[88] Lenin argued that his political opponents had failed to properly appraise the meaning of Tolstoy's death and the demonstrations that followed it. The right-wing press cried "crocodile tears" over the loss of the great writer yet defended the Church's agenda at Astapovo; the liberals glossed over Tolstoy's critique of their bourgeois ideals, mourning the loss of their "great conscience" but ignoring the concrete issues that this conscience had raised. The proletariat, Lenin avowed, would make better use of Tolstoy's legacy, using it to show the workers of Russia the true meaning of Tolstoy's critique of the government, the Church, and private property. Under the tutelage of Stolypin's "lessons," Lenin had concluded in 1908, the Russian revolution would be hardened and would overcome the historical sins of Tolstoyanism.

Indeed, when the public response to Tolstoy's death brought more of these "lessons," Lenin took heart. Answering reports of the demonstrations in Russia, in his "Isn't This the Turn of the Tide?" of November 16 Lenin proclaimed that they were a turning point in the revolution. The larger part of his article, however, is devoted to exposing and reviling the political backwardness of his political rivals in Russia, including the Constitutional Democrats, who not only had failed to seize this political opportunity but had even printed the request of several of their leading representatives in the Duma that the students not demonstrate, as this would cloud the days of grief and show "a lack of sincere affection for his sacred memory."[89]

Lenin's unabashed, even self-righteous, politicization of Tolstoy's death stands out amid the more cautious and concealed designs of his opponents. But his sense of the emblematic significance of Tolstoy and the latent political energy he embodied was shared by other political commentators. His summation of the historical significance of the moment, which became a stock trope for Soviet-era commentators on Tolstoy's legacy, says forthrightly what the authorities feared most—that Tolstoy's political capital would be seized by others, who would turn it toward their own ends.

The Knight's Move

Lenin saw Tolstoy as a linchpin for the revolution—a passive, inert object that could bind together political energies, giving them the mass necessary for political expediency. Tolstoy, Lenin argued, himself was a political ingénue, who had perhaps intuited the crisis in the empire but had no clear vision of the revolution and could instead only reflect it. But if Tolstoy was a mirror, he seemed to reflect different things for different people, depending on the perspective from which they viewed the progression of events. From the moment Tolstoy set forth on his journey, these varying perspectives sent him off in many directions simultaneously. The efforts of the authorities to circumscribe that movement reveal a strategy of containment: they would have wished to merely quiet the publicity, to minimize public awareness of this mirror that seemed to reflect badly on their actions. Efforts to control Tolstoy's movement, and the currents of public opinion that it elicited, were less successful; it was understood that his departure from his home, no matter how single-minded his intentions or how apolitical his itinerary, would appear directed toward many different ends. His movement would not be straight-forward but would produce an abundance of peripheral motion, repercus-sions, and side effects, revealing the hidden strategies of political adversaries and creating openings for their subterfuge. The discourse of radical, liberal, and conservative witnesses to the event reveals their primary concern for this lateral motion and their anxiety over the unforeseen consequences it could produce.

While at times Tolstoy and the tsar were positioned against each other as though they were kings in a chess game between conservative and democratic forces, a closer look reveals that the cultural paradigm suggested by Viktor Shklovskii some years later—what he called the "knight's move"—was sig-nificant to this political endgame. Prefacing the collection of essays to which Shklovskii gave this name, he explained: "In Russia everything is so contra-dictory that we have become clever against our own will and desire." For both the Left and the Right, Tolstoy was like Shklovskii's knight, describing the irregular path by which the Russian masses had been enlightened. Chris-tian pacifism veered sideways toward revolutionary activism, a funeral proces-sion turned into a political demonstration—marching to honor Tolstoy, then suddenly threatening the state; moving to the mournful accompaniment of "Eternal Memory," then to angry shouts of "Down with the death penalty!" As the government responded to the decorum requiring them to honor Tol-stoy, they understood that calls for funeral services were a political gambit that many hoped would create an opening for revolutionary movement.[90]

A *Rech'* editorial found these turns of events natural enough: "And we do not need any explanations to understand why young people, in their desire to express collective sorrow in organizing a civil funeral, suddenly came to the decision to organize today a street demonstration in favor of the ab-olition of the death penalty."[91] At the same time, however, the author of the editorial was wary that political agendas would profane the memory of Tolstoy—a memory that represented what was best in humanity: "But to put together manifestos with this goal, and to connect them to the memory of Tolstoy, raises tragic possibilities that will darken the bright sorrow at the fresh grave, around which hover the best, most pure thoughts of humanity; to risk human life is to reveal the lack of true affection for the sacred memory." Lenin made a special point of ridiculing this editorial in "Isn't This the Turn of the Tide?" where he used it to illustrate the inadequacies of the Consti-tutional Democrats. Meanwhile, on the Right, there was anxiety that the government was not perspicacious enough to discern the enemy's ultimate strategy. L. A. Tikhomirov (the editor of *Moskovskie vedomosti*) wrote in his diary at the time: "The telephone reports on fairly serious "Tolstoyan" unrest in S. Pb. . . . Our caustic [*kislyanoe*] government, if you will, will lead us to a new revolution sooner than I expected."[92] It was a complex game of political chess, the ultimate outcome of which seemed at times to rest on the question of who could convince the public that they were moving the white pieces, and their opponents the black. Every move, it seemed, could not be taken at face value, but was instead some sort of gambit.

Kropotkin, on receiving the news in London of Tolstoy's death, suggested that the society that was revealed by this death was one that would only sink deeper into its contradictory mire without Tolstoy:

> People understood at the same time that L. N. Tolstoy expressed the disease of our age: the oppressive contradictions between the foundations of our social life and the idea of truth for all of those—people of all classes—who have not yet stifled in themselves the voices of conscience, justice, and reason. They understood that with all the strength of his soul Tolstoy sought that key factor that might help truth to conquer the disgracefulness [*bezobrazie*] of our life.[93]

The disorder that followed Tolstoy's death lent credence to this view, and the authorities seemed overwhelmed by the contradictions. *Rech'* ridiculed the government for being overly 'anticipatory' in its measures, of creating revolutionary phantasms:

> The procession on Nevsky, with flags even, on which are painted the slogan "Down with the Death Penalty!" A procession that sings down the whole street "Eternal Memory" to Tolstoy! No, in Russia this isn't simply a disturbance of peace and order. This is already "revolution," and those who sing innocent things and display entirely legal slogans have already concealed terrible thoughts in their minds, and criminal words already circulate on their tongues. They haven't done anything yet, but we know what they want to do![94]

But was *Rech'* any more prescient? Vladimir Maklakov, a leading member of the Constitutional Democratic Party that *Rech'* represented, would see things quite differently ten years later. In a public speech honoring the ten-year anniversary of Tolstoy's death, delivered to an audience in Paris, Maklakov described a naïve Russia that had not understood the implications of this newly politicized life:

> When Tolstoy died the world became different from what it had been before....Something that was in him died for all time. And the Russia that he lived in, for which he wouldn't have traded anything, the humble, beggarly, and uncultured Russia, which didn't foresee that it would soon personally experience the full depth of human vileness and indifference—this Russia felt instinctively that on the day of his death she had lost a protector.[95]

Maklakov, who left Russia after the Bolshevik revolution, could count himself among those feeling this loss, and among those who felt most keenly the ultimate consequences of the political struggle within which Tolstoy's death was situated in 1910.

In the winter of 1910, newspapers and journals overflowed with editorials and letters considering the meaning of Tolstoy's death and civil funeral for Russia, many of them assigning it epochal significance. Some described political confusion and mythomania and worked to mobilize various antipathies that might vitiate the charisma of Tolstoy's death; others depicted order and genuine affection for Tolstoy and celebrated a quickening of Russia's political and ethical consciousness. Thus the death of Tolstoy, as with so many other public figures in Russian history, proved to be a day of national reckoning—a moment of public self-definition as he was internalized and assimilated into history and tradition.

Inasmuch as funeral rituals connect the deceased to a given tradition and to a certain society, the performance of Tolstoy's burial proved to be a determinative factor in this self-conscious process. In contrast to the elaborate national pageant orchestrated for the funeral of Ioann of Kronstadt in 1908, which affirmed the place of church and state in the sacred center of Russia through a public spectacle of reverence for the patriotic son of a Christian Mother Russia, the commemorations of Tolstoy honored a declared enemy of the state. The identifications formed at Tolstoy's funeral united students, peasants, members of the intelligentsia, Tolstoyans, city dwellers, suggesting the formation of a society quite different from the one represented at Ioann's funeral. The civil traditions of the public funeral, which had once accompanied the establishment-affirming rituals of the Orthodox ceremony, now stood defiantly alone. The state was largely disenfranchised from the society that gathered to mourn Tolstoy's passing.

This coup took place not in the streets of Petersburg but at Tolstoy's grave. It was stimulated less by political parties than by changing attitudes toward authority, evolving social relations and sensibilities, and changes to the constitution of the private sphere. The sacred space around the dead was here a public space, and the world's fast attention to Tolstoy's passing prevented the state from controlling its representations and manifestations. Stolypin's agent, sent to assist in the plot of the Holy Synod, was told to exercise the utmost caution to avoid arousing criticism "about government interference in such an intimate matter."[96] While he and the Church's emissaries exploited the sympathies of those family members most kindly disposed to their efforts (Sofia Andreevna and Andrei L'vovich in particular), they could not take control of Tolstoy's deathbed and simulate a reconciliation. As they engaged in this sensitive mission, their communications with their superiors in Petersburg, encoded for secrecy, stood in odd contrast to the public emanations of Tolstoy's last "private" moments. As Tolstoy's death became public, it seems, the state became private.

Tolstoy's renunciation of the traditional funeral liturgy and graveside practices, meanwhile, created a vacuum into which other rituals were drawn. As church and state lost their defining authority, the ceremony became a participatory event, in which the public had the opportunity to place its own mark on the proceedings and to develop its own rituals. When, according to Tolstoy's own wishes, no stone was placed on his grave, visitors quickly developed a tradition of writing their own epitaphs on the surrounding fence (which were subsequently recorded and became, as is often the case with sepulchral inscriptions, part of the lore of Tolstoy's grave). The singing of "Eternal Memory" became ritualized throughout Russia in the various secular gatherings to commemorate Tolstoy, taking the place of the liturgy that would have been performed in the prohibited religious memorials. While the Church made use of the funeral service to remind mourners of their mortality and of the solace of Christian resurrection, the political ceremonies that followed Tolstoy's funeral enjoined the public to demand the abolition of the death penalty. This secularized yet another tradition—the building of churches as memorials to deceased family members. These appropriations repeatedly displaced symbolic supports to the autocratic, Orthodox Russia that had been staggered by one revolution and would soon be toppled by another.

Thus Tolstoy's funeral proved to be a moment of national self-definition over which the state had lost its authority, as meaning was assigned by young students and left-wing activists—by large crowds that were policed, rather than convened, by the ruling powers in Petersburg. The government circumscribed this manifestation of political willfulness but could not entirely suppress a movement attached to the memory of a national hero. An editorial in *Vestnik Evropy* observed that it was the reactionary forces of church and state, rather than Tolstoy or the public, that found themselves isolated during the "Tolstoy days."[97] This reversal might remind the reader of the scene with which this chapter opened, when the crowd at Tolstoy's graveside ordered the reluctant police officer to his knees. During a defining moment of collective sorrow, as the Russian people mourned a national hero, the state was indeed oddly alien to the proceedings. In the theater where this spectacle was performed, the authorities watched anxiously from the wings, uncertain as to how the performance might end. Where once they would have ceremoniously taken center stage to deliver the final soliloquy, they had been demoted to the role of a mute, kneeling police officer. The audience had taken control of the stage and now demanded that the narrative proceed according to its own designs on the life of the hero.

Кочеты. Май 1910 г.

Когда человѣкъ живетъ хорошей жизнью, то онъ бываетъ счастливъ сейчасъ и не думаетъ о томъ, что будетъ послѣ жизни. Счастливъ же бываетъ человѣкъ неизмѣнно тогда, когда полагаетъ свое благо въ исполненіи воли Бога и исполняетъ ее. И потому смерть не лишаетъ блага того, кто исполняетъ волю Бога.

Левъ Толстой.

Фот. В. Черткова. Серія IV, № 12.

21. "When a person leads a good life he is happy now and does not think about what will happen after this life. Unceasingly happy is the person who sees his own good in the fulfillment of God's will and fulfills it. And thus he who fulfills God's will is not deprived of good by death."

killed themselves in a kind of suicide pact, and reports of subsequent suicides concluded that their sensational story, reported widely in the newspapers, had inspired others. Literature, too, was implicated. One of the most commonly cited culprits was Mikhail Artsybashev, whose novels offered a broad tableau of suicidal mania. The hero of his most popular novel, *Sanin,* encourages his comrades to end their senseless and useless lives. The popularity of such literature among adolescents and university students troubled the elder generation and seemed to indicate a deep crisis in the social organism. But while the suicide epidemic was being spread rhetorically, suicide itself seemed to have little explanatory power. Cultural and scientific specialists alike were at a loss to explain its meaning, which, as Durkheim had shown, was generally lost on its victims as well.

In the days after the Moscow suicides, the topic was again discussed in the newspapers. One commentator argued that suicide was motivated by individualism and egotism and stressed the importance of inculcating a sense of the meaning of life among the young.[16] Another pointed to an almanac entitled *Death* by a group of young writers and considered how death had become "fashionable" for youth of the day.[17] In the influential 1909 anthology *Landmarks,* A. S. Izgoev had argued that death was the prime mover of young members of the Russian intelligentsia. The desire to show that they were not afraid of death was the "sole logical and moral basis" for their convictions: the Bolsheviks were more "left-wing" than the Mensheviks precisely because of their more malignant platform.[18] Suicide was a perverse fashion but was perhaps just a logical and fatal extension of this attraction to death.

Lying in bed at Astapovo, Tolstoy was also following this story; it was read to him on November 3 and was the last newspaper clipping to go into his notebook. It was cut from the pages of a newspaper that was devoting a tremendous amount of coverage to his own developing story. Even the newspaper headlines highlighted the intertextuality of these events: one newspaper's report on the Moscow suicides was headed with the title of one of Tolstoy's short stories, "Three Deaths."[19] New layers of proximity were soon to emerge. On the day after Tolstoy died, an eighteen-year-old turned himself into a clinic in a state of great excitement, claiming to have lived a million years and calling the doctor Count Tolstoy; after being held for some time in the hospital, he was released, only to commit suicide by throwing himself from a fifth-story window. A university student killed himself in a Kiev park, leaving a note explaining that he couldn't live up to Tolstoy's moral tenets.[20] Another took his life in a Pskov movie theater, shooting himself at the moment in which a suicide took place in the film and leaving a note explaining, "It's hard to live after the death of L. N. Tolstoy—it's hard to struggle for freedom."[21]

As these young people linked their own deaths to Tolstoy's, he somehow became connected to the long chain of suicides in 1910. The context of these stories would, in fact, become another source of the tremendous resonance of the story of Astapovo with the Russian public. But how did Tolstoy's death reflect on the suicides that were clustered around it on the newspaper pages? As sensational as the Moscow suicides may have been, they were in fact overshadowed by the story of the equally paradoxical departure and death of Tolstoy. A New Year's Day editorial by I. N. Ignatov described Tolstoy's death as the most important event of the previous year, not only because of his great significance as a cultural figure but also because of the way his death reshaped Russian society: "Society itself, under the influence of the death of Tolstoy and the circumstances preceding and accompanying it, has undergone some sort of change, some movement in its feelings and aspirations."[22] His death had awakened an "uneasiness" and sense of expectation among the discontented masses as it revealed to them their demographic majority over the conservative forces in power. Moreover, it ran counter to the contemporary malaise, when people lived without joy and "died without regret, and killed themselves across all class distinctions." The public had been depressed after the failure of the 1905 Revolution and waited for something unexpected to awaken them:

> And at this time, on a solitary fall night an eighty-two-year-old man undertook what is rightly called his last heroic deed [*podvig*]. The thirst for truth compelled Tolstoy to leave Yasnaya Polyana and to seek in the foggy distance something more righteous and worthy. To begin a new life, to shake off from himself the "wizened Adam," to finish with all that which had for decades constituted his usual surroundings, with which he had grown together, and to separate from which is beyond the strength of an even younger and physically stronger man—to undertake this in order to stand even externally, by circumstances, on the level of his most dear ideas—such a deed could stir even a constrained thought and a conscience covered with wounds.

"Some troubled striving has arisen," Ignatov continued. "It has become especially troubling not to search or ponder but simply to wait."

And the young had acted, for the first time since the 1905 Revolution. They took to the streets in mass demonstrations, first protesting against the Church because it forbade memorial services for Tolstoy, then calling for the government to honor Tolstoy by outlawing the death penalty. When they were joined by large numbers of striking workers, it appeared to many that Russia's inchoate revolution had again sprung to life. Even among those with less vested interest in these developments, the renewed activism of the young was seen as a healthy outlet of their pent-up frustrations, a release of those energies that, when turned inward, so often brought violence on the self. As Ignatov indicated, however, this rebellion was like Tolstoy's own final departure—it suggested dissatisfaction with the current state of affairs and a desire for change, but there was no clear itinerary for the revolutionary movement. In Ignatov's view the dying Tolstoy was more vital than the apathetic society awakened by his final act, but it was not clear how lasting this effect would be. The problem was the same one that plagued Michelstaedter: everyone felt sympathy toward Tolstoy's ideals, but few agreed with his belief that they were practicable. The young student in Kiev, who wrote that he was killing himself because his sublimated ideals were so painfully unattainable, pointed to this conflict.

In the same article, however, Ignatov described Tolstoy as being on a search for Truth that represented "all the history of the Russian intelligentsia" and referred to him as the sort of genius that comes along only once in ages, joining others who were likening him to Plato and Buddha. This larger historical perspective placed Tolstoy on a continuum that transcended any chronological rupture that might be troubling Russian society at the time. Tolstoy was a "free spirit" who lived outside the confines of his age: "It is as if he placed himself beyond conditionality and the circumstances of time and even in the physical sense was independent of the arsenal of forces at the command of the present government."[23] This autonomy was precisely what Michelstaedter and his suicidal generation lacked, and its projection onto Tolstoy (he would have been the last to say that he was independent of these circumstances) allowed for the construction of narratives that transcended the historical moment. Tolstoy's final gesture had offered the aesthetic structure to support this coherent self; he seemed to have stepped outside everyday circumstances and to have acted according to some timeless imperative.

At the same time, however, it was a tale that was imbued with native tropes, that was written in a symbolic language intelligible to all, but particularly to Russians. As N. Karabchevskii wrote: "Tolstoy is not an abstraction, digression, or idea coming down on us from who knows where. He is Russian to the marrow of his bones, raised on Russian soil; he is ours, flesh of our flesh and bone of our bone."[24] Other writers echoed this notion: "The little station of Astapovo is like a symbol of Russia, and Lev Tolstoy a symbol of the Russian people. Everything that is best in the Russian people is incarnate in Tolstoy...flesh of our flesh, spirit of our spirit."[25] Within this framework Tolstoy's "liberation" was an experience that could be shared vicariously, a prospect that was enhanced by the oft-cited comments of Tolstoy regarding his wish to die like a peasant. The sublime end to life was not the preternatural death courted by the young but the familiar quietus invoked by the natural world of the common people.

Mikhail Artsybashev, characteristically, did not subscribe to this sanguine view and was quick to identify the ways in which Tolstoy's death conformed to his own teleological uncertainty. Tolstoy's life, Artsybashev claimed, was "a horror for humankind." It was a horror because he was so gifted—so blessed with talent and the experiences of a long, full life—but could find no more meaning in that life than anyone else. Everyone went through life searching for its ultimate meaning, and for many Tolstoy had served as a model for this search, but at the end he had fallen to the "terrible law of the great unknown." He had revealed the bankruptcy of his ideas as he faced death, rising in his bed after a long silence to utter the final words "No . . . the end." Why couldn't he, like his literary character Ivan Ilych, inform those at his bedside that the approaching end was good, simple, and joyful? Artsybashev asked. Why this emptiness, this nothingness that revealed yet again the eternal darkness that plagued humanity?[26]

As Artsybashev wrestles Tolstoy's death onto the apocalyptic plane of his own literary works, his disappointment in the prosaic insignificance of Tolstoy's encounter with death—his expectation that Tolstoy might somehow in his death reveal some great truth—casts Tolstoy as another victim of expressionism. Harrison writes: "And thus surface new visions of the artist-seer, the idea of the messianic restoration of the true nature of life through the redemptive power of the courageous social exception. But more often than not, the project results in the 'savior's' own self-immolation, and the savior ends up discovering that what is ostensibly 'authentic' and 'true' and 'inner' never lies within the realm of the speakable, and may ultimately be just as rhetorical a construct as all it opposes."[27] Artsybashev was not alone in discerning the tragedy in this ultimate unintelligibility. N. Karabchevskii recalled the last words of Hamlet ("the rest is Silence") and saw the basic tone in what Tolstoy had revealed as "terror"—terror that was especially vivid for his generation, who had failed to live according to his precepts.[28] Karabchevskii was internalizing, as did many others, Tolstoy's own guilt and at the same time expressing anxiety over the distance between "rhetoric and persuasion."[29] For Nikolai Berdiaev, this process defined the Tolstoyan ethos and would continue to affect Russian consciousness up to the time of the revolution; in *From the Depths* he argued that Tolstoy's influence was "Russia's internal danger," insofar as he embraced death, rather than life.[30]

These views, however, though not entirely unfounded, were nonetheless strikingly in the minority, and Tolstoy's death was more typically read in quite the opposite way—as a great life-affirming act. Artsybashev was thus quite certain that his reading of Tolstoy's death would shock some of his readers. Although others joined him in viewing Tolstoy's death as a speech act, they did not focus on the empty phrase that so horrified Artsybashev. This did not gain currency as Tolstoy's final statement but was instead displaced by the more didactic and democratic phrase "there are countless people in the world, but you are concerned only with Lev," and the simple, but resolutely Tolstoyan "Truth—I love it very much."[31] These words better fulfilled the expectations of a Tolstoyan testament and suggested that he had found meaning in the face of death. It was necessary only to take a step back from the moment of agony to find death shaping Tolstoy's actions into resonant, coherent moral vision. Where Artsybashev emphasized the ultimate emptiness of Tolstoy's death, others told the story leading up to it, reading his departure as an open-ended gesture describing a rich potential for human agency. Maximilian Voloshin echoed many others when he wrote in *Russkaia mysl'* that Tolstoy's death only enriched the meaning of his life, giving his narrative that final shape it required.[32] His departure had great meaning in this narrative, for from the moment it became known, no one doubted, Voloshin claimed, that Tolstoy had left because he was going to die. As another writer succinctly put it, "Tolstoy left and reached his destination—reached where he needed to go."[33]

How did Tolstoy's death become so articulate, when he himself could not express its meaning as he approached it? Why was it possible to suggest, as did Ignatov, that the dying Tolstoy was more vital than the apathetic society awakened by his final act? Why, when it could even be said that he shared the younger generation's fascination with death and viewed death as a welcome escape, did his death become so expressive of hope and renewal? His story was in many respects every bit as senseless as that of the young suicides: an old man, nearing death, had abandoned the very place where it seemed that he should be—among his family in the comfort of his home.

Tolstoy's literary work provides some illumination on this count. *Anna Karenina* is often classified as a novel of adultery, a family novel, or a society novel, but can also be considered as a work on suicide.[34] It is structured around two suicides—one committed, the other contemplated—that draw the many parallels between Anna and Levin into a conclusive focus. The outcome of these two confrontations with suicide illustrates certain moral imperatives that Tolstoy has in mind, but also narratological principles. Anna's death is tragic—that of a heroine with a fatal flaw—and is attributed all the drama and pathos of a Greek tragedy. Levin's potential death is more problematic—he has no tragic recourse, having achieved everything he has wanted (that most dangerous state for a Tolstoyan hero) and facing no external provocation for his crisis. Levin has the freedom and power that has been denied Anna, yet still he yearns for death. This is the central problem of the end of the novel and of the period in Tolstoy's own life following *Anna Karenina,* as described in *Confession.* The latter work demonstrated that Tolstoy viewed the crisis of Levin as a narrative problem. Tolstoy concluded that he should no longer tell such stories, because they might lead, as did Anna's reading of English novels, to a reflective impasse. Knowing the self, an obsession for Tolstoy, had become a problem: fiction led to knowing oneself as another, to an estranged relationship with the self. Tolstoy's models for life and death are free of this sort of self-consciousness—Alyosha Gorshok types who take both life and death in stride, never imagining that fate might have handed them a different lot.

Tolstoy's later narratives arc sympathetically toward death, but always toward natural death, which is consistently represented as a moment of heightened clarity and enlightenment. The mortality rate in the later fiction remains very high, and his heroes acquiesce to death, but they are preserved from suicide by Christian virtue, Stoic reserve, fear of death, and by a certain narrative restraint. "The Death of Ivan Ilych" is an exercise in working within these narrative strictures. The traditional drama of building toward the hero's death is diffused by beginning the narrative at his wake, after which we step back to journey toward another kind of death.[35] Tolstoy redeems death in a new fashion, in which the catharsis is not that of the sword but that of the sinner in purgatory. We could say that the whole point of the text is to demonstrate that Ivan's death is not tragic but is instead a great spiritual stimulus. Death conquers, as always, but not before it has done its proper work. This work is achieved in the denial of Ivan's possibility to engage in the sort of action that more typically structures narrative.

Similar patterns hold in other programmatic texts of this period: Father Sergius comes close to suicide, but his crisis is resolved by renouncing the life that had led him to despair. The story ends not with a moment of heroic resolve but with heroic dissolution, as Kassatskii renounces the fiction of his identity as a famed spiritual elder and healer to live out his last days in obscurity. This movement is to be read as a return to the essential self, which has been effaced by the fame of the elder "Sergius." "Two Old Men" is not a death narrative, but the same distinction is made: the pilgrim who reaches Jerusalem (his heroic "destination") finds less spiritual fulfillment than the one who stops along the way, caught up in the everyday struggle of a famine-stricken village. The second pilgrim, who leaves the village without ever even telling the locals his name, clearly dwells in that heightened spiritual realm of selflessness.

The desire to transcend everyday life through heroic action is a key problem in these texts, just as it is in *Anna Karenina*. In retrospect we can see that Levin is poised on the edge of a modernist crisis, and Tolstoy explains this in so many words in *Confession* and *What Is Art?* Tolstoy seems to understand that the novel is headed toward a deeper exploration of the alienation that hounds Levin. While he clearly rejects the desire for novelty that moves Anna (her grave error is imagining herself the heroine of an English novel), he has a harder time knowing what to do with Levin. At the height of his crisis Levin has found himself unexpectedly cold to the appearance of his newborn son and is saved at precisely the point where the infant has begun to recognize faces. The undiscerning child is like the proverbial fish circling its bowl with perpetual discovery, failing to recognize any of its landmarks. In this respect he is a reflection of his father, who is trapped in the orbit of self-reflection. Levin sees life as a circle of days, which, if it fills him with delusion, only distracts him from the ultimate limits of his destiny. But as his child begins to recognize his people, Levin is similarly awakened to the possibilities of engagement in life, in experiencing the meaning that he gives it, as he says. This is a tenuous resolution, and Tolstoy felt the need to go further in abandoning the novelistic world he explored in *Anna Karenina*.[36] The rhetorical crisis that caused him to renounce his own novels is in fact predicated by the suicidal despair of Levin.

One could argue that the problematic suicide in the novel is not Anna's but Levin's, even though it is not committed. His wish to die is not motivated by some tragic flaw or circumstance but instead by "weariness of life," or *taedium vitae*, as it was called in Roman law. Historically this has been the most sociologically and morally problematic type of suicide. Lack of a specific provocation points to a general unworthiness in life, a notion that the living find particularly troublesome. In terms of popular narrative, the hero killing him-/herself in the throes of passion over lost love, wealth, health, and so on is a tragic figure, but the death of a hero who has simply become weary of life stimulates an entirely different sort of pathos.[37] In a narrative tending toward this weariness there is no "great time" to which the hero could return. Here suicide is not a momentary acquiescence but a disavowal of time in general—the past as well as the future. Life is not precious but overabundant. Such model narratives as *One Thousand and One Nights* and *Tristram Shandy* lose their sense in a world where evasion of death has no meaning. Where the tragic hero cannot bear to turn another page when honor, love, or fortune has been lost, the existential hero has no interest in the prospect of tomorrow. This is the type of suicide that Levin contemplates.

Dostoevsky acknowledged the inevitability of suicidal ideation in the absence of faith in immortality.[38] Work on narratology has likewise connected portrayals of suicide to the emergence of greater mimesis in realist fiction. Scholes and Kellogg suggest that in this more mimetic narrative environment time displaced fate, which had prevailed in the mythic (or religious) world.[39] In a world where "the hours" are marked without the hands of God or fate, the inexorable tolling of time can indeed seem senseless. In the world of the folktale these repetitions were rites of passage through the cycles of preordained death and rebirth of the hero. The hero fulfilled his destiny by making this journey. Modern heroes act as if cognizant of these repetitions and begin to grow wary, and weary, of making them. They become disenchanted with the forest, shun the gifts of the stranger, and imagine no grail. Like so many Chekhov characters, they have navigated life's passage too many times, only to make their troubling return to themselves. The fin de siècle embodies this sensibility in viewing the close of the nineteenth century as the end of an age, and even of time itself. "It is as though the morrow would not link itself with today," writes Nordau in *Degeneration*.[40] Hardy refers in *Jude the Obscure* to the "coming universal wish not to live."[41]

At the turn of the century this disturbing notion appeared to be realizing itself in the growing trend toward suicide among the young throughout Europe, leading Freud to convene his 1910 conference and his Russian colleague Spielrein to formulate the notion of the death instinct.[42] Tolstoy had also responded earlier that year in a short newspaper piece "On Suicide," and he worked on a longer article throughout the spring and summer of 1910.[43] He emphasized the unnaturalness of suicide, arguing that one could not destroy life. Instead, one could only pervert its form by artificially bringing it to an end. As to the resilience of "real life" (the life of the spirit), he cited the example of a monk at Optina who had lived for thirty years in a state of almost complete paralysis but had served as a model of moral courage and spiritual resilience for thousands of visitors to the monastery. Reading this selection, which was also republished in an anthology on suicide and as a separate pamphlet, one senses that this is another chapter in Tolstoy's long effort to rhetorically master his own "death instinct." He himself had considered suicide on more than one occasion and explicitly connected his religious conversion to his own existential despair. His *Confession* is in many respects an effort to rationalize his failure to take what had appeared to him as the most logical step—suicide, which he acknowledged was the path of honor and strength by which to escape the horrifying knowledge of the ultimate emptiness of life.

Admitting that fear of death had been the impasse preventing him from taking this fateful step, Tolstoy worked in *Confession* to establish a more secure footing for the "life impulse." Death was the animus of psychic trauma, spiritual crisis, and personal transformation, and in the last thirty years of Tolstoy's life his efforts to conquer this anxiety were carried out on many fronts. His anthologies of worldly wisdom and books of daily readings deal extensively with death; they can be read as devotionals of preparation for death and are to this day sometimes used in this function for terminally ill patients. Though he advocated quietism and the acceptance of death as the release from life, he insisted that to end life artificially—whether by means of murder, capital punishment, or suicide—was profoundly immoral. In his later years his fame as a novelist was often superseded by his renown as an advocate of such life-affirming ethical practices as passive resistance, pacifism, and conscientious objection to military service. In a 1909 article he had promised to fight the death penalty to his last breath, which he nearly did—his last article on this matter was finished during his final journey. Dmitrii Merezhkovskii, in his 1910 collection *Morbid Russia* (Bol'naia Rossiia), spoke of a Russia that was "buried alive" and wondered why the aged Tolstoy was the only one willing to resist the government's extensive use of capital punishment.[44]

What binds these ethical positions together is the view that murder in all its forms made death unnatural. Natural death was something that should be met nonviolently but—and this is also important—not with resistance. Tolstoy's later asceticism was still informed by the pessimistic resignation he had found so compelling in Schopenhauer; in private conversation and correspondence he often spoke of his own approaching death as something that he anticipated without fear or regret. This sanguine disposition was not always equally evident in his diaries or confirmed by his behavior (Rilke wrote, "His own attitude to death remained until the end a grandiose and all penetrating *angst*, a fugue of fear, an enormous construction, a tower of fear, an *Angst-Turm*, so to speak")[45]. But it nevertheless entered into the mythology of Tolstoy's death, toward which, his eulogists often claimed, he had walked with great courage and intention. Mikhail Stakhovich wrote: "He felt that his own immense earthly work was fulfilled, that the time had come for his last great spiritual exploit—to go, to go unto death, which leads to God." This image of a natural death, occurring at the close of a long, full life, offered a compelling contrast to the corpses of distraught young artists and lovers strewn about the parks and apartments of Moscow and Petersburg.

Even as he suggested that he would live his last days in the solitude of Father Sergius, *for the public* Tolstoy had again taken up the heroic search, heading into the great wood in search of his destiny. Here he had encountered all the obstacles of contemporary civilization, which had tracked him down and destroyed the peace in which he had hoped to compose himself for his decisive passage from life. In 1907 Simmel had observed that "human beings have been distanced from themselves. Between themselves and their most authentic, essential part there has been erected an insuperable barrier of instruments, technical conquests, capacities, and commodities."[46] Tolstoy's journey was viewed as a return to this self, and his progress was defined by his evasion of the iron age that moved vigorously around him. This was a narrative of escape not from death but from all that was unnatural, artificial and therefore "dead" in contemporary life. Ignatov wrote of Tolstoy being completely free in both the highest sense of the word and in its common sense—from everyday concerns. For Suvorin, he was the freest of individuals.[47] "How much room to act we still have in our time," Rilke wrote. "How many ways remain for us to leave this life."[48]

Perhaps the source of this Tolstoyan vitality and freedom lay in his aesthetic sensibility. Perhaps it was, as some suggested, an artistic impulse that attracted him to the possibility of fulfilling this last representational mission—to exploit the vast signifying potential of death and, possibly, to render his life meaningful. But much of the work in this last narrative, which in many respects was Tolstoy's most successful, was done by others. Rilke wrote that in Tolstoy's death "the inner life of this man rendered itself visible and

immediately transformable into its own legend....He became his own ultimate image in the loftiest meaning of the word."[49] His death was articulate,
in that it so readily transposed into story.

Viktor Shklovskii might have argued that Tolstoy made himself strange—
he caused everyone to look at him with new eyes. But at the same time there
was something deeply familiar in Tolstoy's departure, with its resonances to
his own oeuvre and with Russian folk legend. In this sense his passing was
like that of Halley's Comet (which appeared that year): it travels a circle made
glorious by its seventy-year diameter, an orbit of meaning that is gained by
the predominance of absence in the cycle. It is historically familiar yet experi-
entially strange at the same time—something like the normal cycle of an everyday life, revealing itself just once, in all its unique glory, to those inclined to
look toward the heavens. Like any good hero in a narrative, Tolstoy saves
"the day," a simple orbit around the sun, demonstrating new potential to
abide in the world and to meet death as fate has allotted it to come.

Tolstoy's hope to begin a new life as he neared death spoke much to that
potential, and when that life then lapsed into death it became representation-
ally everlasting, so to speak. His was an end that was a beginning: he had
begun a journey, and because it was not completed there was no arrival, no
disenchantment, no contrast between hope and reality.[50] There wasn't even
a destination—he had left without knowing where he was going and never
even arrived at a decision as to where he should go. What was important was
that he had set off on this journey—much like the hero's journey in folklore,
and this the public viewed as a profound resolution in itself. Somehow Tolstoy had found his own rite of passage through modernity's colliding designs
on his destiny. His natural death became his destiny, toward which he had
moved with powerful resolve.

Here he stood in contrast to those who rushed to stake their own claim
on mortality. They lacked the spiritual and chronological autonomy assigned
to Tolstoy. Coming of age in a time of uncertainty, they identified with its
questions and realized its morbid aesthetic. They seemingly sought too much
in death. To paraphrase Tolstoy, death cannot be charged and taken like an
enemy standard in battle but must come of its own accord and be met peace-
fully, with bread and salt. Death must not be a stranger. Suicide is a gesture
of ultimate estrangement, of alienation from the self. The young student
who made Tolstoy into a lost raison d'être and killed himself in a movie
theater in effect mimicked Tolstoy in making his death into a symbolic coup
de théâtre. Perhaps he hoped that some sense of his death would be found
in the surfeit of meaning that others had attributed to Tolstoy's. More likely
he was viewed as an example of a kind of self-abandon, a death instinct, to
which Tolstoy's last days could be opposed: an old man, still searching for
the authentic self, still searching for meaning, still believing that it could be
found in "the great world."

Finally, among the many chords struck by Tolstoy's departure, one was certainly modernist; dissonant yet somehow in harmony with its age. The tension between his desire to "die like a peasant" and the insistence of the Russian public on observing (and thus participating in) that death is the irony of Astapovo, the source of its expressionist resonance. Voloshin viewed Tolstoy's departure as the last gesture in an ultimately ineffectual struggle to escape the privilege of meaning, the excess of significance that had been allotted him. We find this idea expressed both consciously and unconsciously throughout late 1910. Maxim Gorky wrote of his concern that the country would begin creating legends about Tolstoy, which would be bad for Russian culture; he would not write anything, he explained, for Tolstoy was too great, and any writing would only diminish his meaning.[51] This sense of incommensurability of language and subject, a stock trope in the hagiographical tradition, did not prevent others from building the cult to Tolstoy, as Gorky predicted. As they contemplated his death scene, all the complex social and philosophical questions that it engendered were incorporated into an all-encompassing Tolstoyan self. Writing in *Sovremennyi mir*, N. Iordanskii asserted that Tolstoy was himself more significant than any of the particular social groupings of his time.[52] Ilya Repin proposed that the best way to memorialize Tolstoy would be to build a monument at Yasnaya Polyana "uniting all religious faiths and cults." Rozanov wrote a piece reminding his readers that Tolstoy was profoundly human as a writer (in comparison to the more divine Pushkin, Lermontov, and Gogol), but also that his power to incorporate all of earthly life was unparalleled.

A significant role in these narratives of the ineffable was often assigned to the incoherence in the Tolstoy story, as witnessed by the frequent references to his "indivisibility" and injunctions not to separate him into parts (writer, moralist, teacher, recluse). As these contradictions were incorporated into the panegyric transports of Tolstoy's eulogists, they became part of an elaborate defense against the incursions of modernity. The public celebrated a notion that had so distressed Tolstoy as he wrote his first prose experiment, "The History of Yesterday": that mimetic fidelity was unattainable. This acknowledgment that it was impossible to render all of Tolstoy's meaning seemed a moral victory in the face of modernity's invasive apparatus for self-revelation. The technological powers that had worked so vigorously to exploit his signifying potential could not penetrate these deeper layers of meaning to reveal the completeness of Tolstoy. The church, state, media, and Tolstoyan interpreters had all failed to subject him to their narrative designs. His complex and dissonant legacy was so compelling because it defied the narrative finality that his contemporaries sought to impose. At the heart of that narrative stood a resilient self, comprising the many fragments of a public persona but coherent in its resistance to definition, in its insistence on making its own inscrutable journey toward resolution.

Народы посылаютъ послѣдній привѣтъ великому Толстому.

22. The people send their final greetings to Tolstoy.

Conclusion

The Posthumous Notes of Fyodor Kuzmich

In the months following Tolstoy's death, interest in the writer remained at a peak.[1] Publications poured off the press in response, including numerous editions of previously unpublished letters and works by Tolstoy. The most significant of these was the three-volume collection of his posthumous works edited and published by Chertkov between 1911 and 1912. Some of Tolstoy's best work, including "Hadji Murad," appeared for the first time in these volumes. Among them was a lesser known but fascinating piece—an unfinished frame tale entitled "The Posthumous Notes of Fyodor Kuzmich."[2] It is a Tolstoyan palimpsest of sorts, with Tolstoy writing his own story and morality over that of the legend of the Siberian monk, who was believed by some to have been the former emperor, Alexander I, in disguise.[3]

Just as with his departure, the idea of writing this piece fermented for a number of years in Tolstoy's mind. His first note on the matter appears in his diary in February 1890, and the following year he laid out the plot of the work to A. A. Tolstaya.[4] In 1894 he again outlined the story, this time to Pavel Biriukov. He continued to mention the idea in his notebooks over the next several years but did not begin work on the story. Then, in 1901, Grand Prince Nikolai Mikhailovich visited him in Gaspra and related what he knew of the legend, along with his doubts as to its veracity. This did not dissuade Tolstoy, however, who was interested in the spiritual duplicity of Alexander and noted that, if true, it was "Shakespearian." Again in 1903 the story appears on a list of works to be written, but no work is actually done on the piece until 1905. At this point he read the works of the historian N. K. Schilder, who believed in the legend, and began collecting other background material. The work did not go well initially, but in December Tolstoy grew more optimistic and noted in his diary: "The characteristics of Alexander I came more successfully; if only I can manage to get it at least half done."[5]

Later in the month he again wrote encouragingly of work on the text, but this is the last mention of it in his diaries. Finally, in 1907 he received another book on the legend by mail from Nikolai Mikhailovich and wrote in response that he had had to abandon the project for a time: "And it's too bad. It's a marvelous image."[6]

The manuscript is no less interesting for being unfinished. It includes three sections: a brief framing introduction to the legend's historical background, and then Kuzmich's notes themselves, which begin with a confessional statement and conclude in the form of a deathbed diary under the title "My Life." The introduction outlines the legend of Fyodor Kuzmich and the reasons for doubting that Alexander had in fact died in Taganrog in 1825. The death was mysterious and unexpected and occurred in a remote place; the face of the body displayed in the coffin appeared greatly changed, and the autopsy described a back marked with the sort of bruising that could never have been applied to the body of an emperor. Alexander had often mentioned his desire to abdicate the throne. There are also details in the life of Fyodor Kuzmich that would be consistent with his legend: his similar appearance and posture, regal bearing, reticence regarding his past, refusal to attend confession, and a single page of writing found after his death marked with the initials A. P. (the initials of the former emperor's name and patronymic).

The story's subsequent sections are presented as a final testament and diary written by Fyodor Kuzmich. The diary's introductory passages will remind many readers of Tolstoy's own 1879 *Confession,* where he wrote: "I cannot recall those years without horror, loathing, and heartache. I killed people in war and challenged them to duels in order to kill them. I lost at cards, consumed the labor of the peasants, punished them, was promiscuous, and deceived people. Lying, robbery, adultery of all kinds, drunkenness, violence, murder... there was not a crime that I did not commit, and for all this people praised me and I was and am considered to be a comparatively moral man."[7] In writing the confession of Alexander/Kuzmich Tolstoy could now intensify this hyperbolic self-abjection and corroborate his earlier argument—that public acclaim can obscure, and motivate, great evil. The former tsar writes: "I am the greatest criminal, the murderer of my father, the murderer of hundreds of thousands of people in wars of which I was the cause, a vile profligate, a villain. I believed what they said of me, that I was the savior of Europe, the benefactor of humanity, an exceptional perfection, *un heureux hazard* [a stroke of luck] as I told Madame de Stael." The more humble alter ego of this public figure nonetheless remains intact and capable of spiritual revival, continuing to provide moral intuition no matter how great the self-deception encouraged by public admiration. "I was born and lived forty-seven years of my life amid the most terrible temptations and not only did not resist them but became intoxicated with them, was tempted and tempted others, sinned and made others sin. But God kept his eye on me."

Tolstoy even assigned some of the same codes he used in his own diaries to those of Fyodor Kuzmich. At the end of his first entry the latter writes: "If God allows, I will continue tomorrow," a formulation similar to that found in Tolstoy's diaries, in which plans for the morrow often concluded with the proviso "if I am alive." At the beginning of another, Kuzmich writes "I slept badly [*durno*]," a phrase Tolstoy used to describe a night disturbed by sexual desire. It carries similar meaning here, as he continues: "It is strange to say that the murder of the beauty, the evil Nastasya (she was extremely sensually beautiful) stirred lustful feelings in me. And I did not sleep the whole night."[8] Several other elements in Alexander's story link his experience to Tolstoy's: his distaste for the falsehood of court life is heightened by a visit to the simple household of his former wet nurse (from whose breast, it is implied, he had imbibed her sensibility); he is strongly affected by an absent mother and confronts a major childhood trauma in the death of his nurse. Finally, Tolstoy's depiction of Alexander's eventual escape cannot help but remind us of the author's own; it is preceded, as was Tolstoy's, by growing restlessness, meditative peregrinations, and sleepless nights. During one of these he actually rehearses his escape: "I did not sleep the whole night. Dawn began to break. I awakened the guard, put on my white jacket and summoned the valet. Everyone else was still sleeping. I put on my frock coat, my civilian overcoat, and hat and walked out past the watchmen onto the street."

This spontaneous departure foreshadows a carefully planned one that is to come, but also provides an important Tolstoyan insight. Dressed in civilian clothing, Alexander is able to slip unrecognized into a crowd that has gathered to watch the flogging of a group of mutinous soldiers. After a time he is spotted and realizes that he must leave, but not before he has also recognized himself, as it were, in one of the soldiers passing through the gauntlet. It is Strumenskii, long known for his resemblance to the emperor and even nicknamed "Alexander II" by his comrades. As Alexander returns home, the fife and drum playing as the flogging continues, he feels the moral responsibility to justify what is happening to this double, this other Alexander. He recognizes that he is ultimately the authority that legitimizes this action, and when he cannot answer to his conscience, he is confirmed in a desire he has long held—to abandon the throne for a new life among the people. He returns to his usual morning routine, which includes a report alluding to the Decembrist society plotting his overthrow. After lunch he lies down and falls asleep, only to dream of the flogging, uncertain whether it is he or Strumenskii who is being punished. He leaves the house and goes to the military hospital, where he learns that Strumenskii has survived the beating but is dying. In the days that follow Alexander takes to his own bed with a fever; he recovers, but absent-mindedly cuts himself on the neck while shaving. Feigning a more serious wound, he recognizes his chance and arranges for the body of the dying Strumenskii to be brought to the house and placed in his bed, allowing him to escape.

Tolstoy writes in the story's introduction that Fyodor Kuzmich first became known in Siberia in 1836, and that he continued to wander the territory over the next twenty-seven years. The fictional memoir is written from the perspective of the dying Kuzmich, aged seventy-two. These long years of self-denial and spiritual wandering have led to a more virtuous life for the former emperor, but his redemption is not complete. In his diary Kuzmich confides that he is still confronting the Alexander within, just as Alexander had contained a kernel of Kuzmich. He is still troubled by his sensuality and memories of his former life: "I slept little and saw bad dreams: some sort of woman, unpleasant, weak, presses herself to me and I am not afraid of her or of sinning, but fear that my wife will see. And again there will be reproaches. Seventy-two years and I am still not free."[9] When Alexander/Kuzmich suggests that such dreams, which are not controlled by the deceit of wakeful restraint, reveal his true moral standing, we are to understand that he finds himself still deeply divided. In his notes on the story Tolstoy made the point explicitly: "That he truly wants with all his soul to be good and moral—and wants to reign at any cost. To show the duality of sometimes diametrically opposed inclinations that is characteristic of all people."

As Tolstoy explores the dialectics of identity and plots out an attempt to alter its dynamics, we find him dismissing the notion that Alexander could achieve some final resolution by his departure. No matter how dramatic it might be, it would not "free" him from this struggle.[10] In spite of this, his Kuzmich insists that he has achieved a liberation of sorts, describing his secret abdication as a freedom that divides the "vanity" of his former life from the meaningfulness of the years that followed.[11] It is clear that this vanity is centered in the identity of Alexander as monarch, and that his liberation is from this persona, which has taken on a life of its own in public life. Tolstoy had experienced the same thing; he had become a larger-than-life figure, from whom it was difficult to distinguish his own identity or personality. This public, performed self was so fully developed and ubiquitously realized in the cult of Tolstoy that even the casual reader could identify the problem: how could this celebrity, this self in the age of mechanical reproduction, maintain its integrity? Tolstoy himself addressed this problem directly in his final journal entry: "Maybe I am making a mistake and only justifying myself, but it seems that I have saved myself not as Lev Nikolaevich, but have saved that of which there is sometimes at least a small trace in me."[12]

In November 1910 this self that was not Lev Nikolaevich had been almost fully eclipsed by its persona, by the flesh made word. But his faith in the existence of the self as pure subject, of which only traces are left, is at the heart of this story, even as it is told in the kopeck newspapers. We have read Astapovo as the story of the liberation of Tolstoy's persona into the public sphere, where this mediated self, the product of collective imagination and motivation, made history on a grand scale. It is this public persona that commands attention and continues to be "Tolstoy" in his last days, when he has quit the stage. But we have also traced another journey, toward this unnamed "I," which was seen to legitimate his movement, even as it traversed the public domain, where it was so avidly named and labeled. The public admired both of these selves, wondering if Tolstoy could reach his destination with the media at his heals, whether he could escape his persona when the very gesture of departure was itself so "Tolstoyan."

It is striking now that this eighty-two-year-old man commanded so much attention, that his choice of how and where he might live his last days could have been so significant to his contemporaries. The public response stemmed from the belief that Tolstoy's final days, even in the ferment of his celebrity, might still signify something more than the media discourse and cultural capital they produced. This faith was deeply compelling, in part because it was already becoming antiquated. Tolstoy's contemporaries recognized the quixotic quality of this moral chivalry, this don setting off into the world as a knight-errant: the mills he fought would grind his story into journalistic pulp and convert its moral currency into rhetorical lucre. But they responded with more than idle curiosity as he enjoined a new and modern Russia to recall one of bygone days, in which fathers left spiritual testaments to their children and abandoned their homes to live their last days in solitude with God. His journey was watched with both nostalgia and hope, as if he might be looking for something that future generations would not seek but which might still prove profoundly revelatory.[13] And perhaps they were right. In the century that has passed, who has stepped out onto the road with such suggestive purpose and such an epic sense of moral destiny?

Whether or not Tolstoy could have delivered on this promise, whether or not it had been made with the best intentions or motivations, whither he was going, and why—that all these questions are left unanswered matters little in the end. As Tolstoy wrote of Fyodor Kuzmich, "Let it be proven historically that Alexander I and Kuzmich could not have been the same person: the legend persists in all its beauty and truth."[14] If the Tolstoy who was could not have become the Tolstoy he wanted to be, and if the two have become confused in legend, then perhaps we do not find Tolstoy at all in this story. Perhaps he completes his journey toward solitude in the breach between these questions. In the days of Astapovo much was rendered unto that Caesar that was the public domain, but an even greater part would remain beyond its grasp, mysterious and inspiring. In Tolstoy's view this part belonged to God, and whether or not his contemporaries believed the same, they recognized in it the great spark of the unknown. In their own, modern way, mercantile and pedestrian, they revered this and thirsted for its revelation.

A Word on My Sources

In writing this book two sources were of immense value. The first was a 1928 publication of more than one thousand telegrams sent to and from Astapovo during Tolstoy's eight-day stay there. This Soviet publication was overtly intended to portray the prerevolutionary excesses of church and state, which were revealed in the encrypted correspondence of security agents with their superiors. But the reproduction on the book's inside cover of the pattern from the wallpaper in the room in which Tolstoy died demonstrated the publication's participation in the most typical "cult" behavior, in which any relic of Tolstoy's death might be of interest to the reader.[1] The collection of telegrams itself corresponded to this notion, as, according to the editors, nothing was omitted except for repeated messages. (We thus can read even reporters' corrections to their own work: "Please delete that Tolstoy ate two eggs, incorrect: drank only milk tea.") The telegrams were also interesting from a rhetorical point of view. Here was a vastly important national narrative being formulated on the spot, stimulated by the demands of editorial offices and press agencies that were creating a media event in the fully modern sense of the term. The telegrams represented the raw material of this effort, at times necessarily formulaic in meeting deadlines and providing status reports, but at other times more richly rendered as the reporters sought to distinguish not only the moment, but also their own reception of it, from the everyday.

The second collection was the newspaper archive at the Tolstoy Museum in Moscow, which has a very broad representation of papers from 1910. Although I had at first intended to make the telegrams the core of my study, thinking that they would reveal how narratives of the departure were created most immediately, I found more interesting developments occurring in the editorial offices, where the reports from Astapovo were shaped into stories. To the extent that I was concerned with a process of collective sublimation, this made sense, and the newspapers soon replaced the telegrams as the bedrock of the project. The recurrent headings under which the papers often grouped their reports (*Russkoe slovo* on November 2, for example: "The Clergy on the Departure," "Official Circles," "Loved Ones," "Reactions in the Press") confirmed the categories of investigation that would ultimately organize the book.

The archive also had a card catalogue for journals and books arranged according to date and theme, through which I was able to acquire a fairly complete record of what was published on Tolstoy at the time. I copied everything that did not appear to be derivative or simply factual and did not discriminate against the obscure (small items in small newspapers) or the extreme (such as Black Hundreds newspapers). I sought a chorus that was more wide-ranging than well tempered and was just as interested in discord as in dominant chords. In presenting the material my goal has been to adduce the hue of the event as much as its sense. The chapters, while describing various spheres of representation of the events, roughly correspond to their chronological progression (departure, journey, illness, death) and contain a great deal of material that has not been published or discussed since its appearance in 1910.

This remarkable collection was lovingly gathered by the devoted group who formed the Tolstoy Museum in Moscow after his death. It is itself a monument of the cult of Tolstoy to which this book is dedicated. The newspaper clippings were collected from all over Russia but without indication of the source page numbers, so my citations also lack this information. I must thank the workers in the museum who patiently supported my obsessive desire to read through all this material. I could not have written this book without their help.

Notes

Introduction

1. L. N. Tolstoi, *Polnoe sobranie sochinenii* (hereafter *PSS*), 90 vols. (Moscow, 1928–1964), 58:123–124.

2. Makovitskii created one of the most detailed biographical chronicles ever recorded, based on voluminous shorthand notes made on a notepad hidden in his coat pocket. The longhand result is the *Yasnaya Polyana Notebooks* in four large volumes of small print (*U Tolstogo: Iasnopolianskie zapiski D. P. Makovitskogo* [Moscow, 1979]).

3. "Dnevnik A. L. Tolstoi," Rossiiskii gosudarstvennyi arkhiv literatury i iskusstva (RGALI), F. 508, op. 1, ed. khran. 278, 135. Early flashlights could not sustain their light for long periods (hence the name), so there may have been a practical necessity in effect here as well.

4. T. Tamanskaia, "Na puti v Kozel'sk," *Golos Moskvy*, November 18, 1910 (also printed in V. Ia. Lakshin, *Interv'iu i besedy s L'vom Tolstym* [Moscow, 1986]). From this memoir we know that Tolstoy also met a peasant on the train and asked him about his life. He argued with the student about the benefits of technology, suggesting that the airplane would bring no great benefit to humankind. "People had better just move about on the ground." When he pulled out his electric flashlight as he gathered his things, the student reminded him that he was utilizing technology, to which Tolstoy replied that he could also get along without it, and that the flashlight would never make people better.

5. *PSS*, 84:404. Tolstoy also added in a note that he had instructed Sasha to gather his manuscripts and send them to him. The multiple levels on which this parting letter works is typical of Tolstoy's final days; a deeply personal goodbye is written in the style of a final testament, which is accompanied by an offhand postscript that in effect makes a dispensation regarding his manuscripts according to his recently composed will.

6. *PSS*, 84:404.

7. Makovitskii reports that Tolstoy repeatedly asked military deserters (conscientious objectors often visited Tolstoy because of his opposition to military service) how it was possible to cross the border without a passport. He also asked Makovitskii to inquire about this when he travelled home to Slovakia in 1909 (D. P. Makovitskii, "Ukhod L'va Tolstogo," in *L. N. Tolstoi v vospominaniiakh sovremennikov,* ed. S. A. Makashin [Moscow, 1978] 2:426).

8. Ibid.

9. This excerpt from Aleksandra L'vovna's diary appears in Makovitskii, *U Tolstogo,* 4:480.

10. *PSS*, 58:143.

11. M. V. Muratov, *L. N. Tolstoi i V. G. Chertkov* (Moscow, 1934), 428–429.

12. William James writes of the act of rising from bed in the morning to illustrate the relationship between will and action. He finds himself rising out of bed precisely at a moment when he is *not* thinking about performing this action. For James this demonstrates an important gap between will and action, and one might argue that a similar notion applies here: Tolstoy implies that he leaves not because he has made a rational decision that leaving would benefit him, but because his body can no longer stand the stress of his domestic life.

13. A gathering of friends, associates, and witnesses convened on November 26, 1910, to compare notes and describe the turn of events in detail. Tolstoy's son Sergei presided over the meeting and made reference to the diaries of Makovitskii and other unpublished accounts. A transcript of the meeting was published by Boris Meilakh in 1961: "Novye materialy o L. Tolstom," *Russkaia literatura*, no. 1 (1961): 190–201.

14. A. F. Bobkov, "Neposredstvennye vpechatleniia ot puteshestviia v Iasnuiu Polianu Tul'skoi gubernii na pokhorony L. N. Tolstogo," in *Neizvestnyi Tolstoi v arkhivakh Rossii i SShA* (Moscow, 1994), 355–364.

15. An article in the New Year's Day edition of *Russkie vedomosti* describes the intense public demand for this coverage: "One can state without fear of exaggeration that at that time a significant part of Russia was living merely on news about Tolstoy. There was a long unfamiliar frenzied attention to the newspaper announcements, to the latest news, to minor changes in the content of the telegrams, prompting hope or confirming anxieties. The editorial telephones were busy day and night with readers asking if there was any new information about Tolstoy, if the troubling rumors were true, or if there was any hope for recovery" (*Russkie vedomosti*, January 1, 1911).

16. S. I. Vasiukov, "Populiarnost' Tolstogo," in *Mezhdunarodnyi Tolstovskii al'manakh*, ed. P. Sergeenko (Moscow, 1909), 17.

17. Tolstoy had once complained that "a quiet death under the influence of the rites of the Church is like death under morphine," but for all his efforts to avoid the former, he did not escape the latter. He was given morphine in his last hours at Astapovo.

18. *Gazeta kopeika*, November 27 and 28, 1910; *Rech'*, November 20, 1910.

19. *Gazeta kopeika*, November 25, 1910.

20. See A. B. Gol'denveizer, *Vblizi Tolstogo* (Moscow, 1923), 2:364; also E. E. Gorbunova, "Vstrechi so L'vom Nikolaevichem Tolstym," *L. N. Tolstoi i ego blizkie* (Moscow, 1986), 173.

21. Vladimir Azov, "Pod steklianym kolpakom," *Rech'*, November 4, 1910.

22. "Krylatye sravneniia Sventokhovskogo i Kuprina," *Kubanskii krai*, November 9, 1910.

Chapter 1   The Family Crisis as a Public Event

1. Russian surnames were not traditionally inherited until the fourteenth century, when the nobility adopted this tradition. Peasants, meanwhile, continued to be named primarily after their fathers. As Tolstoy's father was Nikolai, he was reverting to this tradition.

2. Most programmatic in this respect is the figure of Kasatkin in *Father Sergius*, whom I discuss below. It is precisely in the loss of "persona" (represented here by Kasatkin's false identity as the charismatic Sergius) that moral subjectivity can be gained.

3. "Vecherniaia khronika: vesti o grafe L. N. Tolstom," *Novoe vremia*, November 1, 1910.

4. A section of the anthology *The Last Days of Lev Nikolaevich Tolstoy* was titled "The Beginning of the New Life of L. N. Tolstoy." An important allusion here was Nekhliudov's reference to a new world at the end of *Resurrection*. See A. Khiriakov, "Ukhod v mir," in *Poslednie dni L'va Nikolaevicha Tolstogo* (St. Petersburg, 1910), 38.

5. In *War and Peace*, the Bolkonsky family bore a surname and history altered only slightly from that of Tolstoy's maternal family, and in *Anna Karenina*, the name (Levin) given to the moral hero of the story intentionally makes clear his affiliation with the author: Tolstoy's first name, in Russian, is Lev. Levin's proposal to Kitty, one of the most famous scenes in all of Russian literature, was based on Tolstoy's own proposal to Sofia Andreevna Bers.

6. For a full treatment of the public reaction to *The Kreutzer Sonata,* see Peter Ulf-Mueller, *Postlude to the Kreutzer Sonata.*

7. Ian Dubovskii, "U mogily vozhdia chelovechestva," *Maikopskaia gazeta,* November 28, 1910.

8. According to an 1827 article on family law, for instance, the family served as a "representation of the state," under which the father was the monarch, the wife and children his subjects. "If calm, tranquillity, and peace reign in the depths of families," the author argued, "then throughout the state hostilities and revolts fall silent and security dwells." See I. Vasil'ev, "Nechto o semeistvennykh obiazannostiakh v otnoshenii k dolzhnostiam i obiazannostiam obshchestvennym," *Damskii zhurnal,* 17 (1827), 199–200, as quoted in William Wagner, *Marriage, Property and Law in Late Imperial Russia* (Oxford, 1994), 73. This patriarchal perception of the family characterized juridical descriptions of the family throughout the early nineteenth century, according to Wagner.

9. Wagner, *Marriage, Property, and Law,* 133.

10. Ibid., 70. Wagner does not include figures for 1910.

11. Laura Engelstein, *The Keys to Happiness: Sex and the Search for Modernity in Fin-de-Siècle Russia* (Ithaca, N.Y., 1992), 34–35.

12. Rozanov, "Poezdka v Iasnuiu Polianu," in *Mezhdunarodnyi tolstovskii al'manakh: O Tolstom,* ed. P. Sergeenko (Moscow, 1909), 284 (originally published, under the pseudonym V. Varvarin, as "Odno vospominanie o L. N. Tolstom," *Russkoe slovo,* October 11, 1908). Rozanov visited the estate on March 6, 1903. Petr Struve spoke of the same desire to "see" Tolstoy in a letter to A. A. Stakhovich preceding their visit to Yasnaya Polyana in 1909. See Petr Struve, *Stat'i o Tolstom* (Sofia, 1921), 35.

13. *Graf Lev Tolstoi. Velikii pisatel' zemli russkoi* (St. Petersburg, 1903). The editors write: "Pilgrimages to Yasnaya Polyana in recent years have become more and more common. In their memoirs, visitors record one or another comment of the great writer, report one or another detail of his private life at home, which they share with their readers" (46).

14. Tolstoy had named his pedagogical journal of the early 1860s *Iasnaia Poliana,* but by 1910 a journal had appeared bearing that name which had no official affiliation with Tolstoy.

15. "V Iasnoi Poliane," *Golos Moskvy,* 2 Nov. 1910.

16. I. Ia. Ginzburg, "V Iasnoi Poliane," in *L. N. Tolstoi i khudozhniki* (Moscow, 1978), 220.

17. Gippius takes particular interest in the evening meal, noting Tolstoy's estrangement from his family as he quietly eats his vegetarian meal, while everyone else indulges in roast pig and bottles of wine. The next morning, however, in Sofia Andreevna's absence, Gippius notices Tolstoy's facility in approving the lunch menu presented him by a white-gloved servant (part of what impresses her as a smooth daily regime). She informs her readers that the tea and biscuits, of which Tolstoy is partaking, are of good quality. See Zinaida Gippius, *Zhivye litsa* (Prague, 1925), 160–169.

18. "He appeared absolutely marvelous to me. He was just like he was supposed to be. Only not here, in a landowner's estate." Rozanov tours the house, finding it inglorious (Anna Karenina would not have danced there) and spiritually abandoned (like a dog that dies when it is no longer needed by its master). See Rozanov, "Poezdka," 286.

19. *Iasnaia Poliana: Zhizn' L. N. Tolstogo* (Moscow, 1910).

20. *PSS,* 38:18.

21. Much attention was paid to this work. (See, for instance, the review of the year in literature in *Novoe vremia,* January 1, 1911.)

22. A report in *Birzhevye vedomosti* reminded readers that the estate was not only a glorious landmark but also a place of unique repose for Tolstoy, where everything was organized for his comfort. Tolstoy's aging, weakening body needed this care more than anything, the author argued, and it was wondered what could have motivated him to leave (I. N. Potapenko, "Velikoe odinochestvo," *Birzhevye vedomosti,* October 31, 1910). Another report pointed out that these same comforts were antithetical to Tolstoy's beliefs and that he had paid the price of public censure for remaining there because of his tender feelings for his family: Leo, "Poslednii etap," *Severo-zapadnyi golos,* October 31, 1910. On the tenderness of the family, see also "Legenda XX-ogo veka," *Birzhevye vedomosti,* October 30, 1910.

23. Gorbunov-Posadov, editor of the Tolstoyan publishing house *Posrednik*, told an interviewer: "How many times he expressed to us how hard it was for him to live and make use of the relative comforts of life, hearing from all sides the reproaches of his enemies that he only wrote about simplicity but himself enjoyed the services of lackeys" (G. El', "Pochemu uekhal Tolstoi," *Rannee utro*, October 31, 1910).

An article by L. Grossman alluded to these rumors and the disbelief with which they were met: "Somehow the rumors of deep discord in the Tolstoy family, that Sofia Andreevna was prepared to ask the authorities about the establishment of guardianship over her husband, were not taken into account; with some sort of naïve optimism it was supposed that the cloudless happiness of the great writer could not be darkened by the attitude toward him of any writers or critics, or of the government or church" ("Velikii strannik," *Odesskie novosti*, October 31, 1910).

24. "Druz'ia L. N. Tolstogo ob ego ot''ezde," *Rannee utro*, October 31, 1910. Kuz'minskii had evidently conceived this plan after learning that Tolstoy had refused the overtures of other pilots, including the well-known Efimov, to land their planes at Yasnaya. See also *Birzhevye vedomosti*, October 30, and the cover of *Potok* no. 28 (1910).

25. Variants of this idea appeared in other pieces: "Into the world or away from the world? To us or away from us?" "Tolstoy was not going away from the world but on the contrary decided to go into the world." The phrase "Yasnaya Polyana recluse" (*iasnopolianskii otshel'nik*) registered a similar ambiguity, with the Russian word meaning "a person going away from." Had Tolstoy been in retreat from the world at Yasnaya, or did he in fact need to retreat from Yasnaya itself into the world? See *Rech'*, October 31, 1910.

26. *PSS*, 49:32.

27. Chertkov cites Tolstoy's diary of 1884 as early evidence of Tolstoy's disaffection with his family life, and the memoirs of Tolstoy's children likewise point to this period as particularly trying. Tolstoy did not, however, keep much of a diary in 1882 and 1883, so it is difficult to determine when and how this crisis began.

28. Aleksandra was the last of the Tolstoy children to live to maturity. Sofia Andreevna gave birth to one more son—Ivan, who died in childhood.

29. The argument was over the sale of horses from their family property in Samara.

30. "At home two bearded muzhiks—my two young sons—are playing vint. 'She is playing croquet—you didn't see her,' says her sister Tanya." This is the same third person estrangement (bearded muzhiks) that Tolstoy expresses in "Three Days in the Country," in 1910. Accounts of this incident vary greatly among the children: Sergei recalls being there but not even knowing that his father had left until later; Tatiana very vividly recalls the scene of her father leaving, and Ilya describes Sofia Andreevna as being extremely distraught, running out into the garden and refusing to return to the house, though her contractions had already begun.

31. *PSS*, 49:105.

32. "It was no use not going away. It seems that this is not going to pass" (ibid., 113).

33. Ibid., 122. The date for this document is uncertain. It is believed to have been written circa 1884, but Tolstoy in 1896 made reference to a plan made fifteen years ago—probably this one.

34. Sofia Andreevna does not include this letter in her edition of Tolstoy's letters. The manuscript has a note in her handwriting: "an unread and unsent letter of Lev Nikolaevich to his wife" (*PSS*, 83: 548). The extent to which Chertkov's personal enmity toward Sofia Andreevna figures in the editorial machinations of the Jubilee Edition is also an open question. The dating of this undated letter, for instance, might be affected by a desire to construct a particular narrative of the Tolstoy marriage.

35. P. I. Biriukov, *L. N. Tolstoi: Biografiia* (Berlin, 1921), 470. He quotes from the archive of T. A. Kuzminskaia.

36. I. L. Tolstoi, *Moi vospominaniia* (Moscow, 1914), 170.

37. For Tolstoy, the internal dynamics of this conflict became rather complex, as he adopted the contradictions of his family life as his cross to bear. The following comment quoted in the newspapers characterized this dilemma: "If I decide to do something like that [leave home] in my later years, they will say that I wasn't able to withstand my domestic circumstances. But I have shown that I can withstand them, and I waver not because I think it will be difficult, but because I am afraid of lightening my burden" (*Odesskie novosti*, November 5, 1910, citing *Russkoe slovo*).

38. This public-mindedness shapes the discourse of these diaries: they speak to one another, correct and counteract. Tolstoy on occasion addressed his future readers directly, as in the passage from June 19, 1884, in which he criticizes his son Sergei for being envious, then writes: "Someday you will read this, Seryozha, son—you need to know that you are very, very bad. And that you need to work on yourself a great deal and, most important, humble yourself" (*PSS,* 49:105).

39. When the writer Korolenko visited Tolstoy in August 1910, he quickly found himself caught in the middle of this dispute: Sofia Andreevna startled him by immediately divulging personal problems (they were barely acquainted), and Chertkov and Gol'denveizer also took him aside and explained the situation from their point of view (V. G. Korolenko, "Velikii piligrim," in *L. N. Tolstoi v vospominaniiakh sovremennikov* [Moscow, 1978], 2:248).

40. Chertkov was exiled in 1897, along with P. I. Biriukov and I. M. Tregubov, for the distribution of a letter protesting treatment of the Dukhobors. Sofia Andreevna was not above soliciting the support of the state to keep Chertkov out of her husband's reach. According to Makovitskii's notes, Andrei L'vovich received a position as special agent for Stolypin in January 1910, and in July Sofia Andreevna told Gol'denveizer that she was seeking Stolypin's help, through Andrei, to have Chertkov exiled from Russia.

41. The English and Russian editions of the diary differ. This passage from the July 26 entry—"There is certainly some secret plot between Lev Nikolaevich and Chertkov against me and the children"—is omitted in the Russian edition (Moscow, 1936) but included in Maude's translation.

42. The 1851 diary entry included the following: "I fell in love with men very often. . . . Looks always played a major role in the selection, as for example with Diakov. But I will never forget the night when we were traveling together from Petersburg and I felt the urge to kiss him and cry. There was a feeling of lust here, but what it was doing here is impossible to decide. Because in my imagination there were no indecent pictures. On the contrary, I felt a terrible revulsion" (*PSS,* 46:237).

43. "I wanted to show Lev Nikolaevich the source of my jealousy regarding Chertkov and I brought him a page from his early diary, from 1851, in which he writes about how he never fell in love with women but did so many times with men. I thought that he, like P. I. Biriukov and like Dr. Makovitskii, would understand my jealousy and comfort me, but instead he turned completely pale and fell into such a rage as I hadn't seen in a long, long time. 'Go away! Get out!' he shouted. 'I told you I would leave you and I will!'" (*Dnevniki Sof'i Andreevny Tolstoi (1910)* [Moscow, 1936], 142).

Sofia Andreevna also showed the diary to Chertkov's sister-in-law O. K. Tolstaya, Tolstoy's niece E. V. Obolenskaia (Diterikhs, his sister's daughter and the mother of N. L. Obolenskii, who married Tolstoy's own daughter Maria L'vovna), and to Aleksandra L'vovna.

Chertkov's mother wrote: "It never entered my head that I could possibly hear such words of slander from your lips. And I am surprised that your sons have not pointed out to you how you are bringing shame on your whole family at the same time as you pour dirt upon their father." Sofia Andreevna answered: "No one has the right to interfere in the relations between husband and wife. And as to how I am judged by a tiny circle of Tolstoyans—it is really all the same to me. I have forty-eight years of irreproachable life and committed love for my husband, whom I took care of without any outside interference; I helped him and lived one life with him, soul to soul" (*Dnevniki,* 320–322).

44. Sofia Andreevna expresses this concern repeatedly in her diary (see, for example, the entry of July 7, 1910).

45. Sofia Andreevna described her feelings about Tolstoy's private papers in her diary: "I am not concerned that they hide the diaries; that's understandable and entirely legal. And they need to be hidden *from everyone.* What bothers me is that Chertkov and Sasha can read them and I, his wife, cannot. That means he reproaches me and then submits me to the judgment of my daughter and Chertkov" (ibid., 158).

46. In the Russian, Sofia Andreevna unknowingly makes a prescient double entendre here in reference to the *ukhod* ("care," but also "departure") of Tolstoy—it was the doctor, Makovitskii, who assisted Tolstoy in his departure from Yasnaya Polyana.

47. June 22, 1910. The Jubilee Edition, edited by Chertkov, includes commentary that this annotation is explained by Sofia Andreevna's "hysterical condition" at the time (*PSS*, 84:395–396).

48. *Dnevniki*, 130. Sofia Andreevna later inserted, "But afterwards fruitlessly returned. She should have held out."

49. Sofia Andreevna carried on a long campaign to capture on cinematographic film a series of rather forced and artificial sequences showing the Tolstoys in marital harmony.

50. Her doctors, family, and Sofia Andreevna herself all used the term "hysteria" to describe her condition.

51. *PSS*, 58:129.

52. When Sergei L'vovich returned the secret diary to Tolstoy after his fainting spell in early October, Tolstoy told him that it would have been all right if he had read it—so the new diary was still written for public consumption. (Sergei L'vovich reports this in his commentary to Sofia Andreevna's diaries: *Dnevniki*, 349.)

53. *PSS*, 84:411.

54. *PSS*, 57:66. The draft was preserved in his papers.

55. "If you do not accept these conditions for a good, peaceful life, then I will take back my promise not to leave you. I will leave. I will probably not go to Chertkov. I will even make a condition that he not come to live near me, but I will leave without fail, because it is impossible to live as we are living now" (*PSS*, 84:400).

56. *Dnevniki*, 158.

57. Bulgakov's diary indicates how deeply Sofia Andreevna's sincerity was under question: "She raised her eyes upward, quickly crossed herself with little crosses and whispered, 'Lord! Just don't let it be this time, just don't let it be this time!'" He did not believe her prayer was sincere, however, until he later found her repeating it unaware of the presence of others: "And she did this when not in front of others: when I happened to enter the Remington room, I found her saying this prayer."

58. When Tatiana L'vovna confronted her, she gave them back, explaining that she had been afraid that Chertkov would get them. After Tolstoy's death at Astapovo, Aleksandra L'vovna and Chertkov rushed back to Yasnaya Polyana while Sofia Andreevna and the rest of the family stayed with the body; it could be argued that Sofia Andreevna's actions during the fainting spell were justified, or, on the contrary, that Aleksandra L'vovna and Chertkov were only protecting Tolstoy's papers from Sofia Andreevna.

59. Aleksandra wrote in her diary: "Sergei told Mother that she has to change her ways and take treatment if she is ill. That if she doesn't come to her senses, she needs to be taken under guardianship; we will call a family council, summon doctors, seize her property and force her to separate from Father." (This is evidently accurate, as it is cited in Sofia Andreevna's diaries, which were edited by Sergei [*Dnevniki*, 349].) Aleksandra L'vovna, Varvara Feokritova, and Chertkov were all called from Teliatniki (the first two had moved out after prolonged conflict with Sofia Andreevna), and efforts were made to reconcile their differences for Tolstoy's benefit. Sofia Andreevna made peace with her daughter and allowed Tolstoy to renew his meetings with Chertkov.

60. In Bulgakov's description, she runs to the pond, moving fairly quickly with others in pursuit, slips on the bridge, and then rolls into the water. Though she does go in over her head, it is not necessary to resuscitate her. Sofia Andreevna hugged and kissed Bulgakov for saving her, telling him that he had behaved as if he were her own son, an epithet that was particularly evocative under the circumstances. See V. Bulgakov, *L. N. Tolstoi v poslednii god ego zhizni* (Moscow, 1989), 386–388.

61. "We didn't believe that she could make a serious attempt at suicide, but that she could really hurt herself in faking an attempt, because she might misjudge the danger" (S. L. Tolstoi, *Ocherki bylogo* [Moscow, 1956], 249).

62. A servant showed the telegram to Aleksandra L'vovna, who added another one, telling Tolstoy to believe only telegrams signed "Aleksandra." Chertkov refused to meet with her, anticipating that she was just doing this to get him to send a telegram to Lev Nikolaevich.

63. On his arrival on October 28, Andrei vowed that he would learn his father's whereabouts by the next day, intending to appeal for help from the Tula governor (Bulgakov, *L. N. Tolstoi*, 388).

64. Sofia Andreevna was herself in need of much more than this familial support, the children decided, and a Moscow psychiatrist and two nurses were called in to care for and watch over her. The doctor who examined her at the time wrote of her "extreme effort to make herself and her interests the center of attention not only of her family and loved ones but of anyone who happens to cross her path" (S. L. Tolstoi, *Ocherki*, 255–262). This is a psychiatric description of what Tolstoy described as a moral problem in a conversation with Gol'denveizer on July 25, 1910: "It is strange. She is completely lacking in any religious or moral foundation; she doesn't even have any simple superstitions or faith in an icon. In the time since I first became concerned with religious questions, already thirty years now, the contradiction in our views reveals itself more and more sharply, and it has reached the point... There is no truthfulness, no shame, no pity, nothing... only vanity, that people would not speak badly of her" (A. B. Gol'denveizer, *Vblizi Tolstogo* [Moscow, 1923], 2:165). As Sofia Andreevna was often surrounded by sympathy for her husband, one can understand the urgency and immediacy with which she pleaded her case to strangers, for whom she adopted the role of a pitiable, beleaguered wife.

65. *Dnevniki*, 264.

66. Ibid., 266.

67. More details from Sofia Andreevna's story further supported her case: she had gotten up at three in the morning because she heard that her husband was awake. Tolstoy told her that he was not feeling well and was taking medicine. Later she heard a dog go into his room and, fearing that it would disturb his papers, went to check; at this point Lev Nikolaevich said to himself, "Again they are disturbing my papers." She then went to bed and did not wake again until morning, though she usually checked on Lev Nikolaevich every two to three hours.

68. This is probably after the incident in June of that year, relating to the parting letter cited above.

69. The family was more circumspect; in his statement to the press on November 1, Andrei L'vovich described his mother's suicide attempt as an aberration—an effect of the shock of Tolstoy's departure. "The causes for my father's estrangement are rooted in his long-standing views on the so-called intelligentsia lifestyle. Even our modest way of life and furnishings always seemed like an unnecessary luxury to him. Probably Lev Nikolaevich long ago decided to go off somewhere to live a more simple, and perhaps solitary, life. Thus the fact of my father's departure, though it is deeply upsetting to the whole family, is not unexpected. In and of itself the count's departure would not have developed into such an extraordinary event if a complication had not arisen. My mother, expecting less than anyone such a move by the count, took what transpired to heart, and her grief was so great that it could not be assuaged by tears and words of consolation; she even made an attempt at suicide and threw herself into a pond." ("Vecherniaia khronika") He and other members of the family worked to deflect implications that his mother's unstable emotional condition might have been a factor in his father's decision. Sofia Andreevna's sister, T. A. Kuzminskaia, told the press that Tolstoy's departure was nothing more than the "natural consequence" of his beliefs. "K vnezapnomu ot''ezdu L. N. Tolstogo iz Iasnoi Poliany," *Sovremennoe slovo*, October 31, 1910.

70. L. Grossman, "Velikii strannik," *Odesskie novosti*, October 31, 1910.

71. "Poslednii akkord," *Poslednie novosti* (Kiev), October 30, 1910. A report in *Rech'* quoted the writer (and Tolstoy sympathizer) Nikolai Leskov wondering aloud in the early 1890s why Tolstoy continued to live with his family: "What is taking him so long? Such old men shouldn't live with their families. What is there for him there? You need to follow the example of the people in such cases. That is how it is done among peasants who are Old Believers or sectarians. An old man like that will leave everything, will give his property to his oldest son, and head off for somewhere, or live in the bathhouse, or in a special hut" (A. Khir'iakov, "Velikii starik," *Rech'*, October 31, 1910.

72. N. Severskii, "Blazheny alchushchie i zhazhdushchie pravdy," *Volzheskoe slovo* (Samara), October 31, 1910.

73. "Otgoloski 'ukhoda,'" *Russkoe slovo*, November 2, 1910.

74. Gorbunov-Posadov says that the last time he had visited Yasnaya Polyana he had sensed that Tolstoy was on the verge of a major decision. "Lev Nikolaevich does not fall into the category of people who make decisions in moments of sudden spiritual extremes. His decision to

leave his family and live according to his principles was a cherished desire" ("Pochemu uekhal Tolstoi," *Rannee utro,* October 31, 1910). Chertkov, in a letter to *Utro Rossii,* says that Tolstoy left to find solitude, so the fewer people who know the reasons for his departure, the better (cited in *Novoe vremia,* November 2, 1910). Chertkov was also quoted explaining that Tolstoy had wanted to leave for a long time but restrained himself out of pity for his family (*Peterburgskaia gazeta,* November 1, 1910).

75. Respect for the family's privacy was a commonplace in public discourse, if not in practice. *Vostochnaia zaria* reported that "common folk" in Moscow spoke in hushed tones when discussing Tolstoy's family situation (November 9, 1910). The newspapers tried to show their respect as well, as in this newspaper report from a correspondent approaching the Tolstoy house in Moscow, uncertain whether or not news of Tolstoy's departure has reached them: "The correspondent could not bring himself to take on the heavy responsibility of informing the household of the troubling telegrams the newspaper had received" (*Russkoe slovo,* October 30, 1910).

76. Lazurskii was a tutor for the Tolstoy children in 1894. Sofia Andreevna evidently made her unpublished novel *Whose Fault?* (a response to *The Kreutzer Sonata*) available to him, for he was later able to describe its plot to Tikhon Polner, who used it in his *Lev Tolstoi i ego zhena* (1928). Another such insider was I. Perper, who had visited Yasnaya Polyana eleven days before Tolstoy's departure. He reported that Tolstoy had talked a great deal, and with a visibly heavy heart, about marriage, celibacy, and the birth and upbringing of children (*Odesskie novosti,* November 5, 1910).

77. Bulgakov, L. N. Tolstoi, 389.

78. Ibid. On the family receiving sympathy telegrams at Astapovo after false reports of Tolstoy's death on November 4, see *Rech',* November 5, 1910. V. A. Maklakov, another prominent member of the Duma who was also a family friend of the Tolstoys, was misquoted in *Rul'* and sent a letter on November 1 recommending that the family be consulted in the future.

79. The conservative press gave particular privilege to the perspectives of family and friends. A. Stolypin wrote in *Novoe vremia* of the special perspective that a friend of the family might have (in this case Duma member M. A. Stakhovich): "The friendship connecting M. A. Stakhovich to the Tolstoy family over the course of many years, the chain of old, warm memories of his stays at Yasnaya Polyana, of his conversations with Lev Nikolaevich—the sort of conversations one has not with guests but with one's own people, familiar and beloved—and besides this the mature consideration and thinking through of impressions from a passionate and distracted youth: all this leads not to a dry, made-up report but to a heartfelt retelling by an intelligent and feeling man of what he managed to lovingly glimpse of the great soul that was opened up to him" (A. Stolypin, "Zametki," *Novoe vremia,* November 24, 1910).

80. In his letter to Novikov, a peasant in whom he had recently confided his thoughts of leaving Yasnaya Polyana, Tolstoy inquired if Novikov might know of a hut in which he could live. This letter became known to the public by coincidence, when Novikov wandered into the Moscow editorial offices of *Russkie vedomosti* on October 31 looking for work for his son. As he came bearing a note of introduction from Tolstoy, he was asked if he knew of Tolstoy's departure. Novikov had not heard the news but mentioned the letter he had received from Tolstoy. He subsequently brought the letter to Sergei L'vovich in Moscow. It was initially reported by *Russkie vedomosti* on November 2.

81. Tolstoy said this to Makovitskii at Shamordino, according to Maria Nikolaevna. See Al. Ksiunin, *Ukhod Tolstogo* (Berlin, 1935), 93.

82. He received scores of thankful telegrams after Tolstoy's death, and his own death in 1913 received national coverage.

83. "Taking advantage of father's good condition, I decided to ask him about what I absolutely needed to know if his illness were to drag out and become serious and prolonged. I did not close my eyes to the fact that I was bearing a tremendous responsibility: I considered myself obliged to inform my family, as I had promised to do should he become ill. This is why I asked Father if he wanted me to tell them if his illness turned out to be prolonged and serious. Father got very worked up over my words and several times entreated me not to let them know for any reason about his whereabouts or his illness" (A. L. Tolstaia, "Ob ukhode i smerti L. N. Tolstogo," in *Tolstoi: Pamiatniki tvorchestva i zhizni* [Moscow, 1923], 4:158).

84. "At that time there were six doctors tending my father, five of whom were longtime friends of the family. Their unanimous opinion as both doctors and friends was that such excitement was so dangerous that it might kill Father." At the time he wrote these memoirs, Ilya confessed that he still did not know whether or not Sofia Andreevna should have been allowed to see Lev Nikolaevich, but he justified this decision by deferring to his father's will, which he felt was decisively described in Tolstoy's telegram to Sofia Andreevna asking her not to come. "As cruel as such a decision seemed to us, it seemed impossible not to honor his wishes. My mother was tormented terribly by this, but there was nothing to be done" (I. L. Tolstoi, *Moi vospominaniia*, 254.) By the time he published a later edition of his memoirs, however, Ilya had changed his mind and felt that it would have been better for both his mother and his father if she had been allowed to see him before he lost consciousness. (The *Russkoe slovo* memoirs were published in book form by Sytin in 1914, the later edition by the Soviet publishing house Mir in 1933.)

Sergei L'vovich wrote that they had decided to first fulfill the wishes of their father, then of the doctors, and lastly of themselves (*Ocherki bylogo*, 259). The family asked the press to report that they had decided not to visit Tolstoy because they did not want to upset him or give him reason to suspect that his situation was critical (*Novoe vremia*, November 5, 1910).

85. See "Strakh za Tolstogo," *Golos* (Yaroslavl), November 5, 1910. The Tolstoyans were, in fact, in charge. Sergei Tolstoy writes: "Entrance into that home was obtained with difficulty. First you had to knock at the window; someone opened the vent, and the conversation took place through it. Alesha Sergeenko was posted at the door almost without rest, and he admitted only select people" (*Ocherki bylogo*, 260).

86. V. Rozanov, "Gde zhe pokoi Tolstomu?" *Novoe vremia*, November 6, 1910.

87. *Panda*, "L. Tolstoi na obroke," *Novoe vremia*, November 6, 1910.

88. The reactionary papers went further, describing Tolstoy's deathbed scene as "spiritual murder" ("Uzhas smerti gr. L. N. Tolstogo," *Moskovskie vedomosti*, November 16, 1910). In decrying Tolstoy's isolation from his family, these critics often neglected to mention that Aleksandra L'vovna had been at Tolstoy's bedside throughout his illness and had been joined there by Sergei L'vovich and Tatiana L'vovna when they arrived at Astapovo. The family always maintained that they were never hindered by Tolstoy's followers but rather by their concern for his health.

89. P. P., "Posle 48 let," *Novoe vremia*, November 6, 1910.

90. "Ot kogo on bezhal?" *Kolokol*, November 6, 1910.

91. Lev L'vovich evidently had made accusations against Chertkov to the British press even before his letter to *Novoe vremia* appeared (Pavuk-Vovchenko, "Pochemu? K iasnopolianskoi tragedii," *Rannee utro*, November 23, 1910).

92. Lev L'vovich and *Novoe vremia* were known allies in the campaign to neutralize Tolstoy's effect on society. Lev L'vovich had been a follower of his father but had eventually turned against him, speaking out in the press, particularly in *Novoe vremia*, against his father's ideas. It was *Novoe vremia* that had printed Lev L'vovich's answer to *The Kreutzer Sonata*, his 1898 *Chopin's Prelude*, in which he asserted that the best way to corral youthful sexual energy was through early marriage. (See *Novoe vremia*, June 3, 9, and 16, 1898.) One of Lev L'vovich's chief allies at *Novoe vremia*, M. Men'shikov, was also a former Tolstoy sympathizer. In 1898 he had written of Lev L'vovich's relationship with his father: "Life is hard for him [Tolstoy]; he's lonely, and several of his loved ones, like Lev L'vovich, systematically poison his existence. Lev L'vovich again came out against his father in *Novoe vremia* regarding the sovereign's declaration on general disarmament. A revolting, pitiful spectacle" (letter of September 4, 1898, to Annenkova, cited in V. Zhdanov, *Liubov' v zhizni L'va Tolstogo* [Moscow, 1993], 258.)

In 1900, a collection of Lev L'vovich's stories appeared, including his earlier *Tat'ianin den'*, in which he directly attacked the ideas expressed in *The Kreutzer Sonata*. Perhaps there was a complex psychology behind this antagonism toward his father's views; he had caught typhus while working on famine relief on the family's property in Samara and was thereafter in poor health. Aleksandra L'vovna wrote that he used to complain that there was nothing worse than being the son of a great man (*The Tragedy of Tolstoy* [New Haven, 1933], 189).

93. "Otets i syn," *Gazeta kopeika*, November 17, 1910. They also remind readers of Lev L'vovich's earlier letter, in which he explained Tolstoy's departure as motivated exclusively by internal causes.

94. Aleksandr Gol'denveizer wrote that he had at first intended to refute Lev L'vovich's accusations but changed his mind and decided that any polemical discussion of the sort was inappropriate. Instead he limited himself to voicing his displeasure at this blackening of the memory of Tolstoy. A. Gol'denveizer, "Pis'mo v redaktsiiu," *Russkie vedomosti,* November 26, 1910. See also the letters of Khiriakov and A. Sergeenko (*Gazeta kopeika,* November 18 and 25, 1910). Sergeenko wrote that Lev L'vovich's letter would have caused Tolstoy "unbearable spiritual pain" if he were still alive.

95. As quoted in *Rech',* November 22, 1910.

96. Ilya's view resonates with popular opinion in the press that individual perspectives on Tolstoy's legacy would diminish it: "narrow and biased judgements regarding the significance of Chertkov diminish the great memory of my father" (*Gazeta kopeika,* reprinted from *Russkoe slovo*). Ilya claimed that the key to understanding his father was contained in a letter of 1900, in which Tolstoy had written that it was important to live the Christian life under all possible conditions.

97. *Gazeta kopeika,* November 20, 1910.

98. The reactionary *Moskovskie novosti* printed a thoroughly libelous story claiming that until 1905 (not an accidental choice for a year on which to pin this critical change in the regime at Yasnaya), Tolstoy had lived happily at his estate, not denying himself the comfort that surrounded him but instead complaining of any change in his way of life, even though he was living beyond the family means. Then in 1905 Chertkov arrived and began to criticize Tolstoy's lifestyle, provoking him to change and blaming everything on Sofia Andreevna. From that time things got progressively worse, until both Sofia Andreevna and Lev Nikolaevich were nervously unbalanced. It was in this wretched state that Tolstoy had met his death: "Attacks of spite and hatred toward his family and even toward everyone around him continuted to the last minutes of his life. Not long before his death he shouted at Makovetskii [sic], Chertkov and others at his bedside 'Leave me alone! Go to hell! and so forth.' This is how the 'philosopher of love' died" ("Poslednie gody L. N. Tolstogo," *Moskovskie vedomosti,* November 28, 1910). The story had previously appeared in the newspaper *Zemshchina.* Two days later *Moskovskie vedomosti* summarized a similar report, this one from the newspaper *Svet* ("Istinnaia obstanovka smerti gr. Tolstogo," November 30, 1910). They also remonstratively refused to print the letters of Sergei and Ilya refuting Lev L'vovich, claiming that it would be inappropriate to reprint from another newspaper such sensitive family documents. They cared much less about the reliability of their information in printing the aforementioned stories, however.

99. L. L. Tolstoi, "Kto vinovnik?" *Novoe vremia,* November 16, 1910. Chertkov was also of noble origins and grew up in a family home that was visited by both Alexander II and Alexander III.

100. *Novoe vremia,* November 18, 1910.

101. "For now one can only thank Count Lev L'vovich Tolstoy for his courageous revelation of the secret, which amounts to a national crime on the part of Mr. Chertkov, and wish for the full revelation of the dark tragedy that led to the agonizing demise of the great artist of Russia" (*Moskovskie vedomosti,* November 17, 1910). Though the editors maintained this respectful silence, Chertkov's role was obvious to them even before Lev L'vovich's letter appeared, they explained.

102. See Rozanov, "Gde zhe pokoi Tolstomu?"

103. Lev L'vovich alludes to his father's famous work "I Cannot Remain Silent!"

104. Chertkov would eventually fight back in his book on Tolstoy's last days: "What took place around him at Yasnaya Polyana, especially in the governing of the estate, was as if intentionally calculated to grieve, offend, and trouble him in his most sacred feelings" (V. G. Chertkov, *Ukhod Tolstogo* [Moscow, 1922], 29).

105. As reported in *Gazeta kopeika,* November 29, 1910.

106. "[I]f this affair concerned any respected family of reasonable means and good breeding, there is no doubt that pulicizing family problems and arguments would be considered a reprehensible act." (See also *Rech',* November 22, 1910.)

107. "Gr. A. L. Tolstaia i V. Chertkov o literaturnom nasledstve Tolstogo," *Novoe vremia,* January 24, 1911. *Novoe vremia* had summarized her letter in an item appearing on the 23rd,

reporting that it had been received on the previous day. The publication on the 24th was also incomplete, offering excerpts of her letter together with Chertkov's.

108. It was actually Tatiana L'vovna who discovered this crime against literature. The manuscript pages in question were from a draft of *War and Peace.*

109. "Nasledstvo L. N. Tolstogo," *Novoe vremia,* January 28, 1911. Bers wrote that his main impetus for writing the letter was something Sofia Andreevna had said: "All my life I considered our family life the ideal of family happiness, and now in five days all of that has been taken away and nothing but grief, pain, and insult remains from forty-eight years of complete happiness." The arguments against the Tolstoyan side often rested on this inaccurate summation of the course of the Tolstoy marriage, with the couple's final separation coming as a sudden and unexpected aberration.

110. "Zaveshchanie Tolstogo," *Sovremennoe slovo,* February 10, 1911. The reporters consider it their "moral obligation" to answer Bers's charges and impugn them by questioning his conduct: "One can only be surprised that Mr. Bers, who personally has no interest in this affair and knows about it only from third parties, considered it his duty to set forth in the press under his own name all these unjust accusations and claims coming from an unnamed and obviously biased source." *Sovremennoe slovo* used the same strategy in an editorial on Bers's charges, asking if they could be trusted based on the method through which they had been brought forth ("Gospodin Bers," *Sovremennoe slovo,* January 29, 1911).

111. "Gospodin Bers." In another example of this strategy an editorial in *Golos Moskvy* criticized the Tolstoyan Bulanzhe for a "tactless" proposal that Yasnaya Polyana be nationalized so that the family would not be able to interfere with the public visiting the grave (Neznakomets, *Golos Moskvy,* November 18, 1910).

112. One commentator felt it necessary to remind Aleksandra L'vovna publicly: "This is a question not of a family dispute among the relatives of a deceased Tula landowner, but of the works of a great Russian writer" (A. N. V—v, "Russkaia literatura v opasnosti," *Novoe vremia,* January 25, 1911).

113. Maksimilian Voloshin, "Sud'ba L'va Tolstogo," *Russkaia mysl',* no. 12 (1910): 133. Quotation from "U smertnogo odra," *Rech',* November 8, 1910.

114. D. Ovsianiko-Kulikovskii, "V mire—pokoinik," *Rech',* November 8, 1910.

115. I. Leonov, "Dva momenta," *Saratovskii vestnik,* November 14, 1910. In the dispute over her husband's will, Sofia Andreevna found that her best defense was to remind the public of her maternal responsibilities, arguing that Tolstoy's assets were needed to support the large family he had left behind. Once it began to appear that she would lose control of the copyrights, she used a similar argument to defend her unwillingness to agree to the proposed transfer of Yasnaya Polyana to the local peasants. Sofia Andreevna claimed that Lev Nikolaevich had never mentioned wanting to bequeath the estate to the peasants, but that if he had, the family would have "hurried to fulfill his wish"—now, though, since he had given away the rights to his literary works, the family could not afford to give up their land ("Beseda s gr. S. A. Tolstoi," *Russkie vedomosti,* January 16, 1911). Plans were also discussed to nationalize the estate, which the Soviets subsequently did.

116. At times the children could honor themselves by accepting familial responsibility. A letter was written to Pavel Miliukov forestalling any measures on behalf of the Duma to assume the costs of the funeral: "We strongly urge you not bring a measure before the State Duma regarding government coverage of the expenses for Lev Nikolaevich's funeral. If such a measure is proposed, then we urgently request that it not be approved, as we consider this our right, which we do not relinquish" (cf. *Rech',* November 12, 1910).

117. *Sovremennoe slovo,* January 18, 1911.

118. *Sovremennoe slovo,* January 19, 1911. Ten days later, the newspaper repeated its call for a merciful end to this display: "Isn't it time to put an end to this unbecoming and distressing story?" (*Sovremennoe slovo,* January 29, 1911). Similar arguments had arisen when Chertkov appealed to the courts regarding the will in November 1910. A *Moskovskie vedomosti* editorial argued that this action went against Tolstoy's principles. "It goes without saying that the orphaned Tolstoy family would have solemnly fulfilled every last wish of the deceased but for Chertkov and his 'bayonet.'" As soon as the teacher is gone, the student "quickly calls

everyone's attention to the law, to the court, to that bayonet, a campaign against which he had used to insert himself into a stranger's family and to make his improbable claim on the precious and profound secrets of an ancient family hearth." This made the author want to lock himself in his room and read Moliere's *Tartuffe* (*Moskovskie vedomosti*, November 30, 1910).

119. A. N. V—v, "Russkaia literatura v opasnosti." See also *Gazeta kopeika*, February 11, 1911: "L. N. Tolstoy's relations, who have lost hold of a tremendous inheritance, have raised an inappropriate quarrel over his sacred grave and have brought out all their filth onto the pages of the newspapers. There are no two ways to feel about all this."

120. See Sofia Andreevna's letter to *Novoe vremia* thanking the public for their condolences: "There are no words to describe what I have gone through, but the responses of loving hearts assuage my grief" (*Novoe vremia*, November 20, 1910.)

121. Quoted from the reprint in *Novoe vremia*, December 3, 1910. Sofia Andreevna did not refrain from doing a little public relations work regarding the contested manuscripts as well, asking if it was really possible that the Tolstoyans could read everything he wrote, and letters addressed to him, and that his wife could not do the same?. Her volume of letters appeared in 1913. In her introduction, Sofia Andreevna acknowledged that some people might think their publication was premature and made no secret that it was part of an effort to rehabilitate herself before the public:

"Before leaving this life to be united with the one I love in that spiritual realm to which he has departed, I wanted to share with those who love and respect the memory of Lev Nikolaevich that which is so dear to me: his letters to me, and the evidence they provide of our forty-eight years of life together, married happily almost to the end. *All* the letters appear, excepting those touching on living people, and the last six, which the time has not yet come to print. We were separated rarely and only by necessity, and so there are relatively few letters.

"Many will no doubt find the publication of these letters untimely. But what does time matter in such questions? Is it not better that people who knew Tolstoy read these letters, rather than people, fifty years hence, who had no relation to him whatsoever?

"I was also moved to publish these letters by the fact that after my death, which will likely come soon, others will as usual mistakenly judge and describe my relations to my husband, and his with me. So let those who are interested judge according to living and truthful sources, and not by conjecture, judgment, and invention.

"And let people scorn, if they will, one who perhaps was not strong enough to bear on her weak shoulders the duty of being the wife of a genius and a great man."

Sofia Andreevna omitted, incidently, Tolstoy's programmatic letter to her from 1885.

122. "Beseda s gr. S. A. Tolstoi," *Russkie vedomosti*, January 16, 1911. Sofia Andreevna gives the conversation verbatim (although it differs somewhat from what Tatiana L'vovna later described), as if to provide documentary evidence from this most private sphere, to which she herself had been denied access. Her very absence from the scene, she implies, verifies the sincerity of Tolstoy's feelings.

123. N. M. Ezhov also declared in his commentary accompanying the letter that it dispelled any false rumors about Tolstoy's enmity for his wife. In her letter to Ezhov, Sofia Andreevna says that she is writing from her sickbed, and is writing to him in particular because she has sensed his sympathy for her in what he has written for *Novoe vremia*. Ezhov's closing comments are: "Is there any need to comment on this letter? Does it not serve as direct proof of the love and care with which Lev Nikolaevich related to his spouse? And isn't it clear how insulting and illogical all these other articles and conclusions are?" ("Pis'mo grafini S. A. Tolstoi," *Novoe vremia*, November 26, 1910).

124. Al. Ksiunin, "Pochemu ushel Tolstoi," *Novoe vremia*, December 9, 1910. Also published as *Ukhod Tolstogo* (Moscow, 1911).

125. "And here an outsider displaces her, the wife of Tolstoy, saying that she has no place next to her husband, and takes from her that which was her light and air." In an addendum to the article published the next day, Ksiunin quotes from Tolstoy's secret diary: "Chertkov drew me into a struggle, but this struggle is repugnant to me." His source for this passage was probably Sergei L'vovich, who had quoted it at a public meeting to discuss Tolstoy's departure held in Moscow on November 26. (A transcript of this meeting was published by B. Meilakh: "Poslednie dni L. Tolstogo," *Russkaia literatura*, no. 1 (1961): 190–201.)

126. "If some enterprising gentleman wished to live near Tolstoy's estate collecting his letters in anticipation of his imminant death, and was keeping a manuscript at the ready to be published just as soon as Tolstoy breathed his last breath, and thus got it into print when interest in the story was at its very peak, he could not have done this any quicker than Mr. Sergeenko did with the help of Mr. Biriukov. Such is the power of true friendship" (N. Gorbov in *Golos Moskvy,* as quoted in *Novoe vremia,* November 21, 1910).

127. For views on Sergeenko's publication of letters, see "Kak P. S. Sergeenko byli opublikovany pis'ma L. N. Tolstogo," *Rech',* December 30, 1910, and the reponse of *Novoe vremia* the next day ("Sredi gazet i zhurnalov," December 31, 1910). An argument over the publication ensued: Sergeenko explained that the letters in question had been published earlier in *Vestnik Evropy* (June 1904), *Novoe vremia* countered that this publication had included only passages from letters, whereas Sergeenko had published the complete texts.

128. Nikolin, "Opasnost' uvelichivaetsia," *Sovremennoe slovo,* January 25, 1911.

129. They also question Chertkov's editorial qualifications, based on his just-published memoirs of Tolstoy's last days, which had revealed the poverty of his literary talents ("depicting Lev Nikolaevich as a pitiful old man, practically gone out of his mind, and going into repulsive details with his naturalism"). A. N. V—v, "Russkaia literatura v opasnosti."

130. Even Aleksandra L'vovna fell into this category: Aylmer Maude was told that when Sofia Andreevna was nursing Aleksandra, her milk had been ruined by the stress of her marital situation, and so she had had to hire a wet nurse. According to Sofia Andreevna, this was the reason that Aleksandra L'vovna resembled her less than the other children. Aylmer Maude, *The Life of Tolstoy* (Oxford, 1987), 2:150.

Sofia Andreevna had told him this in a conversation from 1909. This distance was probably felt by Aleksandra L'vovna as well. In her memoirs, she recalls that her nanny told her that Sofia Andreevna had visited a Tula midwife and asked for an abortion. When she was refused (because Tolstoy was the father), she then tried to induce a miscarriage. The nurse also told Aleksandra L'vovna that Sofia Andreevna had hired the wet nurse just to spite Lev Nikolaevich. See Aleksandra Tolstaya, *The Tragedy of Tolstoy,* 23–24.

131. "Chertkov o drame L. N. Tolstogo," *Gazeta kopeika,* November 19, 1910.

132. "An endless number of telegrams was sent to Chertkov that were in essence addressed to the Tolstoy family" (Ratibor, "Golos skorbi i negodovanii," *Golos Moskvy,* November 18, 1910).

133. Sofia Andreevna's domestic regime was also under scrutiny. She told the press that for six weeks everything would stay the same at Yasnaya Polyana, after which she would make changes. On November 28, *Gazeta kopeika* reported that Sofia Andreevna would employ just one servant.

134. "U V. G. Chertkova," *Gazeta kopeika,* November 30, 1910.

135. Pavuk-Vovchenko, "Pochemu?"

136. An article titled "Who is the culprit?" ("Kto vinovnik?") appeared in *Russkoe slovo* and was reprinted in full in other newspapers.

137. "Everyone is trying to convince themselves and others that Tolstoy's departure was an individual act, that its causes are found in the singular features of the psychology and worldview of the great writer, and not in the social conditions surrounding him and which provoked him to set off for the unknown distances" (Nik. Iordanskii, "Ukhod Tolstogo," *Sovremennyi mir,* November 1910, 147.)

138. "The members of his family … are simply representatives of that social class and that way of life against which Tolstoy struggled not for life, but to death. They are representative of the Russian ruling class. And Tolstoy went away not from his relations, but namely from that ruling class" (ibid., 148).

139. "Is it even necessary to say and to demonstrate that that neither Chertkov nor anyone else had or could have had any influence. One great power moved the wise old man from his place— that of his own great soul" (G. Petrov, "Torzhestvo styda," *Russkoe slovo,* November 26, 1910).

140. Petr Struve, "Zhizn' i smert' L'va Tolstogo," *Russkaia mysl',* no. 1 (1911): 131.

141. "Legenda XX-ogo veka," *Birzhevye vedomosti,* October 30, 1910. It was rather prescient of the author of this piece to refer to Tolstoy's departure as a "legend" at this juncture.

142. "Only the strong beautiful chord suggested to Tolstoy by some mysterious voice should end this beautiful life. It is quite likely that they will find Tolstoy and he will again be lovingly

settled in the bosom of his family. It would be a pity, a tremendous pity, if that were to happen" ("Poslednii akkord").

143. "His closest relations couldn't follow in his footsteps. His life did not pass in vain for the world. Tolstoy doesn't belong to any party but to the whole world, to which he gave a great example of a righteous life" (as cited in *Russkie vedomosti*, November 2, 1910).

144. Kaled, "Osvobozhdenyi Prometei," *Sankt-Peterburgskie vedomosti*, November 2, 1910. In *Ukhod Tolstogo* Chertkov makes the same argument, supporting it with passages from Tolstoy's diaries.

145. "Iz obshchestvennoi khroniki," *Vestnik Evropy*, December 1910. Similar views had been used to acquit the cross-bearing wife as well—cf. Doroshevich and others on Sofia Andreevna.

146. *Khar'kovskie vedomosti*, November 23, 1910.

147. *Irina De* (Z. L. Shadurskaia), "Zhenskie mysli," *Utro Rossii*, November 2, 1910.

148. Ibid.

149. "Lev Tolstoy strikingly expressed the antagonism between the two principles—the family and life-creation—precisely now when humanity has come to some sort of turning point.... The family collapses everywhere that life-creation appears." Ibid.

150. V. Rozanov, "Prava sem'i v brake," *Novoe vremia*, November 17, 1910.

151. V. Rozanov, "Rodovoe nachalo v istorii," *Novoe vremia*, November 21, 1910.

152. "*It makes no sense to fight your own nature.* It is much more sensible to consider it an expression of that will that exists in every person" (M. Men'shikov, "Urok molodezhi," *Novoe vremia*, November 5, 1910).

153. *Novoe vremia*, January 1, 1911.

154. "And now you have become like unto yourself. You tore off the mask of flesh from your old age, and all its dust will be of interest only to your God" (I. Skantrel [Yves Scantrel], *Sovremennyi mir*, no. 11 (1910), 223. The original article appeared in *La grande revue* on November 12.)

155. Ibid., 227.

156. "You were too great to not be pure, to not be righteous. Too great to lie. And now the superhuman [*sverkhchelovecheskaia*] joy of a smile has illuminated your face; like a rose on a cradle it will never fade—it is the smile of the holy" (ibid., 226). This theme was important in other coverage of the event. When word was first received of Tolstoy's departure, a *Birzhevye vedomosti* editorial titled "A Great Solitude" asserted that like all great people, Tolstoy needed to be alone, and expressed high hopes for the fruitfulness of his retreat. Ibsen's character Stockman had discovered that "The strongest man in the world is he who stands most alone," and Tolstoy too could no longer live "in the framework of convention" (*v ramkakh uslovnosti*) (I. N. Potapenko, "Velikoe odinochestvo," *Birzhevye vedomosti*, October 31, 1910). L. Grossman wrote in an Odessa newspaper that Tolstoy's renunciation was striking for his contemporaries because of its "great solitude" ("Velikii strannik").

157. The correspondence was published in *Novoe vremia*, November 29, 1910.

158. *PSS*, 58:124.

159. Even as he sought this internalized agency, Tolstoy certainly understood that his departure would affect others; the problem became one of not letting these effects determine his actions. The last words in his diary, from November 3, 1910, point to this distinction: "And everything for the good of others and, most important, myself" (*I vse eto na blago i drugim i, glavnoe, mne*) (*PSS*, 58:126).

160. *The Circle of Reading* became a significant element in the lore of his death, as it dealt specifically with death and the hereafter.

161. *Novoe vremia*, December 8, 1910. Tolstoy's former valet, Ilya Vasil'evich, shows visitors the bedroom and study and the room in which all the wreaths are kept. Sofia Andreevna visits the grave every day.

On December 19 *Novoe vremia* offered its readers a virtual tour of the house by Al. Ksiunin, focusing in particular on Tolstoy's bedroom: Tolstoy's favorite little pillow, sewn by his sister, on his bed; family pictures on the walls; and the night table with comforting amenities standing next to his bed. One of the walls features a portrait of Sofia Andreevna in her youth, "surprisingly beautiful." Tolstoy's presence is missed, however: "Yasnaya Polyana looks orphaned. The white house with the glassed-in veranda and low roof is empty and quiet and is beginning to resemble a museum. The person who gave life to the large rooms of the old home has gone forever, and now those intelligent eyes, piercing to the soul, watch only from the walls." Tolstoy's own quarters themselves looked "dead" (Al. Ksiunin, "Iasnopolianskie vospominaniia o Tolstom," *Novoe vremia,* December 10, 1910).

162. Such tours were also offered at the Tolstoys' Moscow house on Khamovniki (*Russkoe slovo,* November 26, 1910).

163. See "Okolo dorogoi mogily," *Russkie vedomosti,* November 19, 1910.

164. A. O—ov, "U dorogoi mogily," *Sovremennoe slovo,* January 7, 1911. Mikhail Kuz'minskii writes that an American by the name of Charles Flint had offered 3 million rubles for Yasnaya Polyana, which the family refused because of the nature of Flint's plans for the property. (He was going to use 230 desiatins for an exposition of farm equipment—the remaining 60 desiatins, containing the estate and Tolstoy's grave, were to become international property.) There was much discussion over whether the estate should be nationalized, but the government balked when it heard that the family would ask one million rubles. The rumored offer by Flint was used to demonstrate the necessity of a state purchase.

165. Michelle Perrot argues that the death of the father was the most significant event in the life of a family at this time ("The Family Triumphant," *The History of Private Life* [Cambridge, 1990], 4:176).

166. "It is hard to say what should have been done in this situation. The only thing certain is that we should have done what seemed best for my father. And that my mother subumissively complied with the recommendations of the doctors was, on her part, a heavy and redemptive sacrifice, the meaning of which it is not our place to judge" I. L. Tolstoi, *Moi vospominaniia,* 255.

167. *Poslednie dni,* 49.

168. Ernest Simmons has suggested the possibility that the Russian government allowed Chertkov to remain at Teliatniki because they understood that his presence was causing a family crisis that might ultimately discredit Tolstoy.

169. I. Leonov, "Dva momenta," *Saratovskii vestnik,* November 14, 1910.

170. "Smert' Grafa L. N. Tolstogo."

171. *Rech',* December 15 1910. "From this it is clear that even as he wrote this letter Tolstoy was considering the possibility that he might never realize his final wish, and his letter will remain only as posthumous evidence of the spiritual torments with which Russian reality surrounded the best son of the motherland."

172. This evidence was presumably from the second entry in Tolstoy's secret diary, which Chertkov himself would later edit for the Jubilee Edition. Faithfulness to the manuscripts offered expiation to both Sofia Andreevna and Chertkov.

Chapter 2   Narrative Transfigurations of Tolstoy's Final Journey

1. "Isn't it more accurate to suggest that the great sinner, before breathing his last, instinctively positioned his fingers so as to make the sign of the cross, but his weakened arm did not have the strength to rise from his blanket and could only move reflexively there. We will comfort ourselves with the thought that the last wish of the dying Tolstoy was to cross himself. We will think that Tolstoy, not managing to formally make peace with the Church, entered eternity having made peace in his soul with Christ." As reprinted in "Gazetnyi den'. Vazhnoe svidetel'stvo," *Russkaia zemlia,* November 9, 1910.

2. Tolstoy had given particular attention to the example of Alexander I, who according to legend had feigned his death and lived his last days in Siberia as the monk Fyodor Kuzmich. He wrote his own, Tolstoyan narrative of the story, which I discuss in the conclusion of the book.

3. One newspaper cited "simple folk" making this connection. "Prostoi narod ob ot''ezde gr. L. N. Tolstogo," *Vostochnaia zaria,* November 9, 1910.

4. "O podvige," *Russkoe chtenie,* November 6, 1910.

5. See also Pål Kolstø, "A Mass for a Heretic? The Controversy over Leo Tolstoi's Burial," *Slavic Review,* 60, 1 (2000): 75–95.

6. See S. Bulgakov, *O religii L'va Tolstogo (Moscow, 1912)*; N. N. Gusev, *Lev Tolstoi pro-tiv gosudarstva i tserkvi (Berlin, 1913)*; Richard Gustafson, *Leo Tolstoy: Resident and Stranger (Princeton, 1989)*; A. A. Kozlov, *Religiia grafa L. N. Tolstogo: ego uchenie o zhizni i liubvi (St. Petersburg, 1895)*; S. Pozoiskii, *K istorii otlucheniia L'va Tolstogo ot tserkvi (Moscow, 1979)*; and G. I. Petrov, *Otluchenie L'va Tolstogo (Moscow, 1978)*.

7. See esp. *The Critique of Dogmatic Theology*.

8. The first text, completed in 1881, was not published in Russia until 1908—and not completely until the Jubilee Edition. Another version of the text, excluding the commentary and the parallel Russian and Greek texts on which Tolstoy based his version, was published under the title *A Brief Account of the Gospels*.

9. Tolstoy viewed this work as a moral duty. (See his preface to *A Brief Account of the Gospels*.) Years later he described this duty to a Japanese student: "Religion is the rational revelation and recognition of all life. Its essence is the same in all religions. The authority of true religion depends not on its miracles but only on the inner justification of the conscience. To destroy all superstition and propound the one rational religion is the greatest and the main obligation of every person" (G. S. Tamura, "Vliianie na menia Tolstogo," in *O Tolstom: Mezhdunarodnyi tolstovskii al'manakh* [Moscow, 1909], 342).

10. This challenge spread to the core of the Church: on August 25, 1910, for instance, the monk Gamaliil wrote to Tolstoy to complain of corruption in his monastery and to solicit Tolstoy's spiritual guidance. Several months later a group of peasants wrote to Sergei Tolstoy that they were praying for their drunken priest, who had refused their request to perform funeral services for Tolstoy (S. L. Tolstoi, *Ocherki bylogo* [Moscow, 1956], 270).

11. An article titled "Who Was Jesus Christ? (Against the Tolstoyans)" takes up this task explicitly, admitting that Tolstoy had presented the most comprehensive challenge to the notion of the divinity of Christ. See Sviashch. Al. Vvedenskii, "Kto byl Iisus Khristos? (Protiv tolstovtsev)," *Missionerskoe obozrenie*, no. 2 (1911): 243.

12. Tolstoy did not invent this role (he adapted it from numerous sources, from antiquity to contemporary figures such as William Lloyd Garrison and Adin Ballou), but he was the first person in the modern age to develop it into a major socio-political force. Gandhi, Solzhenitsyn, and numerous others would follow in this tradition.

13. Pobedonostsev felt that Tolstoy's teaching could have a debilitating effect not only on the Church but also on the larger body politic. He remarked in the late 1890s that Tolstoy's influence had even weakened the moral fiber of the other sects in Russia.

14. Ioann of Kronstadt warned Prince Dmitrii Khilkov, one of the Tolstoyans involved in the propagandizing at Kursk, that he and Tolstoy would suffer "retribution, the likes of which has never before been prepared for a sinner." See P. Sergeenko, *Tolstoi i ego sovremenniki* (Moscow, 1911), 259–260. Ioann later assisted Khilkov's mother in taking custody of her son's children and baptizing them in the Orthodox Church (P. Biriukov, *L. N. Tolstoi* [Berlin, 1923], 3: 345–348). Many other Tolstoyans were in fact imprisoned or exiled for their part in distributing his literature or propagating his ideas.

15. A. Solnyshko, "Tolstoi v adu," *Nauka i religiia*, no. 6 (1968): 78–79. This ritual marked the transfer of the Kursk-Root icon of the "Lady of the Sign" between the local monastery and the city of Kursk; it is depicted in a well-known painting by Repin, *Procession of the Cross in Kursk Province*.

16. Despite such warnings, the famine relief program served thousands. One peasant said at the time that if the Lord was like his priests, and the Antichrist like Tolstoy, he would choose the latter, to whom he was sending his starving children for their own "bread of life." See Jonas Stadling and Will Reason, *In the Land of Tolstoy* (London, 1897), 58–59.

17. See the pages from his diary published in O. Ioann Kronshtadtskii, *O dushepagubnom ereticheslve grafa L. N. Tolstogo* (St. Petersburg, 1905).

18. Arkhiepiskop Nikanor, *Vosem' besed protiv grafa L'va Tolstogo* (Odessa, 1894), 60. Nikanor's book first appeared in 1887; by the third edition (1894) the text had been expanded to contain eight lengthy orations totaling over two hundred pages.

19. Another influential ecclesiast, T. I. Butkevich, echoed these sentiments in an 1891 sermon in Kharkov. He ended with an ominous warning: "But what awaits our fatherland if this

evil is not cut off today but spreads out like the sea across the broad expanses of Russia? How much harm will it bring? What havoc will it wreak? But let this not be! Our Blessed Lord is our hope that this evil will be cut down in good time." The sermon was dedicated to the ten-year anniversary of the ascension of Alexander III to the throne. (The Church's conflict with Tolstoy was always a political matter.) Butkevich also published a series of articles against Tolstoy in the Kharkov journal *Vera i razum,* which actively supported the Church's anti-Tolstoy campaign. See M. L. Gomon, *L. N. Tolstoi i khar'kovchane* (Kharkov, 1993), 128.

20. Antonii Khrapovitskii, then rector of the Moscow Theological Seminary but subsequently the metropolitan who signed Tolstoy's excommunication in 1901, told Tolstoy's wife that the metropolitan wanted to expel Tolstoy from the Church. Already in 1888, however, Archbishop Nikanor wrote N. Ia. Grot that the Synod was seriously considering anathematizing Tolstoy. See S. Pozoiskii, *K istorii otlucheniia L'va Tolstogo,* 81.

21. On January 22, 1892, *Moskovskie vedomosti* printed a scathing commentary, calling Tolstoy's ideas "unbridled socialism." The newspaper retranslated sections of the article back into Russian, recasting Tolstoy's words according to its own tendentious designs. The result was a significant scandal, and other newspapers were forbidden to reprint any text from the article. L. N. Tolstoi, *Sobranie sochinenii v 22-i tomakh* (Moscow, 1978), 17:271.

22. Pozoiski, 82. His source: Rukopisnyi otdel publichnoi biblioteki im. M. E. Saltykova-Shchedrina, Pis'ma Pobedonostseva.

23. Skvortsov later defended Pobedonostsev against charges that the excommunication was a personal vendetta, claiming that during Tolstoy's illness Pobedonostsev had expressed tolerance for the performance of church services for Tolstoy in the case of his death. Moreover, he had written the first draft of the *Poslanie* but had not attended the two Synod sessions when it was edited by the bishops, who changed it considerably ("Pechat'," *Rech',* November 15, 1910).

24. Gomon, *L. N. Tolstoi i khar'kovchane,* 129.

25. "O zapreshchenii pominoveniia i panikhid po L. N. Tolstom v sluchae ego smerti bez pokoianiia." The full text of this letter is provided in Petrov, *Otluchenie L'va Tolstogo ot tserkvi.* The *ukaz* from 1900 prohibiting services is printed in *Tolstovskii ezhegodnik,* 1912, 158.

26. Pozoiskii, *K istorii otlucheniia L'va Tolstogo,* 78.

27. Ibid., 79. His source: Tsentral'nyi gosudarstvennyi istoricheskii arkhiv v Sankt-Peterburge, Arkhiv kantseliarii ober-prokurora sinoda, f. 797, op. 94, d. 133, l.2.

28. V. I. Sreznevskii writes that police archives on public reaction to the excommunication show that most, even if they did not agree with Tolstoy's views, saw the act as something "untimely, unnecessary, stupid, and harmful to the strength and fortitude of the Church." Nikolai Lebedev, a legal advisor to the tsar's cabinet, viewed the move as an unfortunate expression of revenge by Pobedonostsev: "Maybe tens of thousands read Tolstoy's forbidden works in Russia, but now hundreds of thousands will read them. Before they didn't understand his false doctrines, but the Synod underscored them. When he dies Tolstoy will be buried like a martyr, with particular pomp." A. A. Popov, the director of a Kiev preparatory school, concurred: "The excommunication of Count Tolstoy was like shooting at sparrows. The upper classes laugh, and the lower classes don't understand and don't take it into account. In answer to the excommunication Count Tolstoy wrote a will, in which he gives orders to be buried without any church rites. This will be a pretext for pilgrimages." "Otrazhenie otlucheniia Tolstogo ot tserkvi," in *Tolstoi: Pamiatniki zhizni i tvorchestva,* ed. V. I. Sreznevski (Moscow, 1923), 3:111–116.

The sheer volume of the Church's anti-Tolstoyan rhetoric attests to the seriousness with which it approached this crisis. Metropolitan Antonii himself contributed extensively (250 pages of his collected works are devoted to exegeses of Tolstoy), but he was joined by many others. A good survey of this literature can be found in *On the Matter of the Defection of Lev Nikolaevich Tolstoy from the Orthodox Church,* an elaborate compendium offered by *Missionerskoe obozrenie* as a free supplement for its subscribers. The volume went through three editions, growing to 685 pages in the edition published at the time of Tolstoy's death.

29. The government attempted to forestall public manifestations of sympathy for Tolstoy, prohibiting publication of information regarding his journey, but news managed to spread by word of mouth. See Bulanzhe, "Bolezn' L. N. Tolstogo v 1901–1902 gg.," *Minuvshie gody, no.* 9 (1908): 33–68.

30. This scheme has been attributed to Pobedonostsev.

31. Perhaps another reason why Sofia Andreevna was denied access to her husband at Astapovo: a letter from the Bishop of Tauride to Pobedonostsev claimed that she herself intended to tell a priest after Tolstoy's death that he had asked for a final confession and communion so that he could receive a Christian burial. The Church was aware of her support and attempted to exploit whatever influence she might have (Pozoiskii, *K istorii otlucheniia L'va Tolstogo,* 111). The Church's espionage and intrigue continued until the time of Tolstoy's death. Pavel Znamenskii, a priest living near Yasnaya Polyana, made regular reports to the Tula eparchy on the heretic's activities. Another priest, Fedor Glagolev, reported that Tolstoy's brother Sergei had requested the administration of church rites from his deathbed in 1904 after many years of antagonism toward the Church. Tolstoy had taken part in the Orthodox funeral for his brother, carrying the coffin to the church—but had not entered the building itself. Sergei Tolstoy's deathbed repentance gave hope that his brother might also re-enter the Church at the last moment.

32. Klavdiia Lukashevich, *Shkol'nyi prazdnik v chest' L'va Nikolaevicha Tolstogo s risunkami i notami* (Moscow, 1909). When a thousand schoolchildren visited Yasnaya Polyana for an afternoon in 1907, the local priest reported his concern that Tolstoy would have a "corrupting" effect on the guests, "undermining their Christian education" (Pozoiskii, *K istorii otlucheniia L'va Tolstogo,* 114).

33. *Fellowship,* Los Angeles, August 1908.

34. A Saratov collection, *Concerning the Jubilee of Count Lev Tolstoy,* contained the Synod's instructions and anti-Tolstoyan propaganda, a satirical poem written in response to *The Kreutzer Sonata,* and diatribes against the left-wing and "Jewish" press. This same group published a similar collection in 1910. See *Po povodu iubileia grafa L'va Tolstogo (Sbornik statei, perepechatannykh iz gazety "Volga")* (Saratov, 1908).

35. Gomon, *L. N. Tolstoi i khar'kovchane,* 133–134. Ioann of Kronshtadt also worried that he had done more harm than good in explaining the Tolstoyan heresy to a group of peasants.

36. When questioned by the media, Ioann denied that he had ever made such a prayer (Kovalev, "Bor'ba tsarizma i tserkvi s L. N. Tolstym," *Voprosy istorii religii i ateizma* [Moscow, 1960]). Ironically, it was Ioann who would die shortly thereafter, in December 1908.

37. Troitskii wrote on learning of Tolstoy's fainting spell in September. According to Pitirim's successor Parfenii, Troitskii visited Yasnaya twice a year. After a 1908 visit Tolstoy admitted he had spoken rudely to Troitskii and offended him (N. N. Gusev, *Dva goda s Tolstym* [Moscow, 1928], 55–57).

38. Tolstoy's diary entry is from January 21, 1909. The previous day Parfenii arrived with two priests (and accompanied by police officers), spent the evening, and had a long one-on-one discussion with Tolstoy. News of the meeting spread, and Tolstoy gave an interview to a correspondent from *Russkoe slovo* regarding the content of their discussion. When the *Russkoe slovo* story appeared, Parfenii and Tolstoy exchanged letters regarding its inaccuracy but agreed not to issue any further statements about it. While Tolstoy writes in his diary of being unhappy with the meeting, Gusev records that Tolstoy had encouraged Parfenii's visit, thanked him for his courage on leaving, and was pleased by their encounter (*Dva goda,* 242–243).

39. Sofia Andreevna received a letter from Metropolitan Antonii asking her to help make peace between Tolstoy and the Church. Tolstoy's response: "There is no point in speaking of reconciliation. I am dying without animosity or spite. And what is the Church? How can one make peace with an indefinite entity?" (S. L. Tolstoi, *Ocherki bylogo,* 213).

40. Ibid., 211.

41. Ivan Nazhivin, *Iz zhizni L. N. Tolstogo* (Moscow, 1911), 78.

42. These detailed hour-by-hour reports indicate a certain amount of spying, perhaps motivated by idle curiosity regarding a famous guest but also suggesting that the importance of these visits was immediately obvious.

43. "Delo Kaluzhskoi dukhovnoi konsistorii o nerazreshenii sinodom pominovaniia i panikhid po Tolstomu," *Trudy tolstovskogo muzeia: Lev Nikolaevich Tolstoi* (Moscow, 1929), 405.

44. Iosif sent a telegram to Astapovo on November 4 asking if Tolstoy would still be in the station on the 5th, and if not, where he was going next (*Smert' Tolstogo: Po novym materialam* [Moscow, 1929], 93). Whether Iosif was actually considering coming, or if he sent it on behalf

of Varsonofii, is not clear. A telegram from A. V. Kolobov to Obolenskii reports that Iosif had full power to decide if services could be performed for Tolstoy (ibid., 103). Iosif was less cooperative with the Synod than other clerics and was said to be unwilling to make a report on any personal meeting he might have with Tolstoy ("L. N. Tolstoi i sinod," in *Poslednie dni L'va Nikolaevicha Tolstogo* (St. Petersburg, 1910), 96).

45. One church emissary, Archbishop Parfenii of Tula, told the security chief at Astapovo that he had come in response to the personal wishes of the emperor ("Iz materialov o L. N. Tolstom," *Krasnyi arkhiv*, no. 4 [1923]: 352). See also the official report of the head of the Railway Police to the Moscow Police Department in the same source (351). Stolypin's agent N. P. Kharlamov worked closely with agents of the railway police, who also knew of Varsonofii's secret mission.

46. Kharlamov's report (like Varsonofii's) describes these efforts in detail. See "Otchet chinovnika osobykh poruchenii," *Sel'skaia molodezh'*, no. 8 (1991): 33.

47. Andrei L'vovich was repeatedly approached as a potential accomplice for the Church. He had received a position working for Stolypin in Petersburg early that year and served as the inside contact for Stolypin's agent Kharlamov at Astapovo. In spite of his orders to operate in strict secrecy, Kharlamov revealed his identity to Andrei, a trusted ally ("Otchet chinovnika," 32–37).

48. During his visit Tikhon had spoken with Tolstoy's sons (most likely Andrei and Lev, who was visiting from Paris), who were concerned about Chertkov's "almost hypnotic" influence on their father. They had banished Chertkov from the house and now wished to exorcise his spirit ("K poslednim dniam zhizni L'va Nikolaevicha Tolstogo," *Dela i dni*, no. 1 [1920], 293–295). At Astapovo, however, the family was making collective decisions; Andrei reported that his brothers were indifferent and his sisters adamantly opposed to the performance of church services, and that his mother too did not wish to have the services performed against her husband's will.

49. *Poslednie dni*, 95–99. On November 4 Stolypin inquired what measures the Church would take in case of Tolstoy's death and what they had learned about his visit to Optina. The Synod met that day without Antonii; present were Luk'ianov, Flavian of Kiev, Vladimir of Moscow, Tikhon of Yaroslavl, Mikhail of Minsk, and the above-mentioned Parfenii of Tula, who would travel to Astapovo himself as the Synod's emissary. On November 5 *Rech'* reported that the Council of Ministers was unanimous, including Luk'ianov, in believing that the excommunication should be rescinded (several members felt that this was necessary for Tolstoy but also for the good of the country). Only two members of Synod considered this possible, however, and the wishes of the ministers did not prevail.

50. Metropolitan Atonii told a crowd at a lecture in Zhitomir two weeks later that the Synod had considered allowing Tolstoy to be buried according to the *inovertsy* ceremony even if he had not repented but decided against it because there was little chance that those surrounding Tolstoy would allow it. The *inovertsy* ceremony allowed soldiers of other Christian faiths to be buried in a modified service accompanied by the singing of *"O Holy God"* (*"Sviatyi Bozhe"*). This service for those who had defended the "righteous fatherland" had never been intended for someone like Tolstoy, however. The Church instead followed its own *ukaz* from 1900 prohibiting services for Tolstoi, which can be found in *Tolstovskii ezhegodnik* (Moscow, 1912), 158.

51. The funeral of former Duma President S. A. Muromtsev just one month before showed that the public would perform funeral services without the Church's sanction. The day that Tolstoy left his home an article in *Russkaia znamia* entitled "Outrage against the Faith" described how funeral services for Tolstoy had been forbidden by the Church and pointed to the example of Muromtsev's funeral as a case where a "godless" person was unjustly given a church ceremony. This article, appearing before Tolstoy had even taken ill, reveals the Church's abiding concern over the handling of Tolstoy's death ("Nadrugatel'stvo nad veroiu," *Russkoe znamia*, October 30, 1910).

52. The former contain detailed police-like accounts of Tolstoy's actions and conversations at the monasteries, including reports on when he sent telegrams and who visited him. See "K poslednim," 293–295. Parfenii also included copies of the above-mentioned correspondence between Troitskii and Tolstoy. Reports continued to be filed throughout Tolstoy's last days and after. (See also the correspondence of Parfenii and Evdokim with the Tula governor in *Tolstoi i o Tolstom* [Moscow, 1924], 1:84–86.)

53. *Novoe vremia*, November 7, 1910.

54. A dispatch of N. E. Efros to his editors at *Rech'* in Petersburg suggests that the reporters in fact learned of the telegram before the family did: "Apparently Antonii's telegram made a big impression on the family; the countess, hearing the text from the correspondents, sighed deeply, sorrowfully shook her head, with tears in her eyes" (*Smert' Tolstogo*, 98). The decision not to give the telegram to Tolstoy gave the Church evidence to support its conspiracy theories about the group controlling access to Tolstoy's quarters. Most dispatches of reporters at Astapovo place this decision in Chertkov's hands (see telegrams 229, 230, 231, 234, and 238 in *Smert' Tolstogo*); telegram 237, however, describes Chertkov conferring with Aleksandra L'vovna and Dr. Makovitskii about Antonii's message.

55. "Arkhiepiskop Arsenii o L. N. Tolstom," *Pskovskaia zhizn'*, November 6, 1910.

56. "O grafe L. N. Tolstom," *Voin i pakhar'*, November 3, 1910.

57. "Iz materialov o L. N. Tolstom," *Krasnyi arkhiv*, no. 4 (1923): 353.

58. "Doklad nachal'nika peterburgskogo okhrannogo otdeleniia ministru vnutrennykh del o skhodkakh studentov vysshikh uchebnykh zavedenii v Peterburge 8 noiabria 1910 g.," *Literaturnoe nasledstvo* 69 (1961), 2:338.

59. *Gazeta kopeika*, November 29, 1910.

60. *Odesskie novosti*, December 19, 1910.

61. As published in *Russkaia mysl'*, Struve's speech closed with the following: "And inasmuch as I considered it my duty to be silent about this during Tolstoy's lifetime, so now, among everyone who has gathered here, united in thought and feeling, to religiously honor the departed Tolstoy, I consider it my duty to bear witness about the great fact of his religious life. It is great because herein the most difficult victory was upheld, here was accomplished the greatest triumph: of man over death" (*Russkaia mysl'*, no. 1 [1911]: 132). Struve later published the speech in *Stat'i o L've Tolstom* (Sofia, 1921).

62. "Sovremennaia khlystovshchina," *Novoe vremia*, November 18, 1910. As the crowd dispersed, the reporter had overheard references to the participants in this ceremony as *khlysty*. (The *khlysty* practiced self-flagellation and came to represent the excesses of Russian sectarian religious practice.)

63. These may well be the original texts from the evening, but this is not indicated in the publication.

64. *Russkaia mysl'*, no. 1 (1911): 176–179.

65. Ibid., 176.

66. Ibid., 179.

67. *Rech'*, November 9, 1910.

68. G—t', "Oshibka ierarkhov," *Rech'*, November 9, 1910.

69. Tolstoy was often described as a giant father figure but here became a wayward son in need of the maternal indulgence of the Church. ("Can it be that a mother cannot pray and weep for the loss of a native son, who has turned away from her and not succeeded in making his peace with her? ... So let the Orthodox Church, following the testament of our Lord Jesus Christ, forgive our brother, the deceased Lev, and call us to pray for the calming of his sinful soul and to call for the eternal memory and rest of our great brother and her own son" ["Sviashch. Mikhail Kvitnitskii, "Golos sviashchennika," *Rech'*, November 9, 1910]).

70. Staroobriadcheskii episkop Mikhail, "Tolstoi i tserkov'," *Rech'*, November 9, 1910. Also in *Zhizn' i smert' L. N. Tolstogo* (Moscow, 1911), 70–75.

71. Sviashch. I. L., "Otluchen li Tolstoi?" *Utro* (Kharkov), November 7, 1910. Stolypin's agent Kharlamov revealed that funeral services were in fact performed for Tolstoy in many cities because of confusion over the Church's position. A number of papers reminded readers that other branches of the Christian faith and other religions were charitably disposed toward Tolstoy. On November 5, *Odesskie novosti* offered comments by Lutheran, Catholic, and Reformed Evangelical ministers, as well as by a rabbi and a mullah; a preface explains that they were unable to get an opinion "for print" of an Orthodox priest—perhaps an oblique reference to church censorship.

72. Reported in *Rech'*, November 6, 1910.

73. "Ot kogo on bezhal?" *Kolokol*, November 6, 1910. Citing a report in *Rech'* that Chertkov was in control of Tolstoy's bedside and had prevented transmission of Antonii's telegram, *Kolokol*

asked: "Doesn't this mean that a certain revolutionary-anarchist clique is holding Tolstoy captive, and that his flight to a monastery was an attempt to free himself from it, but it soon captured its prey?" *Kolokol* also published a letter from the monk Erast describing Tolstoy's visits to Optina and Shamordino that was picked up by other right-wing papers and became a key document used to support the reconciliation theory. The letter describes Tolstoy's ecstatic feelings for Optina and his regret that he did not visit the elders for fear that they would not receive him because of his excommunication. It is full of dramatic details of Tolstoy's remorseful state, describing his various pained facial expressions and a long tearful embrace of his sister at Shamordino.

Erast's account was undermined by the investigation of *Novoe vremia*'s Aleksei Ksiunin, who interviewed all the principal witnesses to the visit and found that much of Erast's account was inaccurate. He reprinted Erast's report, then followed it with an edited version based on the corrections of Tolstoy's sister. In her interview with Ksiunin, Maria Nikolaevna did maintain, however, that her brother was interested in living at Optina. Ksiunin's report, though correcting Erast's and countering charges that Tolstoy had been dragged away from the monasteries, largely supported the Church's version of events; by moderating the extremes of some accounts, he made the repatriation theory more plausible. Though Maria Nikolaevna's account of one of Tolstoy's comments to her ("I would gladly remain there to live and would carry out the most difficult penance if only they would not make me to go to church and cross myself") was the source of much speculation, she believed that he had come simply to rest and collect his thoughts. See Al. Ksiunin, "Poslednie dni L. N. Tolstogo–v monastyriakh," *Novoe vremia,* November 24, 1910. Ksiunin's investigations were also published in book form: *Ukhod Tolstogo* (St. Petersburg, 1911; repr., Berlin, 1935.)

N. A. Pavlovich has argued that Optina could not have been a "rest stop"—that it was out of the way, and there was a direct road from Kozelsk to Shamordino. Makovitskii has Tolstoy saying, "it's good in Shamordino" when they first talk of moving on (D. P. Makovitskii, U Tolstogo: *Iasnopolianskie zapiski* [Moscow, 1979], 4:408, 411).

74. Arkhimandrit Petr, "Ot chego on bezhal?" *Russkaia zemlia,* November 20, 1910. The author identified another culprit in the un-Christian rituals at Astapovo: "'And did you see any peasants?' I asked. No, he didn't see any peasants, but he did notice a fair number of Jews at the station." Orthodox antisemitism leads to another Crucifixion narrative of Astapovo.

75. I. K. Surskii, *Otets Ioann Kronshtadtskii* (Belgrad, 1924).

76. *Istinnyi oblik L'va Tolstogo, nravstvennyi, religioznyi i politicheskii (po sochineniiam i po lichnoi zhizni)* (Saratov, 1911).

77. Tolstoy appears on the *levyi*/left side, which not only suggests his political lefthandedness but also resonates with his name, *Lev* in Russian.

78. This ugly piece (which probably deserves to be forgotten, rather than quoted) likens Tolstoy's death to Vera Komissarzhevskaya's, who "also died a black death." (She died of smallpox while on tour in Central Asia.) See "Negoduiushchee osuzhdenie dozvolennogo koshchunstva (Istinnoe izobrazhenie smerti Tolstogo)," *Istinnyi oblik,* 45.

79. N. Varzhanskii, *V chem vera L. N. Tolstogo* (St. Petersburg, 1911).

80. N. L. Lazarev depicted Tolstoy as an estranging nihilist: "from the reading of Tolstoy's works a person feels abnormal and always strongly disturbed and cannot receive calming and quieting of the spirit." In this Tolstoyan world nothing was as it was supposed to be: "According to him the state is not the state, the law is not the law, religion is not religion, Christian mystery is not mystery, Orthodox Church hierarchy is not clergy, marriage is not marriage, family is not family, soldier is not soldier, and many other absurd notions." Could a person find anything proper in Tolstoy's works on which life could be built? See N. L. Lazarev, *Zhivaia mysl' v XX veke (1905–1912 gg.)* (St. Petersburg, 1913), 86–87.

81. Episkop Nikon, *Smert' grafa L. N. Tolstogo (Dnevniki iz Troitskogo slova)* (Sergiev Posad, 1911).

82. *Dukhovnaia tragediia L'va Tolstogo,* 163.

83. "Kto takoi byl Lev Tolstoi?" (Kiev, 1911), 4. The pamphlet closes with the blessing of the monastery and the stamp of the monastery censor.

84. *Kem byl Tolstoi (Po luchshim otzyvam russkoi pechati)* (Moscow, 1911). Pictures of a grandfatherly Tolstoy with children figure prominently here.

85. *Gde zhe pravda? (K voprosu dnia o L. N. Tolstom)* (Ryazan, 1910).

86. Antonii viewed this contradiction as a native tendency seen in many Russian writers but felt that it ran deeper in Tolstoy than in Dostoevsky or Turgenev, who remained profoundly Russian in spirit. Tolstoy's call for "individual rebirth" (*vozrozhdenie lichnosti*) naturally appealed to the Russian spirit (which rejected German nihilism) but came into conflict with his pantheistic tendencies (Mitropolit Antonii, "V chem. Prodolzhalo otrazhat'sia vliianie pravoslaviia na poslednie proizvedeniia gr. L. N. Tolstogo," *Nravstvennoe uchenie pravoslavnoi tserkvi* (New York, 1967), 251).

87. Ibid., 267.

88. "What could be more offensive than to be praised only to insult or frighten others? And if we recall that this burial buffoonery was carried out by the same elements of society who five years ago shouted and wrote about him in the press like a crazy old man, a senile aristocrat, like a gentry rag unworthy of attention, then judge for yourselves how his current veneration is any different from when someone raises a discarded pillow and some worn-out clothes on a high post and sticks it in the yard to scare away the crows" (ibid., 268).

89. Sviash. Nikolai Chepurin, "Zhizn' i deianiia gr. L'va Nikolaevicha Tolstogo pred sudom ego ucheniia." *Missionerskoe obozrenie,* nos. 1 & 2 (1911): 30–35, 255–262. Chepurin was among the many decrying the glorification of Tolstoy by the "Jewish-journalistic clique."

90. "Sektanstvo v 1910 g.," *Missionerskoe obozrenie,* no. 1 (1911): 196–197.

91. Pravoslavnyi sviashennik, "Kuda on prishel?" *Missionerskoe obozrenie,* no. 4 (1911): 975–979. Contrary to the Church's claims, the gravesite remains to this day an international place of pilgrimage, where thousands of admirers of both author and moralist come to pay homage.

92. "Khroniki: Provintsial'noe obozrenie," *Vestnik Evropy,* no. 12 (1910): 405. In April 1912, Germogen made a report to the Synod recommending the excommunication of Artsybashev and other writers ("Poslednie izvestiia," *Russkie vedomosti,* April 10, 1912).

93. "Russkaia zhizn'," *Rech',* November 14, 1910.

94. *Novoe vremia,* December 18, 1910.

95. Iliodor went too far with these and other actions, and soon the Synod voted to remove him from his local Tsaritsyn. Nicholas II interceded on his behalf, however, and Iliodor was invited to join the Tula diocese of none other than Parfenii, who had struggled so valiantly to regain Tolstoy's Orthodox faith. Parfenii was said to have thought that Iliodor's energy, boldness, and charisma would be of great value in his struggle with sectarianism, which was widespread in his eparchy. Nicholas agreed to allow this move. His patronage of the reactionary priesthood (Iliodor and Ioann of Kronshtadt are examples) is worthy of further research. See *Novoe vremia,* January 23 and 29, 1911.

96. *Izvestiia Tolstovskogo muzeia,* nos. 3–5 (1911): 194. As a representative of the Council of the All-Russian Fraternal Union (Sovet vserossiiskogo bratskogo soiuza), Iliodor had also sent a telegram in November 1910 to A. I. Guchkov, upbraiding him for his blasphemous entreaty on behalf of Tolstoy ("May the Good Lord open unto him His heavenly kingdom") in the Duma.

97. Even their popular sobriquets, Ioann's *velikii pastyr'* (great pastor) and Tolstoy's *velikii pisatel'* (great writer), made this comparison. Tartu University institutionalized the equation by simultaneously conferring honorary degrees on Ioann and Tolstoy. Ioann returned his diploma, explaining that he didn't want to share the honor with the Anti-Christ. This marvelous letter deserves quoting: "I don't wish to be a member in any way of a corporation, however revered and highly educated, which would place me, by a most insulting misunderstanding, next to the godless Count Lev Tolstoy, the most evil heretic of our unfortunate times, who has exceeded all other heretics in his high-mindedness and pride. I do not wish to be next to the Anti-Christ. Beyond this, I am surprised that the university would associate so carelessly with the Satanic writer and would so slavishly sing his praises" (P. Sergeenko, *Tolstoi i ego sovremenniki* [Moscow, 1911] 263–264).

98. *Poslednie dni i blazhennaia konchina O. Ioanna Kronshtadtskogo: Vysochaishii reskript i chudesa u grobnitsy* (St. Petersburg, 1911). Though Tolstoy avoided directly responding to his attackers, he did comment on Ioann's funeral in "Nomer gazety," his reading of a single edition of a newspaper (*Slovo,* January 16, 1909). The newspaper in question included an item on the campaign of Nicholas II to have Ioann canonized and the decision of the Holy Synod to

make his remains a national shrine. Not mentioning Ioann by name, Tolstoy wrote that it was impossible to believe that "a person called the Russian emperor" and a group of men "who have claimed the right to make decisions about the religious practice of others" felt that it was proper, in the twentieth century, to sanction and stimulate the veneration of inanimate objects. Of all the evil deceptions that were countenanced by the autocracy, this sort of religious superstition was worst of all, because it was used to motivate all the rest; people could be susceptible to such deception only if they had lost consciousness of their spiritual selves and believed in a fraudulent code taught by the official Church, as opposed to the moral teachings of Christ. The article was not published in Tolstoy's lifetime.

99. Lazarev, *"Zhivaia mysl' v XX veke (1905–1912 gg.)*, 207.

100. See "Pamiati L. N. Tolstogo," *Novoe vremia,* November 9, 1910. Men'shikov acknowledges that he is comparing Tolstoy to his "greatest enemy."

101. M. Men'shikov, *Novoe vremia,* December 23, 1908.

102. Kassii, "Misticheskaia vlast'," *Novoe vremia,* December 24, 1908.

103. Although mass confessions were not allowed according to the official doctrine of the Church, an exception was made for Ioann, who claimed to have the power to forgive sins en masse.

104. "Kuda on prishel?" 976.

105. Krest'ianin A. Golubtsev, *Polnoe razoblachenie iasnopolianskogo eretika Tolstogo: Golos prostoliudina* (St. Petersburg, 1910).

106. Ibid., 1.

107. Ibid., 2.

108. "Bor'ba tsarizma i tserkvi s L. N. Tolstym," *Voprosy istorii religii* 8 (Moscow, 1960): 376.

109. Lipsky actually surveys the riches of Tolstoy's literary works, then describes the failings of the religious ones. See Sviashch. Nikolai Lipskii, "Kogda umer velikii Tolstoi?" *Vera i razum,* nos. 21–22 (1912): 505.

110. N. Varzhanskii, "Po povodu 'otpevaniia' L. N. Tolstogo," *Missionerskoe obozrenie,* no. 4 (1913): 673. There is also a report of a priest performing services at the grave in the memoirs of Ia. G. Briuner in *L. N. Tolstoi v vospominaniiakh sovremennikov* (Moscow, 1955), 2:627–628. The editors write that it is "soon after" the funeral, though this time frame is not quoted from Briuner's account; he may, in fact, refer to the event of 1912.

111. N. Kuznetsov, *K voprosu o molitve za gr. L. N. Tolstogo: Otvet sviashchenniku sovershivshemu otpevanie na mogile gr. L. N. Tolstogo* (Sergiev Posad, 1913). Also in *Bogoslovskii vestnik,* no. 3 (1913): 591–625.

112. This compromise was also offered by Metropolitan Antonii in the 1910 speech described above, where he explained that Christians wishing to pray for the salvation of Tolstoy's soul were welcome to do so individually—there was no prohibition against that, and the church fathers had even encouraged it (he cites Feodor the Studite, Makarii Velikii, and Isaac the Syrian).

Despite these ancient precedents, the Tolstoy problem related to the more general challenge faced by the Church in modernity, which increasingly pitted the individual against the institution. Kuznetsov pointed to the priest's doubts about the propriety of Tolstoy's excommunication and complained of the tendency of church officials to argue about the canonical correctness of the Synod's acts, which he related to modernization and bureaucratization that had disturbed the ancient principles of the Church (*K voprosu o molitve,* 607). (There were other modern problems to be addressed: the journal in which Kuznetsov's piece originally appeared also contained an article on the question of life on Mars.)

113. Varzhanskii, "Po povodu 'otpevaniia' L. N. Tolstogo," 678.

114. Arkhimandrit Illarion, "'Velikaia mogila,'" *Vera i razum,* no. 24 (1913): 858.

115. *Dukhovnaia tragediia L'va Tolstogo* (Moscow, 1995).

116. A. Stolypin, Tserkov'-shkola v Astapove," *Novoe vremia,* November 11, 1910. He cites the tsar's reaction to Tolstoy's death as the true reaction of the people.

117. *Russkaia mysl',* no. 1 (1911): 219.

118. *PSS,* 82:216.

119. A. P. Sergeenko, *Rasskazy o L. N. Tolstom* (Moscow, 1978), 256–257.

Chapter 3   The Media at Astapovo and the Creation of a Modern Pastoral

1. *Novoe vremia* made this report, based on a telegram from Dmitrii Obolenskii, a family friend of the Tolstoys; it was immediately picked up by all the other papers.

2. Telegram of Savelii Raetskii to *Utro Rossii* from November 7, 7:45, in *Smert' Tolstogo: Po novym materialam,* ed. V. I. Nevskii (Moscow, 1929), 220.

3. Vladimir Azov, "Pod steklianym kolpakom," *Rech',* November 4, 1910; also in *Kubanskii krai,* November 9, 1910.

4. Andrei Haikin, "Desiat' chasov v odnom poezde so L. N. Tolstym: k zlobe dnia," *Odesskii listok,* November 7, 1910.

5. A. Iuzhanin, "Razrushennaia legenda," *Voronezhskii telegraf,* November 5, 1910 (article dated November 1).

6. *Smert' Tolstogo,* 20. On Orlov's telegram to the family, see T. L. Tolstaia, *Vospominaniia* (Moscow, 1976), 422.

7. *Smert' Tolstogo,* 24.

8. Sergei's economy of words no doubt relates to their cost. The International Telegraph Union set discounted rates (half of the regular tariff) for the press in 1903, placing the journalists at a further advantage over Tolstoy's family and friends.

9. Eventually it was decided that the doctors should provide regular bulletins to the press to avoid this melee but also to prevent inaccuracies in their reports, several of which had occurred in the first days of Tolstoy's illness.

10. *U Tolstogo: Iasnopolianskie zapiski D. P. Makovitskogo* (Moscow: Nauka, 1979), 4:417. Among the telegrams sent to Astapovo which have been preserved, there are indeed four which were sent to Ozolin within hours of Tolstoy's arrival at Astapovo. The first three of these were sent by *Russkoe slovo,* which gave details of the sort of information it was looking for (conversations with Tolstoy, Aleksandra, and Makovitskii, how Tolstoy arrived, where he was, what was his condition, etc.) and encouraged him to send as many telegrams as possible, not worrying about the cost (*Smert' Tolstogo,* 19). Ozolin at first refused to help and was praised for his devotion to Lev Nikolaevich, but he too evidently soon joined his family in leaking information to the press. In a telegram sent by Saveli Raetskii to *Utro Rossii* on November 3, the following comment was crossed out: "In a personal conversation the stationmaster Ozolin gave us a lot of interesting information" (*Smert' Tolstogo,* 45).

11. Kn. D. D. Obolenskii, *Novoe vremia,* November 2, 1910.

12. The telegram was sent to Ozolin but was seen by Aleksandra. Two days later A. Avrekh was reporting the incident to his editors: "*Novoe vremia* made a big faux pas, having sent a telegram to the stationmaster urgently asking him to confirm Tolstoy's death. The telegram fell into Aleksandra Tolstaia's hands and made a terrible impression" (*Smert' Tolstogo,* 205. The actual telegram from *Novoe vremia* can be found on 31.) Ironically, on November 6, *Novoe vremia* ran a report on young boys selling false bulletins announcing Tolstoy's death in front of Moscow theatres. Such false reports contributed to the impression of a media debacle.

13. V. Doroshevich, "Sofiia Andreevna," *Russkoe slovo,* October 31, 1910. Later, when Sofia Andreevna arrived at Astapovo, *Russkoe slovo* instructed Orlov to rely on her as "their friend."

14. Sofia Andreevna told a reporter: "I am terribly grateful to the newspapers—it is only thanks to them, from the telegrams, that I found out that Lev Nikolaevich was sick. My loved ones were hiding this from me" (*Gazeta kopeika,* November 5, 1910).

15. There was not enough temporary housing for the reporters, so, like the Tolstoy family, they were given a railroad coach as temporary quarters. They evidently belonged there every bit as much as the family.

16. Raetskii, in *Smert' Tolstogo,* 42.

17. Reporters repeatedly wrote their editors requesting papers for the Tolstoy family and often reported their reactions back to their editorial offices. When *Novoe vremia* sent its telegram inquiring prematurely about Tolstoy's death, its correspondent wired back to be more careful, as the family was very displeased (*Smert' Tolstogo,* 82–83). Similar reports on the family's negative reactions came after a November 4 article in *Novoe vremia* by Mikhail Men'shikov, "A Lesson to

the Young," which suggested that Tolstoy's situation might dissuade young people from choosing a radical lifestyle.

18. Sergei Iablonovskii, "Ushel," *Voronezhskii telegraf,* no. 248, November 5, 1910.

19. Jeffrey Brooks, *When Russia Learned to Read* (Princeton, N.J., 1985), 130.

20. Ibid., 130–140.

21. *Gazeta kopeika* (1908–1917) was the first to sell for a kopeck and was the model for the other papers. Its circulation in 1910 was about 250,000; it also appeared in a Moscow and a weekly edition. Its publication marked "the birth of a new popular press, which soon created its own reader" (*Den',* no. 160, June 17, 1913). See *Tovarischestvo izdatel'skogo dela "Kopeika"* (St. Petersburg, 1910).

22. Iuzhanin, "Razrushennaia legenda."

23. V. A. Anzimirov, *Na mogilu* (Moscow, 1910). One of these described Tolstoy's reception at the gates of Eden, where he arrives simultaneously with a nameless peasant who would have fit well into one of Tolstoy's later stories. Looking over the Book of Life, God finds the peasant undistinguished by good works or moral growth but mercifully decides that there was nothing more that could have been expected of such a man. Turning to Tolstoy, however, the angels struggle to bring to judgment the entire account of his good works ("They carry and carry the scrolls, but still there are lots of them remaining on earth") and finally enlist the help of the Archangel Michael. When they are finished, God looks at the evidence and is well pleased: "His heavenly countenance shines joyously." Tolstoy is not admitted into heaven, however, but is sent back to earth to finish his work, after which he will return to heaven to live as God's beloved son.

24. Iablonovskii, "Ushel."

25. "Sredi gazet i zhurnalov," *Novoe vremia,* October 31, 1910.

26. "Telegraf," in Brokgauz i Efron, *Bol'shaia entsiklopediia.*

27. In 1910 there were more than eight hundred newspapers, but only fifteen dailies. *Russkoe slovo* was one of the most widely read, with a circulation of 759,000 in 1916. (See Brooks, *When Russia Learned to Read.*) *Gazeta kopeika* and *Moskovskii listok* were of the more popular style. *Novoe vremia,* Suvorin's vehicle, was conservative, while *Moskovskie vedomosti,* an official government newspaper, was considered reactionary.

28. The family agreed unanimously that photographers should be allowed to take pictures of the body; five photographers and two cinematographers were involved. Cinematography was only beginning to become a part of the news media. Charles Pathé, Paris, produced his first newsreel in 1909; and one of his agents was on hand at Astapovo. Film of Tolstoy's death and funeral was shown in Moscow on November 10.

29. *Vel',* "Dokanali," *Sankt-Peterburgskie vedomosti,* October 31, 1910.

30. The aviator M. M. Efimov had sent a telegram to Tolstoy on October 23 asking if he could come to Yasnaya Polyana.

31. *Vel',* "Dokanali." Repin, Sergeenko, and Teneromo had been admonished before, possibly by the same writer, in the 1908 issue of *Satirikon* commemorating Tolstoy's eightieth birthday.

32. The catchphrase that was created by the press to describe the move was an "exodus from the world into the world" (*ukhod ot mira v mir*), the somewhat contradictory logic of which was resolved in the notion that Tolstoy had left the world in which he had lived and which was familiar to most of his readers, that of "worldly life," to enter what he called the "great world" (*bol'shoi mir*)—the broad expanses of the peasant world toward which he had gravitated for many years.

33. Tolstoy's "incomparable greatness" was a consistent theme in the eulogies that followed his death and was often defined by his world renown. Reference to the number of publications of his work in other languages was used to quantify his fame and genius, as was the reaction of the worldwide press to events at Astapovo. Tolstoy was Russia's first universally known celebrity, and much attention was paid to how the foreign press handled the story. Several of the larger papers ran regular columns in their daily Tolstoy sections titled "Reactions in Europe" or "Reactions from around the World." These sections measured world views on Tolstoy but also on the Russian press and public; it was understood that the eyes of the world were on Russia and were perhaps judging its actions.

34. *Skitalets,* "Svetlyi strannik," *Rannee utro,* November 4, 1910. *Skitalets* wrote about poverty and labor issues for the penny papers.

35. M. Liubimov, "V glushi polei," *Golos Moskvy,* November 3, 1910.

36. Al'min, *Bessarabskaia zhizn',* October 31, 1910.

37. Iablonovskii, "Ushel."

38. "Malen'kie zametki," *Utro* (Kharkov), November 2, 1910.

39. Azov, "Pod steklianym kolpakom."

40. "Zametki," *Minskii golos,* November 4, 1910. This piece presumably was written several days before it appeared. Similar in tone is a piece appearing in *Saratovskii listok:* "He left, and don't look for him. Don't look for him! He himself has asked us not to look for him and to leave him in peace. Isn't it our duty to fulfill the will of the one who is setting off on a journey from which there is no return? It was not just empty words when Tolstoy said that he would not return. He left, but don't try to trace his elderly steps. Give him peace now, and he will live forever!" (Svoi, *Saratovskii listok,* November 2, 1910).

41. A. Lisovskii, "Ne ishchite ego!" *Iuzhnaia zaria,* November 3, 1910. Some newspapers saw what was transpiring as something much less than holy. Christian and conservative papers criticized the liberal and popular press for using Tolstoy's departure to stir up antichurch and antigovernment propaganda. (This was particularly true after Tolstoy's death, when student and worker response to the prohibition of public commemorations of the event erupted into political unrest in the capital and other major cities.) One Odessa newspaper commended its own respectful silence about Tolstoy's departure, and from its superior position pointed an accusing finger at the "Jewish newspapers," which were full of frivolous stories, announcements, and conjectures about Tolstoy (*Russkaia rech'* [Odessa], November 3, 1910).

42. The anonymous interviewee is said to run a publishing house and is thus probably Ivan Gorbunov-Posadov, at that time an editor for Posrednik (S. R., "Begstvo iz velikogo plena," *Utro Rossii,* October 31, 1910).

43. *Smert' Tolstogo,* 22.

44. A. L. Tolstaia, "Ob ukhode i smerti L. N. Tolstogo," in *Tolstoi: Pamiatnik tvorchestva i zhizni,* V. I. Sreznevskii (Moscow, 1923), 4:177.

45. Azov, "Pod steklianym kolpakom."

46. *Mariupol'skaia zhizn',* November 3, 1910.

47. Liubimov, "V glushi."

48. A. V. Gol'denveizer, *Vblizi Tolstogo* (Moscow, 1922), 2:348.

49. S. L. Tolstoi, *Ocherki bylogo* (Moscow, 1956), 261.

50. Gol'denveizer, *Vblizi Tolstogo,* 2:348.

51. *PSS,* 84:408.

52. As noted in the introduction, Makovitskii had been making copious notation of Tolstoy's words and movements for several years; he kept small cards in the pocket of his jacket, on which he continually (and surreptitiously) jotted down conversations and comments, as well as anything else that seemed remotely worthy to posterity.

53. V. Nevskii, "Vvedenie," to *Smert' Tolstogo.* For unknown reasons, this introduction was not published in the book itself but is maintained as a separate booklet in the Lenin Library.

54. *Smert' Tolstogo,* 204.

55. Walter Benjamin, "The Storyteller," in *Illuminations,* ed. Hannah Arendt, trans. Harry Zohn (London, 1970), 94.

56. V. V. Rozanov, "Konchina L. N. Tolstogo," *Novoe vremia,* November 8, 1910. The editorial appears without Rozanov's name.

57. "Tolstoy with his very being was a great censor: the 'regulating' effect of his literature is immeasurable" (ibid.)

58. Aleksandr Blok, "Solntse nad Rossii," in his *Sobranie sochinenii* (Moscow, 1960–1963), 5:303 (emphasis Blok's).

59. Iuzhanin, "Razrushennaia legenda."

60. D. Brazul, "Smert' L. N. Tolstogo," *Kubanskii krai,* November 9, 1910.

61. Ibid.

62. D. Brazul, "Mnogogrannost' L. N. Tolstogo," *Kubanskii krai,* November 9, 1910.

63. E. Kuz'min, "Tvorimaia legenda," *Kievskie vesti,* October 31, 1910. The author seems to refer to one of Tolstoy's last works, where he refers to "airplanes, dreadnaughts, thirty-story buildings, gramophones, cinematographers, and all of the unnecessary foolishness that we call science and art." See his "Blagodarnaia pochva," *PSS* 38:36.

64. Iablonovskii, "Ushel." Another writer saw Tolstoy rejecting "civilization" and all the wonders of modern technology (S. Gruzhdev, "L. N. Tolstoi i tsivilizatsiia," *Kubanskii krai,* November 9, 1910).

65. K. Sukhovykh, untitled editorial, *Kubanskii krai,* November 9, 1910.

66. Brazul, "Smert'."

67. P. Iuliev, "Nasha voploshennaia sovest'," *Russkaia pravda* (Ekaterinburg), November 4, 1910.

68. Liubimov, "V glushi." Liubimov saw Tolstoy as "the conscience of humanity, the world's conscience, suffering the torments of our mistakes and the worthlessness of the world."

69. A. Aprelev, "Bez liubvi i ponimaniia," *Volyn'* (Zhitomir), November 4, 1910.

70. "Tolstoy is our conscience," another writer chimed in, "and he couldn't come to terms with our vain fussing, with our godless pettiness, with our life, spattered with dirt and blood" ("Zamolchite!" *Viatskaia rech',* November 6, 1910). The press made a public record of even trivial crimes of pettiness against Tolstoy: one writer complained of the banality that was ruling the day, demonstrated by reference to remarks overheard in a cafe about Tolstoy's stop at Shamordino (snickering comments on what he could be doing in a convent) (Neznakomets, "Melochi zhizni," *Odesskie novosti,* November 2, 1910).

71. "Malen'kie zametki," *Utro* (Kharkov), November 2, 1910.

72. A. Iuzhanin, "Razrushennaia legenda."

73. "Zamolchite!"

74. *Saratovskii listok,* November 2, 1910.

75. As cited without reference in L. Anninskii, *Tolstoi i kinematograf* (Moscow, 1980), 60.

76. Rozanov, "Konchina."

77. *Kaspii* (Baku) October 31, 1910.

78. A. Belyi, "Lev Tolstoi," *Russkaia mysl',* no. 1 1911: 92.

79. As quoted in Iv. Chuzhanov, "Tolstoi i tolpa," *Odesskii listok,* November 7, 1910. Merezhkovskii warns the Russian public not to drive Tolstoy to his death.

80. Belyi, 94. He continues: "The magnetic force emanating for years from Yasnaya Polyana and changing course in a number of directions was by no means limited to Tolstoy's words and visible actions; it consisted of his silence. . . . And now it has become clear that the very silence of his artistic genius was only the deepening of his genius, the agonizing attainment of the last and highest point."

81. Ibid.

82. *Skitalets,* "Svetlyi strannik."

83. Kuz'min, "Tvorimaia legenda."

84. Lisovskii, "Ne ishchite ego!"

85. Iablonovskii, "Ushel."

86. V. Obninskii, "V Astapove," *Utro Rossii,* November 4, 1910. See also *Sibirskaia zhizn',* November 1, 1910: "Even if Tolstoy, like Gogol, renounced what he had believed for decades, that would not mean the justification of falsehood and violence, but that his powerful mind did not stand up to the contemporary vileness."

87. Aprelev, "Bez liubvi i ponimaniia."

Chapter 4   Tolstoyan Violence upon the Funeral Rites of the State

1. This circular was issued before the Synod had reached its decision regarding the performance of services (N. P. Kharlamov, "Otchet chinovnika osobykh poruchenii," published by L. Riabchenko in *Sel'skaia molodezh',* no. 8 (1991): 35).

2. "Politicheskaia bor'ba vokrug smerti Tolstogo," *Literaturnoe nasledstvo,* 69 (1961), 2:386.

3. A. B. Gol'denveizer, *Vblizi Tolstogo* (Moscow, 1923), 2:365.

4. While "the state" was not nearly so monolithic an entity in 1910 as it had been prior to the 1905 Revolution, I will take advantage of my Tolstoyan context here and define it as that

toward which he was invariably opposed—the political and ecclesiastical power structures which drew their authority from traditional, hierarchical relations.

5. *Krasnyi arkhiv,* no. 6 (1935): 211.

6. *Vestnik Evropy,* no. 11 (1910): 342.

7. A. Al'tshuller, *Aleksandr Evstaf'evich Martynov* (Moscow, 1959), 195.

8. Nicholas Tyrras, "On Dostoevsky's Funeral," *Slavic and East European Journal,* no. 2 (1986): 276.

9. *Pobedonostsev i ego korrespondenty* (Moscow, 1923), 1:556–557. Tolstoy's funeral is often called the first national civil funeral in Russia—to be more precise, it is the first in which the civil ceremony did not accompany the Orthodox one but instead stood alone.

10. Igor' Volgin, *Poslednie dni Dostoevskogo* (Moscow, 1991), 472. The police did confiscate a set of chains that was brought to the procession to represent Dostoevsky's time in prison.

11. A. S. Suvorin, "O pokoinom," *Dostoevskii v vospominaniiakh sovremennikov* (Moscow, 1964), 2:423–424.

12. *Perepiska L. N. Tolstogo s N. N. Strakhovom* (St. Petersburg, 1911), 306.

13. Quoted in Marcus C. Levitt, *Russian Literary Politics and the Pushkin Celebration of 1880* (Ithaca, N.Y., 1989), 152. He cites Iu. Nikol'skii, "Delo o pokhoronakh I. S. Turgeneva," *Byloe,* no. 4 (October 1917): 148–149.

14. On the censuring of Tolstoy's Turgenev speech, see V. A. Gromov, "K istorii zapreshcheniia rechi L. N. Tolstogo ob I. S. Turgeneve," *Iasnopolianskii sbornik* (Tula, 1988), 43–53.

15. "Vnutrennee obozrenie: Pokhorony S. A. Muromtseva kak 'priznak vremeni,'" *Vestnik Evropy,* no. 11 (1910), 342–348.

16. L. A. Tikhomirov, "Iz dnevnika L'va Tikhomirova: Period stolypinshchiny," *Krasnyi arkhiv,* no. 1 (1936): 178. In 1881 Bernhard von Werder had said that in thirty years no one would remember Dostoevsky's name; his funeral had been large simply because opportunists wanted to demonstrate their general discontent (Tyrras, "On Dostoevsky's Funeral," 276).

17. "Iz materialov o L. N. Tolstom," *Krasnyi arkhiv,* no. 4 (1923): 361.

18. Reports from a correspondent appearing in a Kharkov newspaper prompted the following message to the local governor: "The interior minister wishes to recognize this sort of article as inappropriate for an official organ and has ordered that in the future announcements on the health of Count Tolstoy should not be presented as articles with discussions of various types but limit themselves to the facts regarding the progression of his illness" (M. L. Gomon, *Lev Tolstoi i khar'kovchane* [Kharkov, 1993], 143).

19. See P. E. Shchegolev, ed., "Pokhorony L'va Tolstogo do ego smerti," *Byloe, no.* 2 (24) (1924): 111–114. The body was to be transported on one of two routes, as per the choice of Tolstoy's family: on a postal train, with a planned forty-minute delay, so as to minimize the stop in Kharkov ("to limit the stop to fifteen minutes and leave Kharkov on time, regardless of the delay in the mail"), or on an express train from Sevastopol to Sinel'nikova, which would be attached to a military train to Belgorod, then to a postal train (again with a planned delay to minimize the stop in Kharkov).

20. Two working titles for this text, "The Desire of the People" and "What the Majority of Russian People Above All Desire," point to Tolstoy's role as a spokesperson for the masses. His tendency to engage ruling authorities on a personal level and to consider political questions from an ethical viewpoint gave voice to the mass sympathies that transcended political organizations. His pacifist writings against the Russo-Japanese War expressed the visceral morality that led a group of mothers to lie down over the tracks to prevent a train from leaving Kharkov with a detachment of soldiers (at the same train station that had demonstratively welcomed Tolstoy in 1901).

21. Even in private conversations about the executions, Tolstoy repeatedly referred to Stolypin in terms of his moral agency, more than in terms of policy. He spoke differently about Stolypin's role in breaking up the peasant commune (*mir*)—here he was more concerned that the *peasants'* integrity was being undermined by Stolypin.

22. Tolstoy had actually mentioned Nicholas II, Stolypin, and the head of the Justice Department by name in his first draft of "I Cannot Remain Silent!" but it is still quite clear in the final draft to whom he refers.

23. In keeping with his attempt to establish a level of personal responsibility, Tolstoy asked that he himself be put in prison, so that then at least he would know that killings being carried out were not to his benefit.

24. D. P. Makovitskii, *U Tolstogo: Iasnopolianskie zapiski* D. P. Makovitskogo (Moscow, 1979), 4:101.

25. Ibid., 4:118. Tolstoy's son Andrei L'vovich began working for Stolypin in early 1910. This relationship requires further investigation in light of the events of 1910.

26. Among these instances prior to 1910: 1862 (Yasnaya Polyana school), 1881 (assassination of Alexander II), 1883 (Turgenev speech), 1891–1892 (famine relief), 1897 (Dukhobors), 1901–1902 (illness, post-excommunication), 1908 (eightieth birthday).

27. A great number of Tolstoy's works were published abroad (many by Chertkov in England) before they were published in Russia. Under the new censorship laws after 1905, editors were allowed to publish Tolstoy's works but were often subsequently fined for doing so.

28. Cezarre Lombroso, *Moe poseshchenie Tolstogo* (Geneva, 1902), 12–13.

29. Gusev was arrested in Tolstoy's own home on August 4, 1909, charged with distributing revolutionary propaganda, and sent to Cherdyn' for two years. See N. N. Gusev, *Dva goda s L. N. Tolstym* (Moscow, 1973), 283–304; also Tolstoy's "Zaiavlenie ob areste Guseva."

30. The government's reaction to the Tolstoyan campaign on behalf of the Dukhobors clearly illustrates this policy: while Pavel Biriukov and the Chertkovs were exiled in 1897 for distributing pamphlets on the persecution of the Dukhobors, Tolstoy, who had published a major novel to support the campaign and had written many of the offending tracts himself, was left untouched. Visiting the two in Petersburg just before their exile in February, Tolstoy was under tight surveillance throughout his stay, but government archives show that the focus was often on those with whom he consorted. (The latter included the same Men'shikov who, as an editorialist for *Novoe vremia*, was such a prolific commentator on Tolstoy's last days. Though by 1910 he held a negative view of Tolstoy's influence, in 1897 he was a proponent of Tolstoy's ideas.) Although the authorities' surveillance was so complete as to contain a report of Tolstoy's visit to a barbershop ("At 9:20 a.m. Count Tolstoy set off for the barber, where he had his hair and beard trimmed"), the government itself would not touch a hair on his head. See *Tolstoi—pamiatniki tvorchestva i zhizni* (Moscow, 1923), 4:192–193.

31. "Tsirkuliar ministra vnutrennikh del P. A. Stolypina o prazdnovanii iubileia L. N. Tolstogo," *Tolstoi i o Tolstom: Novye materially*, ed. N. N. Gusev, vol. 1 (Moscow, 1924), 82–83.

32. While at Optina, Tolstoy had been questioned in regard to his passport, which he did not have with him; the issue was resolved when others vouched for his identity. This incident, and in general the question of whether or not Tolstoy would be allowed to cross the border (if, as was reported, he intended to travel to Bulgaria) without proper papers became an item in the newspapers. See an untitled item in *Odesskii listok,* November 3, 1910.

33. The agent was told that the issue was of great concern to Nicholas II. See N. P. Kharlamov, "Konchina L'va Tolstogo," *Nauka i religiia*, no. 11 (1985): 42.

34. An agent arranged this by virtue of his acquaintance with one of the operators. At Zaseka (the station near Yasnaya Polyana), the government installed its own telegraph machines for use during the funeral. Various police reports that have been published suggest that all the correspondence was being monitored: "The heads of both telegraph stations assured me that not a single telegram was sent that was biased or that depicted the situation from a distorted or unfavorable perspective" ("Raport Iu. E. Freiberga v Shtab korpusa zhandarmov," in "Politseiskie doneseniia o pokhoronakh L. N. Tolstogo," *Istoricheskii arkhiv*, 6 [1960]: 75). See also "Raport o prebyvanii gr. Tolstogo na st. Astapovo," in "Iz materialov o L. N. Tolstom," *Krasnyi arkhiv*, no. 4 (1923): 348.

35. "Raport o prebyvanii," 340–343.

36. The local minister of internal affairs in Tula reports this (ibid., 358).

37. As Tolstoy had dictated to N. N. Gusev in 1908: "although all this is entirely meaningless, this is so that no rites are performed during the burial of my body. A wooden coffin, and whoever wants may carry it and take it to the Zakaz, opposite the ravine, to the place of the 'green stick.' There is at least some reason to chose this location over any other" (N. N. Gusev, "Ukhod Tolstogo," *30 dnei*, no. 9 [1928]: 20). The family digressed from Tolstoy's wishes by

accepting funeral wreaths, which were examined in advance by Special Agent Kharlamov and the local governor and chief of police to make sure that their messages were not "inappropriate." (Two or three were removed out of one hundred.) After Dostoevsky's funeral it was forbidden to carry wreaths in the funeral procession—they were collected on a special cart so that they could be inspected ahead of time.

38. A security official met with a representative of the Moscow students: "In conversation with him I categorically insisted that there be no manifestations, flags, antigovernment or anti-religious speeches, no carrying of wreaths, and no inappropriate inscriptions on ribbons. I supported this demand by reference to the expression of this wish by the family of the deceased count" (B. Meilakh, *Ukhod i smert' Tolstogo* [Moscow, 1979], 292–293. His source: "Dela kantse-liarii Tul'skogo gubernatora, sekretnogo stola, o sostoianii zdorov'ia gr. L. N. Tolstogo," Arkhiv Tolstogo.) According to one police report, at this point the Tolstoys were on quite friendly terms with the police ("Raport Iu. E. Freiberga," 75).

39. Meilakh, *Ukhod i smert' Tolstogo*, 294. This is another illustration of the degree to which dissimulation and fear of dissimulation figure into the events surrounding Tolstoy's death.

40. Ibid., 293. His source: "Zapisi vospominanii Ivana Shuraeva," Biblioteka muzeia-usad'by L. N. Tolstogo Iasnaia Poliana.

41. S. Ia. Elpat'evskii, in *Zhivoi Tolstoi*, ed. N. N. Apostolov (Moscow, 1928), 559.

42. There was an order from Petersburg prohibiting anyone from going to Yasnaya, but the stationmaster telephoned Stolypin and told him there would be a riot if they did not allow the students to go. Permission was granted for two trains for students, but no more. When the students attending the funeral returned to Moscow, they found local trams waiting for them—this had been arranged so as to disperse the crowd as quickly as possible.

43. S. L. Tolstoi, *Ocherki bylogo* (Moscow, 1956), 270. Among these late arrivals were Mili-ukov, Rodichev, and Stakhovich from the Duma, as well as a deputation from Moscow University, including the rector, Manuilov.

44. "Za nedeliu," *Rech'*, November 15, 1910.

45. V. Ia. Briusov, "Na pokhoronakh Tolstogo. Vpechatleniia i nabliudeniia," in *L. N. Tolstoi v vospominaniiakh sovremennikov* (Moscow, 1978), 455.

46. Ibid., 459.

47. Another member of the crowd could not restrain himself and made a brief but effusive speech, which was considered "unnecessary" by observers (cf. Briusov and S. L. Tolstoy).

48. S. L. Tolstoi, *Ocherki bylogo*, 269.

49. A. F. Bobkov, "Neposredstvennye vpechatleniia ot puteshestviia v Iasnuiu Polianu Tul'skoi gubernii na pokhorony L. N. Tolstogo," in *Neizvestnyi Tolstoi v arkhivakh Rossii i SShA* (Moscow, 1994), 364.

50. "It made a particularly strong impression on me that the coffin was carried by peasants, simple muzhiks in torn homespun coats, sheepskins, with their wind-tussled hair. If you didn't pay attention to the rest of the public, it seemed that they were burying a simple muzhik, just like the ones who were carrying him (Bobkov, "Neposredstvennye vpechatleniia," 355).

51. Preshelets, "Pokhorony," *Kievskie vesti*, November 11, 1910. Briusov felt that the funeral "was worthy of Tolstoy, or, more accurately, worthy of Russia" (Briusov, "Na pokhoronakh Tolstogo," 459).

52. The song had also been used effectively in the civil funeral service for the actress Komis-sarzhevskaia in a Petersburg theater the previous year. It was sung by the actors of the theater, and a Kiev newspaper reported that there had never been a more moving ceremony (Preshelets, "Pokhorony"). During the Dostoevsky procession through Petersburg, the crowd had sung "O Holy God," another piece from the liturgy, but as Dostoevsky was receiving a Christian burial, this was not a breach of burial sacraments.

53. Briusov, "Na pokhoronakh Tolstogo," 457.

54. *Russkaia zemlia*, November 16, 1910. The students were disciplined, and order was restored.

55. Kharlamov, "Konchina L'va Tolstogo," 44.

56. "Telegrammy nashikh korrespondentov," *Novoe vremia*, November 18, 1910.

57. Meilakh, *Ukhod i smert' Tolstogo*, 298.

58. One editorial explained: "Russia is too deeply involved in international relations to completely ignore public moods, especially when their unanimity nullifies even territorial boundaries" (*Rech'*, November 9, 1910).

59. *Poslednie dni*, 94.

60. V. Korolenko, "Umer," *Rech'*, November 8, 1910.

61. Tikhomirov, "Iz dnevnika," 183.

62. *Rech'*, November 6, 1910.

63. *30 dnei*, no. 9 (1928): 25 (Source: S. Iu. Witte, *Vospominaniia*, v. 3 (Moscow, 1923)).

64. Tikhomirov, "Iz dnevnika," 181.

65. Another of the government public relations efforts failed as its proposal to pay the funeral expenses was rejected by the Tolstoy family. The Tolstoys' letter refusing the money was printed in *Rech'* on November 12. Tikhomirov comments at length in his diary on Stolypin's impolitic position, particularly in relation to the proposal of an American banker who wanted to buy Yasnaya Polyana and build a "people's university" there, which might become nest of rebellion ("Iz dnevnika," 183).

66. "Gosudarstvennaia duma," *Russkie vedomosti*, November 9, 1910. The paper gives a detailed report of this speech and reactions from other Duma members.

67. *Poslednie dni*, 94.

68. *Moskovskie vedomosti*, November 9, 1910.

69. *Rech'*, November 11, 1910.

70. The singing of "Eternal Memory" was also prohibited.

71. The head of the Moscow Security Department received orders from Petersburg on November 20, 1910, to send two reliable agents to report on the activities at Yasnaya Polyana and Chertkov's estate. An agent known as "Blondinka" was sent to Yasnaya Polyana and filed a report on gatherings at Tolstoy's grave, as well as on the activities of Chertkov and Makovitskii among the local peasants (N. Sitnikov, "Velikan i pigmei," *Molodaia gvardiia*, no. 10 [1974]: 58).

72. Meilakh, *Ukhod i smert' Tolstogo*, 317.

73. Borei, "Malen'kie zametki," *Novoe vremia*, November 12, 1910.

74. M. Men'shikov, "Igra v pozhar," *Novoe vremia*, November 13, 1910. Men'shikov's fulminations continued three days later in an article entitled "A Struggle for Civilization." Here he claimed that capital punishment was a bulwark of civilization, and that "Jew-Masons" were using the doctrines of Tolstoy and falsifying the teachings of Christ in order to "disarm" and "disempower" the government by taking away its last deterrent to crime (M. Men'shikov, "Bor'ba za tsivilizatsiiu," *Novoe vremia*, November 16, 1910).

75. Kassii, "V Tolstovskie dni," *Novoe vremia*, November 16, 1910.

76. This is a case of the priest calling the kettle black, for the Church had sought to create its own public relations coup at the side of Tolstoy's deathbed.

77. "Iz obshchestvennoi khroniki," *Vestnik Evropy*, no 12 (1910): 439.

78. "Khronika—provintsial'noe obozrenie," *Vestnik Evropy*, no. 12 (1910): 404. (For a contrasting view, see Men'shikov, "Urok molodezhi," *Novoe vremia*, November 4, 1910.)

79. "Vnutrennee obozrenie," *Vestnik Evropy*, no. 12 (1910): 351.

80. "Graf L. Tolstoi v gosudarstvennom sovete," *Moskovskie vedomosti*, November 11, 1910. The piece is unsigned, but was written by the paper's editor, L. A. Tikhomirov, as indicated by his diary.

81. Two days later the focus was still on this session of the State Council: "The last session of the State Council will remain one of the darkest pages of our age. The chair, from his side, used every means to reconcile the thirst for victory of those maintaining this position. Behind the scenes pressure was used to persuade the Right to at least not make a show of their shameful attitude toward a national treasure" (editorial, *Rech'*, November 11, 1910).

82. "In every other country such a death would have served as a powerful push toward the unification of all society around the dear grave" (ibid.).

83. Editorial, *Rech'*, November 12, 1910.

84. *Rech'*, November 11, 1910.

85. A large part of Lenin's article concerns the appraisals of Tolstoy being made "in the legal press" on the occasion of his eightieth birthday: conservatives and liberals are both tendentious and misunderstand the anniversary.

86. V. I. Lenin, "Lev Tolstoi kak zerkalo russkoi revoliutsii," in *Lenin o Tolstom* (Moscow, 1928), 49. Originally published in *Proletarii*, September 11, 1908. Lenin ridiculed the Tolstoyan "milksop" who publicly reviled himself for not practicing moral perfection and devoted his energies to eating rice cutlets instead of meat (51).

87. V. I. Lenin, "L. N. Tolstoi i sovremennoe rabochee dvizhenie," in *Lenin o Tolstom* (Moscow, 1928), 69. Originally published in *Nash put'*, November 28, 1910.

88. V. I. Lenin, "L. N. Tolstoi," in *Lenin o Tolstom* (Moscow, 1928), 59. Originally published in *Sotsial'demokrat*, November 11, 1910.

89. Lenin is quoting the editorial in *Rech'*, November 11, 1910.

90. Kharlamov wrote in his memoirs: "those who called for these services were not believers, nor were they moved by religious convictions. Spiritual motivations were obviously completely alien to everyone pronouncing their desire for prayers for Tolstoy's soul, with the exception of Sofia Andreevna. They were pursuing exclusively demonstrative ends, of course" (Kharlamov, "Otchet," 35).

91. *Rech'*, November 11, 1910.

92. Tikhomirov, "Iz dnevnika," 181.

93. P. Kropotkin, "Tolstoi." In *Zhizn' i smert' L. N. Tolstogo* (Moscow, 1911), 125.

94. *Rech'*, November 12, 1910.

95. V. Maklakov, "Lev Tolstoi (Uchenie i zhizn')," in *O L've Tolstom: Dve rechi* (Paris, 1929). In January 1921 Maklakov delivered a speech in Paris explaining Tolstoy's antipathy to Bolshevism, which had been obscured by Soviet practices of honoring Tolstoy on the recent ten-year anniversary of his death. Maklakov suggested that the Soviets celebrated his passing because Tolstoy would surely, had he been alive, have opposed their revolution. This was yet another case, for Maklakov, of Tolstoy's death being used as a political opportunity. See V. Maklakov, *Tolstoi i bol'shevizm* (Paris, 1921).

96. Kharlamov, "Konchina L'va Tolstogo," 42.

97. "Iz obshchestvennoi khroniki," *Vestnik Evropy*, no. 12 (1910): 436–437.

Chapter 5   On or about November 1910

1. Untitled item, *Russkie vedomosti*, March 3, 1912.

2. This pattern would continue into the early Soviet period, when Tolstoy would for a time serve as the leading prerevolutionary model for the Socialist Realist novel.

3. Peter Stansky, *On or About December 1910* (Cambridge, 1996) and Thomas Harrison, *1910: The Emancipation of Dissonance* (Berkeley, 1996).

4. Virginia Woolf, "Mr. Bennett and Mrs. Brown," in *The Essays of Virginia Woolf* (New York, 1988), 3:384–389. Shaw, incidentally, was corresponding with Tolstoy at this time.

5. Stansky is not alone in focusing on the effect of striking visual phenomena on the British public of the day: George Dangerfield's seminal study of the same period, *The Strange Death of Liberal England* (New York, 1935), begins by pointing to Halley's Comet streaking across the horizon.

6. That this anxiety was spread throughout Europe is attested by Harrison in a quote from Henry Adams from February 1910: "Every reader of the French and German newspapers knows that not a day passes without producing some uneasy discussion of supposed social decrepitude: falling off of the birthrate; decline of rural population, lowering of army standards; multiplication of suicides; increase of insanity or idiocy; of cancer; of tuberculosis; signs of nervous exhaustion; of enfeebled vitality; 'habits' of alcoholism and drugs; failure of eyesight in the young, and so on, without end" (Harrison, *The Emancipation of Dissonance*, 6).

7. Ibid., 17–18.

8. Georg Lukács, *Theory of the Novel*, trans. Anna Bostock (Cambridge, 1971), 12.

9. Harrison, *The Emancipation of Dissonance*, 97.

10. Ibid., 15–16.

11. N.—, "Tsep samoubiistv," *Russkie vedomosti*, November 2, 1910.

12. "Tri smerti," *Russkoe slovo*, November 2, 1910.

13. The tomb utilized the death mask of Tarasov and is itself an important monument to the morbid fascination of this period in Russian history. It is beautifully preserved and is now under the protection of the Russian government as a cultural landmark.

14. In the November 15 edition of *Rech'* such a column appears alongside an editorial on Tolstoy's death, in which the author dismisses the notion that the latter could itself be viewed as a kind of suicide. This notion had evidently been suggested by the right-wing press and was easily refuted by reference to Tolstoy's work on his article refuting the death penalty during his last days.

15. A. Izmailov, "Novye knigi: O samoubiitsakh," *Russkoe slovo,* November 6, 1910. This was a review of a collection containing articles by Bishop Mikhail, Rozanov, Kareev, Lunacharskii, Ivanov-Razumnik, Aikhenval'd, and Abramovich.

16. A. D., "Novoe issledovanie o samoubiistve," *Utro Rossii,* November 4, 1910. The review concerned the Munich edition of Robert Gaupp's *Uber den Selbstmord* (the text had not been translated into Russian). It opened by decrying the "bloody nightmare" of the suicide epidemic that had overtaken Russian society.

17. Izmailov, "Novye knigi."

18. A. S. Izgoev, "Ob intelligentnoi molodezhi," *Vekhi* (Sverdlovsk, 1991), 111.

19. *U Tolstogo: Iasnopolianskie zapiski D. P. Makovitskogo* (Moscow, 1979), 4:423. The article "Tri smerti" appeared in *Russkie vedomosti, November 2, 1910.*

20. "Samoubiistvo tolstovtsa," *Birzhevye vedomosti,* November 30, 1910.

21. "27-ogo dekabriia...," *Pskovskii golos,* December 31, 1910.

22. I. N. Ignatov, "Smert' Tolstogo," *Russkie vedomosti,* January 1, 1911.

23. Ibid. Michelstaedter included Tolstoy in his list of artists and thinkers whom he considered "persuaded selves"—people who "found their homes in the world only by feeling that they did *not* belong" (Harrison, *The Emancipation of Dissonance,* 76).

24. N. Karabchevskii, "L. N. Tolstoi," in *Poslednie dni L'va Nikolaevicha Tolstogo* (St. Petersburg, 1910), 221.

25. Tan, "Zhizn' cheloveka," in *Poslednie dni,* 196.

26. Mikhail Artsybashev, "O Tolstom," in his *Sobranie sochinenii,* 3 vols. (Moscow, 1994), 685–700. (See especially 692–693 and 698.)

27. Harrison, *The Emancipation of Dissonance,* 16.

28. Karabchevskii, "L. N. Tolstoi," 219.

29. Tan, "Zhizn' cheloveka," 195.

30. N. A. Berdiaev, "Dukhi russkoi revoliutsii," in *Iz glubiny* (Moscow-Petrograd, 1918).

31. There are many variants to the former statement, which are described in N. Gusev, "Kakie byli poslednie slova L. N. Tolstogo?" *Tolstoi i o Tolstom: Novye materialy* (Moscow: Tolstovskii muzei, 1924), 1:77–80. Gol'denveizer recorded it as: "Remember one thing: there are masses of people in the world besides Lev Tolstoy, and you are all looking only at Lev" (*Pomnite odno—est' na svete propast' narodu, krome L'va Tolstogo, a vy vse smotrite na odnogo L'va...*) (A. B. Gol'denveizer, *Vblizi Tolstogo* (Moscow, 1923), 2:356). The second phrase is also often cited, though it was not intelligible to Sergei, to whom it was spoken, and had to be interpreted by the ever-ready Makovitskii, who recorded it as "Truth...I love much...they all" (*Istina... liubliu mnogo...vse oni...*) (S. L. Tolstoi, *Ocherki bylogo* (Moscow, 1956), 264).

32. Maksimilian Voloshin, "Sud'ba L'va Tolstogo," *Russkaia mysl',* no. 1 (1911): 135–138.

33. Tan, "Zhizn' cheloveka," 197.

34. As it is a commonplace that Tolstoy is obsessed with death, it is indeed surprising that more attention is not paid to this aspect of *Anna Karenina.*

35. It is significant that this resolution is achieved in solitude and is not communicated to others. Ivan Ilych's existential crisis is resolved by a despair that causes him to renounce life—not unlike what a suicide might feel—but here it is redemptive, because life is taken from him.

36. The salvation of Levin to a significant extent prefigures this development in the sense that it is essentially a "Christian" approach, rather than the Stoic one that was more appealing to Tolstoy intellectually.

37. The suicidal death of the hero is similar to the death of the author suggested by Roland Barthes—a figurative death of "the hero as such," in the sense of relinquishing the heroic role within the narrative.

38. In *Diary of a Writer* Dostoevsky acknowledged: "It is clear, then, that suicide—when the idea of immortality has been lost—becomes an utter and inevitable necessity for any man who, by his mental development, has even slightly lifted himself above the level of cattle." *Sochinenii v 30-i tomakh* [Moscow, 1971–1989], 24:49.) Elsewhere he imagines the logic of a suicide: "Since I cannot eradicate nature, I am eradicating myself, solely out of weariness of enduring a tyranny of which no one is guilty." (Ibid, 23:148.)

39. Robert Kellogg and Robert Scholes, *The Nature of Narrative* (Oxford, 1966), 234–236. In his *Theory of the Novel* (1914–1915) Lukács views the novelistic hero as a psychological seeker who might reveal "the concealed totality of life," whereas the epic hero represents a totality that is already full shaped. "Thus the fundamental form-determining intention of the novel is objectivised as the psychology of the novel's heroes: they are seekers" (60).

40. Max Nordau, *Degeneration* (New York, 1968), 5–6.

41. Thomas Hardy, *Jude the Obscure*, ed. C. H. Sisson (Harmondsworth, UK, 1981), 411.

42. Sabina Spielrein, a student and colleague of Jung and Freud, was born in Rostov in 1885 and died there in 1942, executed with her two children by the invading Nazis. Spielrein's work on "the death instinct" was conceived in 1910 and first published by Freud in 1912.

43. The short piece "O samoubiistve" ("On Suicide") appeared in *Russkoe slovo*, March 9, 1910, then again as a pamphlet published by Sofia Andreevna. The longer piece was entitled "O bezumii" ("On Madness") and was never finished or published in Tolstoy's lifetime. See *PSS*, 38:395–418. In a diary note as he worked on the latter piece, Tolstoy writes: "It is impossible that there would not be suicide when people do not know what to depend on, when they do not know who they are and why they are living, and are at the same time certain that it is not possible to know this" (*PSS* 58:47). He begins the article by writing that he is receiving two to three letters per day from young people contemplating suicide.

44. D. S. Merezhkovskii, *Bol'naia Rossiia* (Leningrad: Leningradskii universitet, 1991), 202.

45. R. M. Rilke, *Briefe aus den Jahren 1914–1921* (Leipzig, 1937), 93.

46. Georg Simmel, *Philosophy of Money*, ed. David Frisby, trans. Tom Bottomore and David Frisby (New York, 1990), 484.

47. See Suvorin's obituary (*Poslednie dni*, 192), in which he refers to Tolstoy as his own literary autocracy.

48. R. M. Rilke, letter to Clara Rilke, November 18, 1910. As cited in Anna A. Tavis, *Rilke's Russia: A Cultural Encounter* (Evanston, Ill., 1994), 93.

49. Ibid.

50. If Tolstoy had lived, the results might have been quite inglorious: being tracked down by his wife, gloomily returning to Yasnaya Polyana hounded by the press, etc.

51. This statement is rather ironic in light of Gorky's later memoirs on Tolstoy, which have become central documents in the corpus of these legends.

52. Nikolai Iordanskii, "Lev Tolstoi i sovremennoe obshchestvo," *Sovremennyi mir*, no. 12 (1910): 91. See also his discussion of contemporary civilization (100).

Conclusion

1. Interest would remain quite high well into the 1920s, when Tolstoy was often cited as the most popular Russian author in Soviet surveys.

2. The edition was published simultaneously in Russia and by Chertkov's Tolstoyan press in England, Svobodnoe slovo [Free Word]. The full text of the story under discussion here was published only abroad; a censored version appeared in the Russian edition.

3. A similar legend would circulate about Tolstoy, even before the publication of this story. In early January 1911 the newspapers reported of rumors that Tolstoy was alive and had surfaced in Siberia. See for example "Legenda o Tolstom," Birzhevye vedomosti, January 10, 1911. (The same story was picked up by numerous other papers on January 10–12.)

4. Anna Tolstaya subsequently sent Tolstoy a postcard of Fyodor Kuzmich, with a note that she was sending a picture of the hero of Tolstoy's future legend.

5. *PSS* 36:585.

6. *PSS* 36:586.

7. Tolstoy, "Ispoved'," *PSS,* 23:4.

8. *PSS,* 36:61. This lust, directed at the dead body of a beautiful woman, revisits that convergence of sexuality and violence that Tolstoy had explored in *The Kreutzer Sonata,* "The Devil," and *Father Sergius.*

9. Alexander's inability to liberate himself from lust, along with his antipathy for his wife and resentment of his mother, places this text in the terrain that Daniel Rancour-Laferriere has described in his *Tolstoy on the Couch: Misogyny, Masochism, and the Absent Mother* (New York, 1998).

10. Fyodor Kuzmich begins his memoirs in thanks for his solitude but noting that he is left alone with God and his "criminal memories."

11. "Having understood the vanity of my former life and the significance of that life which I lived and live as a wanderer, I will try to relate the story of my terrible life" (*PSS,* 36:65).

12. *PSS,* 58:124.

13. One reason for public responsiveness to the story of Tolstoy's departure is found in the third figure in the narrative of Fyodor Kuzmich—that of the soldier Strumenskii. It is this third Alexander who awakens the emperor to his moral potential, and it is his mortified flesh that allows, and is redeemed by, Alexander's spiritual rebirth as Fyodor Kuzmich. This sacrificed body is promised another sort of redemption in the last days of Tolstoy, who himself assumes the identity of this rebellious foot soldier. This was understood as a deliberately democratic act, a demonstrative renunciation of his aristocratic wealth and privilege for the benefit of others. No matter how personal the motivations for Tolstoy's act may have been in the end, the spectators could see themselves as its symbolic beneficiaries, and this lent the days of Astapovo much of their vast resonance and broad-ranging dynamics.

14. *PSS* 36:586.

A Word on My Sources

1. The collection of telegrams represents one in a long series of efforts (to which this book can be added) to offer a more complete and *vérité* account of what transpired at Astapovo—an enterprise described by Vladimir Chertkov (with his own characteristically obsequious excess) in the introduction to his book on the *ukhod:* "In the story of Tolstoy's departure with which we are here concerned even the most exhaustive research cannot encompass all the infinite number of circumstances, internal and external, that motivated this event. Alas, the circumstances that provoked and contributed to his departure even in those realms of Tolstoy's private life that are open to investigation are too numerous and various for any one person to give an exhaustive account" (V. G. Chertkov, *Ukhod Tolstogo* [Berlin, 1922], 22).

Index

Page numbers in italics indicate illustrations